D0251499

CNBC
24/7 TRADING

CNBC Profit From It Series

CNBC is the recognized global leader in business news, providing real-time financial market coverage and business information to more than 150 million homes and offices worldwide.

Now, bringing their expertise to a collaboration with Wiley, CNBC and Wiley are proud to launch the "Profit From It" book series—a publishing partnership dedicated to demystifying the markets for individual investors and active traders.

Available November 2000:

CNBC 24/7 Trading: Around the Clock, Around the World
by Barbara Rockefeller

Available February 2001:

Money and Power: The History of Business

Available March 2001:

CNBC Creating Wealth: An Insider's Guide to Decoding the Market

CNBC
24/7 TRADING

Around the Clock, Around the World

BARBARA ROCKEFELLER

JOHN WILEY & SONS, INC.
New York • Chichester • Weinheim • Brisbane • Singapore • Toronto

Library of Congress Cataloging-in-Publication Data:

Rockefeller, Barbara, 1946–
    CNBC 24/7 trading : around the clock, around the world / Barbara Rockefeller.
        p.   cm.
    Includes bibliographical references.
    ISBN 0-471-39314-2 (cloth : alk. paper)
    1. Electronic trading of securities.   I. Title.
  HG4515.95 .R635 2001
  332.64—dc21

                                       00-064920

Printed in the United States of America.

10 9 8 7 6 5 4 3 2 1

FOREWORD

CNBC's coverage of the markets conveys a frontline view of the events and developing trends that shape the financial markets and investors' financial future. Yet, even professionals covering financial and business news sometimes find it difficult to keep up with the pace of change in today's financial world. New technologies, new products, and new sources of information continually expand the investment possibilities. An old Chinese proverb says, "May you live in interesting times." Today's investors couldn't hope to live in a more exciting era. TV and the Internet bring to private traders' desktop computers information that was formerly the exclusive domain of Wall Street professionals. News, price quotes, technical analysis tools, fundamental analyses of every stripe—all these are available to the average investor at midnight just as they are at noon. For investors with the skill to distill and analyze this information, the options have never been more plentiful—nor more overwhelming.

Spotting trends, ultimately, is one of the most important jobs of any good investor or trader. And one of today's most talked-about trends is the move toward continuous, round-the-globe trading. Today's investors have more opportunities—and challenges—than ever before, thanks largely to the instantaneous communications that have revolutionized everything from how they get market information to how they place their trades. The markets are now, literally, at their fingertips, and not just in one time zone from 9:30 A.M. to 4:00 P.M. With today's technology, information and markets on continents around the globe are almost as immediately accessible as our own. Or so it seems.

Gone are the days when the ring of the closing bell on the New York Stock Exchange (NYSE) ended the trading day for almost all investors. Increasingly, that sound is becoming symbolic of the end of one session and the beginning of another—the extended-hours and overseas markets that comprise the new world of 24/7 trading. We are used to Europe's winding down its trading day just as we're getting into the meat of ours. But now, when New York closes, the Asian markets are gearing up for business, and Europe's next-day opening will overlap Asia's closing. Savvy investors see these markets (as well as the ever-expanding domestic after-hours session) not as peripheral concerns but as fresh opportunities—essential elements of their trading and investing portfolios.

The emergence of this round-the-clock, round-the-world market is the central theme of *CNBC 24/7 Trading*. This book embraces the reality that the markets never stand still, and that successful investing demands both discipline *and* flexibility: discipline to learn and master sound investing and trading principles, and flexibility to recognize and take advantage of new opportunities as they arise. This book is a guide to the emerging 24/7 marketplace, a roadmap to the potential rewards for investors who can grasp that marketplace's opportunities and understand its risks.

CNBC has been on the forefront of not just bringing the markets directly to investors, but making them accessible and understandable. It's one thing to be bombarded with facts, figures, and theories; it's quite another to make sense of this information and be able to use it to advantage in the market. But that's what CNBC is about: synthesizing and clarifying the information that's moving the markets, and cutting through the noise so that the faces and forces that impact investing become tangible and intelligible.

In the past several years, we have witnessed the transformation of the markets. They used to be side dishes on the news menu. Now they are featured entrées—a part of mainstream culture. People whose market experience a few short years ago may have been limited to checking the stock quotes in the morning paper before deciding whether to put their 401(k) funds in stocks or bonds now have the ability to analyze events as they unfold and then act on that analysis in the market.

It has been fascinating to see how we've all reacted to the information revolution. What surprises many people is that business and market news doesn't have to be dry or boring—far from it! The public has realized that the economy and the markets are more than lifeless statistics; they're the pulse of our society, the engine that makes everything run. They tell us where we are and give us insight into where we're going; they encompass every aspect of our culture. Earnings surprises, price/earnings ratios, and profit taking have entered the popular lexicon. People who wouldn't have known what impact the Federal Reserve had on monetary policy a half-dozen years ago now debate the likelihood and relative merits of a quarter-point or half-point interest rate change.

One thing hasn't changed, though, no matter what a market's hours are, and no matter which country's securities are being traded. To be able to profit from a market, investors still need to listen to what that market is telling them. In short, they need to be able to spot trends and opportunities, regardless of whether they are buying a stock for the long term on the NYSE during regular trading hours, trading another in the extended-hours market through an electronic communication network (ECN), or taking a short-term position in an overseas fund or in American Depositary Receipts (ADRs). Investors can use any number of approaches to find these opportunities—including fundamental or technical analysis (or a blend of the two)—but the goal is always the same: Find repeatable patterns that offer trades with the best reward at an acceptable level of risk.

But with these new market opportunities come additional responsibilities. 24/7 trading requires that investors think at a higher level, one that takes into account factors like the fluctuations in international currencies and interest rates, and the liquidity concerns that are inherent in extended-hours and foreign stock trading. The importance of self-education can't be underestimated. Profits never come without hard work. Simply understanding that the investment arena is now continuous and global doesn't guarantee prospering in it. Information technology may have removed some of the major hurdles, but the playing field is not entirely level. Individual investors still don't have the same kind of access to information and markets as the pros, nor do they have the intense training of many professionals, and nowhere is that more evident than in the new 24/7 markets. There are realities to trading around the clock; success demands study and dedication.

This book provides the tools for success, from defining your investment style and risk level to learning ways to find, in the 24/7 market, opportunities that fit your profile.

The key to investment success is being prepared for opportunities when they arise. In the emerging 24/7 global market, this is where you can start preparing.

Welcome to the market that never sleeps.

SUE HERERA
CNBC Anchor

ACKNOWLEDGMENTS

The efforts of many people went into the making of this book. CNBC and Wiley would like to thank the author, Barbara Rockefeller, for undertaking such a massive project. The author would like to extend a special thank you to Angel Europa who contributed to the research on risk.

The following individuals from CNBC provided input and feedback on the book: Bill Bolster, Bruno Cohen, Andrew Darrow, Patti Domm, Sue Herera, Howard Homonoff, Charles MacLachlan, Doug McMahon, Elisabeth Sami, and Kimberlee Smith.

At Wiley, the following individuals contributed to the effort: Jeffrey Brown, Mary Daniello, Robin Factor, Peter Knapp, Meredith McGinnis, Joan O'Neil, and Pamela van Giessen.

CONTENTS

GETTING ORIENTED IN THE NEW 24/7 WORLD

What does "24/7" mean? In everyday conversation, it means being ready for whatever comes, 24 hours a day, seven days a week. The term was originally used by the police, military, and hospitals to describe emergency situations, and many investors today want to be able to act—and therefore trade—in the same round-the-clock way. In investing, "24/7" means having an ability, almost all the time, to see and act on live prices and events.

Nasdaq chairman Frank Zarb says, "In a few years, trading securities will be digital, global, and accessible 24 hours a day. People will be able instantly to get stock-price quotations and instantly to execute a trade, day or night, anywhere on the globe, with stock markets linked and almost all electronic." Zarb thinks as many as 500 companies will be tradable 24/7 within three to five years.

The advent of 24-hour trading doesn't mean you *must* trade 24 hours a day, only that you *can*. The entire world is at your fingertips, day or night. So if you have a flash of blinding insight at 4:15 A.M., you can act on it immediately instead of having to wait for "the market" to open—"the market" being, for most readers, the U.S. markets.

Another insight might arrive at 4:15 P.M. It may come from a news release, a morning newspaper you don't read until the afternoon, or a corporate earnings announcement embargoed until "after the close." The New York Stock Exchange is open for business from 9:30 A.M. to

4:00 P.M., Eastern time. So if you are in San Francisco, Tokyo, or Istanbul, the "regular" hours of the NYSE are inconvenient to begin with. Even for investors in the Eastern time zone of the United States, keeping up with prices and events during a workday can be difficult. Many working people can't watch CNBC at the office and can't access financial sites on the Internet at their desks. In other words, unless you work in the finance industry and can watch CNBC and track financial Web sites during the workday, you're probably trading during evenings, nights, and weekends—when, obviously, the NYSE and other U.S. markets are closed.

HOW INVESTING HAS CHANGED

The world has more than 40,000 stocks. Today, you have access to more than half of them, and the day is coming soon when you will be able to buy and sell any stock, anywhere in the world, 24 hours a day. The emerging 24/7 capability is more than just a marvel of electronic communication; it is a transformation of the investment process itself. Consider these changes:

- Real-time financial and business news that used to be available only to Wall Street players is now available to you via the Internet and CNBC.

- The customer of the stock exchange is becoming the individual, not just the broker.

- Competing investment theories and strategies are discussed and evaluated in public for all to see.

- Analysis techniques—fundamental and technical—are being integrated into individuals' trading platforms.

- The average investor is becoming more knowledgeable about corporate finance and less easily stampeded into herdlike behavior.

You, the individual investor, are empowered by these changes. CNBC, the new e-brokers, ECNs, and news and analysis Web sites all encourage you to challenge what you read and hear, and to seize the new opportunities. This is good news. Your challenge is in finding a systematic approach to the new market order, and sorting through the news that *you* will want to act on. Access to the news and to expert advice offers tremendous opportunity, but it can also be overwhelming. The goal of this book is to help you navigate the new 24/7 trading world in which we live, so you will be better prepared to see developing opportunities and seize the profits they produce.

HOW 24/7 TRADING CAN BENEFIT YOU

Let's assume that you've heard about this 24/7 capability and you want to know how it can benefit you. The emerging 24/7 capability offers three kinds of opportunity:

1. You can trade U.S. securities outside the regular stock exchange hours, and take advantage of breaking news.

2. You can trade foreign securities that are listed in the United States and other countries, and arbitrage price differences.

3. You can trade foreign securities that are listed only in their home countries.

> **liquidity**
>
> Liquidity is the term describing the number of market participants who are active in a market at any one time; a liquid market has many participants and an illiquid market has few participants. Liquid markets are characterized by small bid-offer spreads and few gaps, while illiquid markets typically display wide bid-offer spreads and many gaps.

24/7 trading offers enormous opportunities—particularly with respect to truly diversifying a portfolio by adding foreign securities. But it can also be challenging because of the difficulties of researching securities on which little or no information is available, and because of the lack of **liquidity** (a subject we'll cover throughout this book). In the 24/7 world, you will be especially challenged by the need to assess risk without knowing as much as you'd like about what you're considering buying, or about the availability of other market players. That world can also be daunting, frustrating, and sometimes horrible—for example, when you want to sell a stock after an exchange's regular hours. The goals of this book are: to demystify and decode what 24/7 trading is all about, and to help you get started.

"Trade like a professional" is the latest buzz phrase. It means, simply, that you can conduct trading activities that used to be reserved exclusively for institutions and professional investors. The first key to breaking the institutional barrier was the electronic communication network (ECN). ECNs have been around for more than 30 years but only recently became available to the public via the Internet. The second key is the real-time business and financial news, analysis, and research available via television and the Internet. Together, these two keys unlock the gateway to a level playing field on which the average investor has the same access to the news—plus the same virtually instant execution capability—as Wall Street professionals.

These wonderful developments are transforming the investment environment in individual investors' favor, but they are not the whole story and do not fully level the playing field. An ability to see streaming live quotes does not also confer understanding, experience, and knowledge of how to think about this information. The ability to execute a trade in seconds does not also imbue the trader with wisdom about the risk and reward of the trade. Mere information is not knowledge, and knowledge is not wisdom.

This is not to say that a dedicated individual can't perform as well as professionals, or better. Just keep in mind that information flow and execution speed are not the only tools needed to trade like a professional. You, the individual investor, actually may have an advantage over the professional because your mind is not cluttered with theories or encumbered by institutional constraints. But the most common disadvantage facing individual investors is that many of them may fail to think and act systematically—a discipline that is imposed on professional investors by their formal training and the firms they work for.

INVESTING IS DIFFERENT NOW: MORE INFORMATION ENHANCES DECISION MAKING

The ability to analyze price history and to calculate measures of future risk and return is the single most valuable element of progress offered by the new tools: financial TV and the Internet. It is what makes it different this time—not the news itself, but the ability to research the implications of the news for risk and return, and to act on that research virtually in real time. For example, a value investor buys Security A with an expected future return of 20 percent and a risk factor of x for the intended holding period. A momentum investor buys Security B with the identical return and risk factors for the intended holding period. They are performing the same investment act using the same decision tool. It is irrelevant whether Security A is "old economy" or Security B is "new economy." Only one thing matters: They know the basis of the decision—the trade-off between risk and return over a given investment horizon. Fresh news can provide fresh perspective on risk, return, or a holding period.

Financial news, electronic trading, and the Internet do not repeal the laws of supply and demand, negate the business cycle, or eliminate fear and greed as the emotional motivation for much financial activity. 24/7 trading does, however, allow the opportunity for anyone to get the news—including price news—and to make rational investment decisions at the highest level of analytical excellence. The average investor gains the ability to use the same tools as the professionals.

INVESTMENT INFORMATION IS EVERYWHERE, BUT CONSIDER YOUR SOURCE

According to a poll reported in *Time* magazine in April 2000:

- 23 percent of Americans check their stock prices every day.
- 28 percent check their stock prices every week.
- 29 percent check their stock prices about once a month.

Yet everybody has a different interpretation and judgment of what is seen and heard. Like the blind man and the elephant, we can only feel and picture what experience has set us up to expect. The advent of 24/7 trading, with the upcoming availability of foreign stocks and increased extended-hours trading, adds more noise. And when we're feeling overwhelmed, it's cold comfort to know that most other heads are spinning, too.

Investment information is everywhere, and many investors are struggling to keep up with it. We all know about information overload. Financial service companies advertise everywhere, not just in financial publications; they even advertise in publications like *National Geographic* magazine. If you subscribe to a financial newspaper or magazine, sign on to a financial Web site, or just have a brokerage account, chances are your e-mailbox is stuffed with updates, late-breaking news, analyses, and the like. This is good news because it means we have more information at our disposal. But the abundance of Web sites offering stock market news and analyses and chat rooms means that we face the challenge of sorting through it all. Sometimes it can be difficult to know what is wheat and what is chaff.

Chat room participants and message board posters may or may not have enough knowledge to make a defensible recommendation, but institutional analysts are supposed to be savvy professionals. Now their work is accessible to the public on Web sites. Here are just a few Web addresses:

- www.multex.com is a site specializing in professional brokerage house analysts' reports. Many are free. Others are on a fee basis, generally $10–$100.

- www.zacks.com is a site for earnings estimates. You can screen the universe of stocks for earnings surprises, earnings over *x* percent, and so on.

- www.firstcall.com (Thomson Financial) is another site for earnings information. Most of the services are fee-based but some are free. The site carries earnings data, company research from 700 institutions, corporate news, owner and insider information, and newsletters, including recently launched newsletters in Latin America.

- www.bulldogresearch.com is a new Web site that was launched in the spring of 2000 to keep track of institutional stock analysts, see how their recommendations worked out, and rank the advisors. This site complements Mark Hulbert's performance tracking of some 175 investment advisory newsletters in the *Hulbert Financial Digest*, now in its twentieth year.

- www.insiderscores.com describes what company insiders are doing and how their trades have compared to subsequent price moves. The content is not strictly analysis, but it's helpful all the same.

- www.flextrader.com tabulates the "voting card" on a large universe of stocks according to 22 different technical trading systems. Technical systems can be considered an alternative or a supplement to fundamental research.

- cnbc.com includes an earnings center showing actual and estimated earnings (color-coded for beat, missed, and in line), stock and fund screeners, and many other features. Stocks can also be organized by industry/sector. Pick "electronics/semiconductors" and get the whole list with a graphic depiction of the one-day gain or loss (in green or red). Click on a name from the list and get a chart with prices of the last 10 trades, insider trading, and other information.

Many professional analysts have a particular point of view: Stocks should be bought for their fundamental value and should be held for very long periods of time. Others have a different point of view: Stocks should be evaluated according to the condition of the economy, or a technical chart, or even the stars. These latter points of view can be described as "contrarian." They do not put fundamental value first, nor do they consider the proper holding period to be years or decades. To divide the equity analysis world into conventional and contrarian camps is not strictly accurate, but it helps to organize the vast amount of information flowing into your mind. Let's look at each camp.

Contrarianism has an innate appeal. We all like to think that we are unique and too savvy to be merely a member of some herd. The problem is that most of us are hostages to a worldview or perspective that was developed before the electronic revolution. Everywhere, we see the phrase "It's different this time"—or the equivalent of "It's never different, so toe the line." Another phrase, this one from the 1960s, comes to mind: cognitive dissonance, defined as trying to hold as true two equally reasonable and plausible but contradictory ideas.

Now let's look at what the conventional camp believes. First, we need to consider the debate on what is a "rational" investing strategy. The conventional camp says it is irrational to hold a stock with a P/E ratio of 150 when, historically, the average P/E is 16. A technical analyst, however, can equally well assert that it is irrational to sell a stock *that is still rising* just because its P/E fails to pass a fundamental test. In this case—and in many other cases of cognitive dissonance in the market today—the pivot point of the argument is the intended holding period. The conventional camp believes in holding stocks more or less forever, in which case someone who buys when the P/E is at 150 will be looking at losses someday, when the price reverts to the historical mean. The technician believes that the stock should be sold when its price turns down and that the investor should not be held hostage to a specific idea of a long holding period.

Thus, both sides in the conventional/contrarian debate can be right about *some* things, but neither side is right about *all* things. Two seemingly mutually exclusive points of view can each be true, depending on the context and on the assumptions of the speaker or writer. Therefore, in an application of "consider your source," it's important to know the worldview of the speaker or writer and to understand his or her interpretation of the facts. In this book, we try to distinguish specific views and analyze the strategies.

WALL STREET IS NOT THE CENTER OF THE UNIVERSE

It is now recognized that Wall Street is *not* the center of the financial universe—which is why you're reading this book and why you're interested in 24/7 trading. The U.S. stock market is the single biggest stock market in the world, but, as Table I.1 indicates, it actually represents less than half of the world's market capitalization.

Non-U.S. companies and markets sometimes outperform the United States, even in technology. For example, Vodafone Airtouch (VOD) is the world's largest mobile telecommunications company (UK), with 38 million customers in 23 countries. Europe and Japan, in fact, are far ahead of the United States in wireless telephony. In both cases, a single standard was adopted to cut through squabbling and disputes among competing companies, such as Vodafone and Ericsson (ERICY) from Sweden and Nokia (NOK) in Finland. As a result, more than 60 percent of households in Sweden own mobile phones, and more than 40 percent in Italy and Japan. The United States comes fifth, just after the United Kingdom, but a little ahead of Germany, France, and Spain. The United States doesn't even lead in Internet penetration.

TABLE I.1
WORLD CAPITALIZATION MARKET WEIGHTS
As of December 31, 1999

Region	Market Capitalization (in Billions of U.S. Dollars)	Percentage of Total
United States	$15,370	44.8%
Europe	9,553	27.9
Japan	4,693	13.7
Emerging markets	2,715	7.9
Pacific ex-Japan	1,215	3.5
Canada	763	2.2
Total	34,309	

Source: Morgan Stanley Capital International Indices.

A little over 40 percent of U.S. households are wired to the Internet versus almost 60 percent in Sweden.

Foreign markets sometimes outperform Wall Street, too. Morgan Stanley Capital International has an index for Europe, Australasia, and the Far East (EAFE) which is used as the benchmark for global equity fund managers. It has beat the U.S. market in 14 of the past 25 calendar years. In three of those years, the U.S. market took a net loss, but in two of those three years, the EAFE Index did better. The best year for the EAFE was 1986 (up 70 percent). The best year for the United States was 1995 (up "only" 38 percent). The worst year for the United States was 1974 (down 8 percent). EAFE's worst year was 1990 (down 23 percent). EAFE, of course, covers practically the whole world except the United States. Breaking down the performance to more manageable portions, the United States is still the winner over 10-year and 20-year time frames, as shown in Table I.2.

It goes without saying that a 10- or 20-year average conceals the high flyers that are dragged down by the dogs. A portfolio including the best foreign stocks would have done better than a portfolio of the medium and worst U.S. performers.

TABLE I.2
ANNUALIZED RATES OF RETURN

MSCI National Indices	10 Years (12/31/89–12/31/99)	20 Years (12/31/79–12/31/99)
Japan	−0.7%	13.0%
Germany	12.9	14.8
United Kingdom	14.2	16.7
United States	19.0	18.1

Source: Morgan Stanley Capital International Indices.

New issues are often among the best performers, at least initially; many fall later. In 2000, for the first time, European equity offerings surpassed those in the United States by a significant amount. Europe had $116.8 billion in new offerings in the first six months of the year, compared to $97 billion in the United States. Europe is surpassing the United States in mergers, too. The U.S. merger market was $874 billion in the first half of 2000, just slightly ahead of the first half of 1999. The actual number of deals fell 13 percent. Meanwhile, worldwide merger volume rose to $1.9 trillion, a 26 percent increase over the previous year. Deals in which a European company was the acquirer accounted for 40 percent of all global deals in the first half of the year.

> **price/earnings ratio**
>
> The price of a stock, divided by its earnings per share; often called a P/E ratio or multiple.

Many foreign stocks have lower P/Es (**price/earnings ratios**) than U.S. stocks. *Forbes* magazine (July 24, 2000) has calculated the P/E of its list of 500 international stocks as 19, compared to 27 for the S&P 500. In the United Kingdom, Sweden, and Switzerland, the average P/E is 20. In South Korea and Mexico, the average P/E is 10. Lower P/Es may or may not mean greater price appreciation potential but they are worth knowing about.

DIVERSIFICATION THROUGH GLOBAL INVESTING REDUCES RISK

Trading around the clock and around the world is also appealing because the world is becoming a smaller place. Stock exchanges everywhere are merging and forming alliances. The changes in how stocks (and now options, futures, bonds, and currencies) are traded have been mind-boggling. Consider these recent alliances:

- The Paris, Amsterdam, and Brussels exchanges announced in April 2000 that they are merging.
- Nasdaq-Japan officially opened in June 2000, and Nasdaq-Europe, in partnership with Europe's new Ix exchange, is

scheduled to begin operations in early 2001. Partnerships have been established in Hong Kong, Quebec, and Australia, and global agreements are being pursued for Asia, Latin America, and the Middle East.

- The NYSE announced, in June 2000, that it is participating in discussions to explore the feasibility of a Global Equity Market (GEM) with the Australian Stock Exchange, Euronext (Amsterdam, Brussels, Paris), the Hong Kong Exchanges, the Bolsa Mexicana de Valores, the Bolsa de Valores de São Paulo, the Tokyo Stock Exchange, and the Toronto Stock Exchange.

The total market capitalization of the world's publicly traded stocks was over $20 trillion at year-end 1999, and the new NYSE alliance will encompass 53 percent of all stocks traded in the world. By the time this book goes to press, more mergers and alliances will be on deck. Mergers and alliances are helpful to individual investors because they result in standardization of terms and conditions (such as the time from the transaction date to the settlement date).

The main reason investors seek investments beyond standard U.S. market hours and outside the U.S. borders is: diversification reduces risk. Most people are aware of the diversification principle. It was devised in 1952 but, so far, its practical application by individual investors has been elusive. Many investors believe that "diversification" simply means investing in different types of assets (at its simplest, this means stocks versus bonds) or investing in different types of securities within an asset group (e.g., small caps as well as large caps in the same industry).

But the diversification principle really pertains to risk levels and the **correlation** of securities. When the return on two securities is not correlated (i.e., when one goes down, the other does not follow), the risk level of the portfolio containing them may be lower than it was before the two securities were added. Even if two high-risk

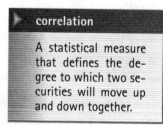

correlation

A statistical measure that defines the degree to which two securities will move up and down together.

securities are added to a low-risk portfolio, if the two new securities are inversely correlated (i.e., when one goes up, the other goes down),

portfolio theory

Investment practice that permits investors to classify and estimate the expected returns and risks of securities.

the risk of the entire portfolio may go down. Professional fund managers and financial planners use these ideas, named **portfolio theory**. Yet it is extraordinarily difficult to find a readily understandable way to use the theory when the goal is to take full control of investment decisions yourself.

The overriding assumption in this book is that you want to do it yourself, or you want a deeper understanding of 24/7 markets and their risks and rewards, so you can work with an advisor toward the best possible portfolio diversification. If you ask a financial planner or a broker about investing in individual foreign stocks, you will generally be told that you should be looking at an international mutual fund, or maybe ADRs or iShares (international shares, formerly WEBs: World Equity Benchmark funds that track country indices but trade like stocks in the United States; we'll discuss these in more detail in Chapter 8) because they are less risky and easier to trade. And there are ample opportunities in ADRs, exchange-traded funds, and international mutual funds.

HOW THIS BOOK CAN HELP YOU GET STARTED IN 24/7 TRADING

The 24/7 market is changing on a daily basis. It would be virtually impossible to cover all aspects of the market—from stocks and bonds to futures and options and foreign exchange—in one book. Here, we focus on the 24/7 stock market in an attempt to ground you to what is available today, what isn't, and to help you prepare for the capabilities that will emerge tomorrow.

This book is organized in two parts. Part One offers guidelines on how to research and buy after hours and around the world. We will look at where and how to find information and will help you learn to analyze it. Chapter 1 helps you identify what your investment strategy really is and then guides you in assessing your risk comfort level.

Chapter 2 examines the extended-hours markets in the United States and discusses the logistics of investing in foreign markets. Chapter 3 examines one of the key issues surrounding 24/7 investing—liquidity. Chapter 4 delves into today's hot topic—risk. You will learn to assess the risk level of your investments and identify your ideal risk level.

Part Two gets into the nitty-gritty of around-the-world investing. Chapter 5 provides guidance on how to find new stocks that you may be interested in buying, and how to screen them to ensure that they're right for your portfolio. Chapter 6 offers some background on why you might invest in foreign markets, and delves into the thorny issue of diversification. Chapter 7 describes the increased risk you assume when you invest in foreign stocks—sovereign risk, operations risk, legal risk, and more. The emphasis is on avoiding catastrophic loss. Chapter 8 explores the opportunities at home—how to invest in foreign stocks through U.S. markets via ADRs, exchange-traded funds, iShares, and international funds.

Appendix A provides a technical analysis primer for readers new to this type of analysis. The basics of foreign exchange are offered in Appendix B to aid you in getting your bearings in the 24/7 global market of many currencies.

Finally, a guide to CNBC resources is included in Appendix C.

Throughout this book you will find references to many Web sites. These are top sites as selected and reviewed by leading business publications such as *Online Investor, Barron's, Forbes,* and many others. They were reviewed by the author and a team of researchers for practicality, ease of use, and relevance. The goal was to provide you with free (or inexpensive) sites. Where there was a lack of free or lower-cost resources, we provide you with information on resources the professionals use.

PART ONE

Doing

Research

and

Analysis

Around

the

Clock

CHAPTER 1

GETTING STARTED IN 24/7 TRADING

Getting started in 24/7 trading requires you to review all of the factors that contribute to the way you invest and your choice of investment vehicles. What's your investment style? Do you want quick returns, or are you more interested in long-term capital gains? Are you a value investor or a momentum investor? What's your risk comfort level? You should carefully consider all of these issues—and more—before getting started in the extended-hours market or in researching and buying foreign securities. This chapter provides some food for thought to help you answer these questions.

"TWO-BASKET" INVESTING

As a practical matter, most people split their portfolios between two baskets. One is held for the long term and the other is actively traded. The actively traded basket is usually considered to carry more risk, sometimes to the extent of being designated "mad money." Trading 24/7, which encompasses extended-hours trading and trading in foreign stocks, is usually—and logically—consigned to the actively traded basket. Long-term holdings can more easily be bought and sold during the regular working hours of the exchanges, when there is maximum liquidity. Foreign stocks, unless they are in the form of ADRs, iShares, or mutual funds, are traded during the exchange hours of their home countries. Aside from the Americas and a few hours of overlap with Europe, foreign stocks are traded outside regular U.S. market hours.

With the two-basket model, we assume that the composition of the long-term basket changes very little and the actively traded basket changes continuously, depending on how much time the investor spends on it. There is a tendency to regard the long-term basket as low-risk by virtue of its having a long term and low turnover. This may or may not be true in the statistical sense. Similarly, the actively traded basket may or may not carry a higher risk. A stock doesn't become low-risk because it is consigned to the long-term basket; its riskiness is inherent and measurable. Likewise, a stock isn't high-risk because the investor chooses to trade it actively. A long-term basket comprised of high-risk stocks can easily have a more variable return than an actively traded basket that is managed with discipline. Thus, theoretically, we could design a low-risk long-term basket consisting entirely of foreign stocks and pair it with an actively traded basket of Fortune 100 stocks—the exact opposite of how we usually imagine the two-basket model to be distributed.

One goal of this book is to demonstrate that each *combined* portfolio has a distinctive risk–return profile. Trading 24/7 forces investors to examine the riskiness inherent in each stock and in how the stocks are combined to form a portfolio. Together, the long-term basket and the actively traded basket constitute a portfolio, and investors may be surprised when they evaluate the risk and expected return of the combined portfolio.

The evaluation process may change the way you think about investing and trading in general. You may choose to reallocate funds between the two baskets. You may decide to trade more actively—or less actively.

WHAT'S YOUR INVESTING STYLE?

Choosing an investment style is the first important decision you have to make. Active trading is inherently different from buy-and-hold investing—not in the analytical process, but in understanding risk and applying trading rules. If you're trading 24/7, you're most likely an active trader. Electronic domestic and international extended-hours trading makes execution efficient, but it also magnifies conceptual and execution errors. These are *your* errors when you're doing it yourself, so you will need to tread carefully. Extended-hours trading and international trading are qualitatively different from in-hours domestic trading or investing. For example, when you're buying a Chinese dot-com at midnight, you do not have the same investor protections that you have when you buy 100 shares of IBM from your local U.S.-registered broker at noon. "Trade like a professional" means more than being able to click "okay" on a computer screen.

The good news is that once you develop a global worldview, you will be able to see opportunities more clearly and steer clear of profit-draining investments and strategies. You can take charge of your portfolio or decide against doing it yourself and hire a professional. This book focuses on how to trade yourself or, at a minimum, how to gain the information you need to speak confidently and knowledgeably with financial professionals. You can make sensible deductions about risk by performing your own research via the Web, cable news networks like CNBC, and newspapers and magazines. You can understand and conquer foreign exchange risk. You can use technical analysis to avoid bad timing (at the very least) without becoming a slave to charts. You can become an evolved trader who calculates both the upside and the downside risk in advance, and exercises the discipline to exit trades at preset limits. Professionals know that losses are inevitable; the trick is to trade in such a way that gains far outweigh losses.

WHAT'S YOUR TARGETED HOLDING PERIOD?

Investing is a dynamic process, whatever the pace of your portfolio turnover. It is a *process* of getting from point A (your initial equity) to point Z (your ending equity). When you view investing as a lifelong process, the distinction between "trading" and "investing" becomes a thin line. Many people think of "trading" as an irresponsible, high-risk speculative endeavor, whereas "investing" connotes a more disciplined, low-risk approach to "saving." Although speculators may *seem* to have a higher risk tolerance, they may, in fact, have a *lower* risk tolerance, which accounts for their short holding period (especially if they use **leverage**). In other words, they trade more actively to lower their risk by being out of the market some of the time. Traders and investors have the same goals and engage in the same thought processes and actions; they simply have a different expected holding period. Short-term traders can be highly disciplined and risk-averse, and long-term investors can be reckless and take more risk than they realize. For you, the important tasks in 24/7 trading are: assess your risk realistically, estimate your profit goals, and determine your holding period.

> **leverage**
>
> In trading and investing, the use of borrowing, including borrowing on margin, to increase return without expending additional capital.

Determining your own expected holding period is the hardest decision you will ever make. Let's say you research the Widget Company and it looks like a bargain, based on the product, management, earnings outlook, competition, and some key ratios. You believe its price will rise 20 percent over the next year. You buy the stock. It rises 20 percent in the first *week*. Now what do you do? You have achieved your expected return. Should you take your profit and look for another bargain, or will you be captive to your expected holding period of one year? You have a major investment in this company, in terms of the time you spent researching it. If you take your profit early, you have to do research again; besides, maybe Widget will rise 40 percent.

But remember: *The only reason to invest is to make money.* This brings up the issue of the pace at which you make money. Some investment advisors like to use a version of the fable of the tortoise and the hare. The tortoise makes 10 percent per annum over a 25-year investing life and ends up with more than the hare, who makes 100 percent one year and loses much of it the next year. This may be a comforting story, but it doesn't always hold up to scrutiny.

If the tortoise and the hare start out with equal equity and the hare makes 100 percent in the first year, he may be permanently ahead. The mere fact of having doubled his equity changes his behavior. The wealthy person will bet less, in any situation, than the poor person, simply because the expected return if he wins is such a small proportion of his total wealth that it is not worth *any* risk of loss. The poor man, on the other hand, tends to underestimate the risk of loss because the gain that is possible if he wins is a significant chunk of his total net worth. In a way, the millionaire is financially conservative (risk-averse) because he is rich, and he remains rich because he became conservative.

Meanwhile, if the tortoise started in a down year and lost 50 percent in that first year, he has to make 100 percent to get back to his starting equity. How can he lose 50 percent? Easy. The tortoise made a decision to hold his securities for a long time because he fancies himself a long-term investor. He believes his stocks will come back after a big fall, and beliefs become wishes. But the tortoise's strategy is flawed because his basic assumption is a statistically normal return of 10 percent per annum over the next 25 years, and that doesn't take into account a bad first period. He can never catch up. The 100 percent return he needs, to get back to his starting equity, is unlikely to occur *according to his own assumptions about expected return.*

This outcome raises several very thorny questions to which there is no single correct answer. One solution is to assume that the 10 percent per annum target will be achieved over the longer time frame by catching up with a higher rate of return in later years. In other words, a statistically abnormal higher rate later on will compensate for the statistically abnormal lower rate in the first period. It is risky to assume two statistically abnormal events, but, historically, we do find occurrences of **reversion to the mean.** Their frequency encourages many investment advisors to recommend that the best practice, in the face of a first-period loss, is to "stick it out"—an approach that focuses on the characteristics of the security

> **reversion to the mean**
>
> The tendency of a security to go back to or "revert" to its average price, especially after a sudden upward spike or downward dip in price.

itself. If the stock is a good long-term "value" stock on a fundamental basis, it will revert to its rising trend line. The "buy and hold" money management rule derives from the high quality of the security.

Another approach is the **stop-loss order,** a money management tactic that derives from the investor's personal tolerance for loss, whatever the quality of the underlying security. For example, suppose you determine in advance that if you have a 10 percent loss in Security A, you will sell it, even if everyone says it's the best stock in the world and is sure to recover.

> **stop-loss order**
>
> An order to a broker to buy or sell a security at a specific price; this limits the loss in an existing position if the price moves in an unfavorable direction.

Setting stop-loss limits is difficult because you need to blend your personal feeling about losses with the statistical variability of the security. It's hard to exclude consideration of the security's quality. You will feel differently about exercising a stop-loss rule when the stock is a blue-chip rather than a dot-com. Exercising stop-loss limit rules is agonizing. Emotional neutrality becomes very difficult to maintain.

In sum, the outcome of the first period of investing can be crucial to the total outcome of a lifetime of investing, and, equally important, critical to the evolution of the mind of the investor. A big up-front gain is always arithmetically superior to small and steady gains—unless there is a catastrophic loss.

Fortunately, the new investing environment is alerting people that there is a trade-off between expected return and holding period. If you are an unlucky soul who has had a bad first year and thus must play catch-up just to get back to your starting equity, you have the choice of selecting from the high end of a menu of expected returns, even if, temporarily, that gives you more risk than you normally would take. More than 40,000 securities in the world today trade on recognized exchanges. Somewhere out there is a combination of securities that will likely return your equity to its starting point. In short, you might first want to determine your expected return, and then derive a flexible holding period that suits you. The 24/7 trading environment offers an opportunity to trade in different time frames, beyond the two-basket approach.

RISK IS ALWAYS PERSONAL: WHAT'S YOUR RISK COMFORT LEVEL?

If you perform extensive research on a stock and have determined that it is a "value" stock according to conventional fundamental criteria, is it OK to buy the stock on **margin?** It's important to know where you fall on the holding period continuum if you use leverage—whether you have a margin account or you incurred other debt to get a "stake" for trading stocks. The risk of a specific trade may be quantifiable, but your perception of risk is always personal. The classic numbers game illustrates the point. Suppose you choose a three-digit number from 000 to 999 and $1 gives you a chance to win $500 in the next 24 hours. The probability that you will win is 1 out of 1,000, or 0.0001. What is the expected return? Pascal told us the answer back in 1653: It is the probability of winning multiplied by the reward, or 0.0001 × $500 = 50 cents.

> ### margin
>
> The cash you have in your brokerage account as a proportion of the current value of stocks. When you buy stocks "on margin," you are borrowing up to 50 percent of the purchase price from the broker. After the purchase, the broker revalues the stocks in your account and you must have at least 25 percent of the current market value of the stocks in cash. Some brokers may require more than 25 percent. If the cash you put into the account is less than 25 percent of the value, the broker may have the right to sell some of your stocks without notifying you in order to comply with SEC rules. See www.sec.gov/consumer.

Some people think it makes sense to bet $1 to get 50 cents. Most people do not. They may pay the $1 anyway, for the entertainment value, but that's like spending money to go to the movies; it's the price of a fantasy—in this case, the fantasy of winning. People don't delude themselves that numbers games or lotteries are the same as "investing." But Pascal's little formula for expected return is *exactly* what we should probably be using to evaluate investments.

When you are in "investment mode," you can think in terms of *return.* Return per unit of time is the benchmark, but once you focus on return itself, you will find that the unit of time becomes less important. If 20 percent per year is your target and you make 20 percent in the first week of owning a stock, you have achieved the return you expected. That it took less than a year is less important. Putting time limits on your investment emphasizes the less important criterion. If making a million dollars is your target, you may think it would be nice to make the first million in the first year, instead of making a little each year for 24 years and completing the entire million in the twenty-fifth year. But making a million in any year—from a modest starting point of, say, $100,000—necessarily requires taking extraordinary risk—akin to "betting the ranch" on a single throw of the dice. You may choose to do precisely that, and the probability of winning may be considerably higher than 1 in 1,000, as in the lottery example above, but such a gamble would be an exceptional one-time bet. A good example of such a bet was George Soros' sale of British pounds ahead of a major devaluation of the currency. He was knowledgeable and experienced in currency trading, and he correctly analyzed the political and economic situation. Soros' gain from that single trade was reported in newspapers at the time at $1 billion.

Aside from exceptional cases like this, in nearly all circumstances we have to keep in mind the tortoise-and-hare fable. It can and does happen that "value" investors who are investing their savings get stuck with a losing first year and never catch up. It also can and does happen that a speculator puts together a brilliant portfolio using leverage that beats "the market" with lower risk because his or her holding period is short. Logically, the safest investment strategy of all is to be in the market and to put the stake at risk for the shortest possible time. The longer you stay out of the market, the safer your money. The longer you are in the market, the more risk you are taking.

The logic of this observation may be bothersome to those who believe in buying value stocks with an indefinitely long holding period. This is an insoluble paradox facing the financial industry today. On the one hand is evidence that buy-and-hold is a winning long-term strategy when the stocks selected are true "value" stocks and do not lose that status because of big-picture changes in the economy, or other evolutionary events that are difficult or even impossible to observe until after the fact. The advent of 24/7 means that the universe of "value" stocks has now been increased manifold because foreign stocks are now directly available. The analysis and monitoring that are needed to ensure that they are now, and will remain, value stocks have been increased many times, too.

On the other hand, active trading has the virtue of keeping you out of the market some of the time, which, by definition, reduces your total risk regardless of the inherent risk characteristics of the individual securities being traded. If you buy a very risky stock and its price varies an average of 10 percent per day but you hold it for less than one day, you are taking less risk than if you buy a stock and its price varies only 2 percent per day but cumulatively could vary by more than 10 percent over a longer holding period. Many investment advisors recommend against active trading, in part because they perceive that the average investor does not adequately take into consideration the risk of loss in any single trade and does not exercise the discipline needed to cut losses short. This is why many day-traders end up losing money. The 24/7 environment is even riskier than the standard daylight environment because there is reduced liquidity in extended-hours trading, and less information (and less timely information) is available in trading foreign stocks.

When you enter the 24/7 environment, you are automatically taking more risk, whether you are seeking value stocks for your long-term basket or trading opportunities for your actively traded basket. The benefit of embracing the 24/7 trading world is that it forces you to consider those extra risks and, in the process, to evaluate risk in general and your own perception of risk and return.

WOULD YOU CREATE YOUR OWN MUTUAL FUND?

Every analysis of stock market returns uses equity index benchmarks. The S&P 500 is foremost among them. It is stated as a fact by some that "You can't beat the market," at least not over any extended period of time. If you buy an index-tracking mutual fund, you are buying all the companies, so of course you can't beat the market. The market *is* all the companies. But, if you stop and think about it, at any point in time, an index-tracking fund reflects "market sentiment" as well as the composite value of the market. **Market sentiment** is determined by real corporate events such as earnings, but also by developments in the overall economy, such as inflation and the level of interest rates. The market can be temporarily up or down on external factors that momentarily distort the true value of the underlying holdings. In fact, the true value is hardly ever achieved; the market is never in equilibrium. The track records you see for index-following funds require a long holding period to show high annual averages. Depending on where you enter and exit, and on how long you hold such a fund, your actual return can be very different because of these effects.

> **market sentiment**
>
> A catch-all phrase that refers to the ephemeral mood of the majority of market participants. It ranges from extremely bullish (many institutions and individuals buying stocks and the main indices rising with strong momentum) to extremely bearish (many institutions and individuals selling stocks and the main indices falling). In both cases, volumes are high. It is possible to have bullish or bearish market sentiment in one sector (such as high-tech or biotech) while the overall market sentiment, as seen in a broad index, lacks an extreme of emotion.

Mutual funds—which outnumber U.S. stocks by some 11,000 to 7,500—come in two basic varieties: (1) passive index tracking funds or (2) actively managed funds that are periodically rebalanced (some more frequently than others). Actively managed mutual funds try to identify hidden treasures within a sector or class, and combine them in such a way as to maximize returns while reducing risk. Rebalancing is where the professionalism comes in. The analysts employed by funds spend all day, every day, either digging into companies' financial statements or engaged in heavy-duty quantitative analysis. Still, an investor's return depends on a buy-and-hold strategy, even if the experts are changing the mix of securities within the fund from time to time.

Today, investors have another choice: concocting their own mutual fund at Netfolio.com or Folio(fn).com. The first step is to define what kind of risks you're comfortable with. The program then screens the universe of stocks to assemble a basket of stocks that should, together, give you the return that is desired at the risk that is named. For this, you pay a flat fee per year and no transaction commissions, but you are expected to stick with your portfolio through thick and thin (and hope to get the expected return that you specified at the beginning of the exercise). In short, you have no ability to respond to "market sentiment" on a short-term basis without rebalancing the portfolio, exactly as professional fund managers do. If you choose to rebalance the portfolio more than once a year as the investment environment changes, you must pay the fee every time (and come to deeply appreciate the many diverse analytical requirements of the professionals).

Each kind of fund—index-tracking, actively managed, or do-it-yourself—has its own advantages and disadvantages. To buy index-tracking mutual funds is to be at the mercy of market sentiment at any given point in time whenever you need to liquidate some of your stock market holdings. To buy funds that rebalance and then hold for a long time is to get the benefit of professional expertise, but also to trust some strangers to perform in the future as they have in the past. Creating your own mutual fund gives you control over both strategy and tactics, but it is expensive (if you rebalance more than once a year) and requires a good analytical mind.

The cost of mutual funds is a hairy subject that is fraught with hot debate. The standard passive index fund is perhaps best represented by the Vanguard Index 500 Fund, which returned 20.9 percent per annum in the seven years that ended June 30, 2000 (according to a letter in *The New York Times* on July 30, 2000, from John Bogle, founder of the Vanguard Group). Five advisors tracked by *The New York Times* over the same period had returns averaging only 15.7 percent, a difference of 5.2 percent. Bogle states that 3.2 percent of the difference can be attributed to the higher costs of the advisors (for performing periodic rebalancing), compared to the Vanguard index-tracking fund. In fact, on a cash basis, the Vanguard index-tracking fund returned a hypothetical $188,750 on an initial investment of $50,000. The others returned an average of $138,500, showing that the index-tracking fund made $50,000 more, *the amount of the original investment.* Those who say passive index tracking is boring and lacks the excitement of stock picking may be right, but they can't deny that the returns may be consistently superior. Bogle points out that "the magic of compounding" is critically important. Even if the advisors and the index-tracking funds earned the same 10 percent per annum over the next 13 years (for a total of 20 years), the index fund would still be ahead, $652,000 to $478,000.

Clearly, it is not easy for the professional or do-it-yourself investor to beat the indexes over a long period of time, systematically. 24/7 trading offers more opportunities to beat the index, but it requires more active trading: exploiting short-term opportunities in the extended-hours market, or venturing overseas, or both. Choosing a portfolio of individual stocks, whether you include mutual funds or not, is the most difficult investing task, albeit the one with the greatest flexibility. You will need to acquire the same mindset as professional fund managers and learn to use most of the same analytical tools. Truly professional fund management is a full-time job, and professional firms have the added benefit of being able to hire specialists in everything from financial statement analysis and analyses of market and economic environments to statistical modeling. As a practical matter, you cannot expect to duplicate all these skills and absorb all that knowledge.

What you can do, however, is learn enough about the risk/reward trade-off to avoid the worst drawbacks of amateur investing. To buy and sell stocks indiscriminately without ever knowing the risk and return of your total portfolio is dangerous. To buy and sell in the context of portfolio management is to aim for professionalism and, hopefully, increased reward.

WHAT ASSUMPTIONS HAVE YOU MADE ABOUT 24/7—AROUND THE WORLD—INVESTING?

To manage risk and return yourself, you need to choose your assumptions about how the world and its stock markets behave. It is generally assumed that international investing is riskier than domestic investing. This can be true or not, depending on the specific stocks chosen and the holding period over which they are owned. Another assumption you need to question is whether multinational companies' stocks provide all the international diversification you may want. They may or may not, depending on the company. A portfolio that contains U.S. companies with big international operations doesn't necessarily reap the benefits of global diversification. When you buy a stock, you are only indirectly buying its future sales and revenues. More immediately, you are buying the market's perception of the *stock today,* and that is colored by perception of the overall *market today.* If the international component of sales and revenues do not affect the stock price, then your assumption is probably incorrect. In fact, many multinational companies' stocks behave like domestic companies' stocks. For instance, Figures 1.1 and 1.2 show that Coca-Cola and McDonald's, both major multinationals, trade very much in line with the S&P 500.

Global firms may or may not have steadier sales and revenues because of their international operations. They have an additional risk not shared by purely domestic companies: currency risk (which is covered

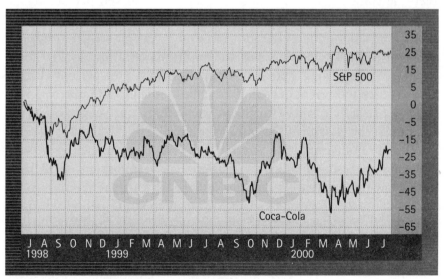

Figure 1.1   Coca–Cola and the S&P 500 (% change)
Data: Reuters DataLink; chart: Metastock.

Figure 1.2   McDonald's and the S&P 500 (% change)

Data: Reuters DataLink; chart: Metastock.

in detail in Chapter 7). For example, a company selling into Japan has seen the value of the yen bounce from 120 to 80 yen per dollar and back again. American shareholders care only about the consolidated (company-wide) dollar value of sales and revenues. In 1995, when it took only 80 yen to buy a dollar, the results of operations looked good. By May 1999, it took 120 yen to buy a dollar—a 50 percent change. Even if sales and revenues were identical to those in 1995, the company *appeared* to have results 50 percent worse than four years earlier, just because of the change in the exchange rate.

It gets more complicated, too. The 50 percent reduction in sales and revenues is stated only on a translation or accounting basis. A Japanese company may have bought its dollars for future remittance to the parent company in advance of the actual accounting period when the translation effect was to take place. Such a currency hedge affects the true cash flow of the company. Some international companies excel at hedging currency risk, and some don't bother to try, on the premise that "Nobody can forecast exchange rates." Unless you read the small print in the footnotes of the annual report, you won't know whether you are taking a desirable or undesirable risk when you buy a multi-national company's stock.

ARE YOU WILLING TO INVEST IN EMERGING MARKETS AND GROWTH REGIONS?

Business cycles come and business cycles go. When South Africa is booming, Thailand may be tanking. As of mid-2000, Europe claimed that it was entering a period of outstanding growth that would outshine growth in the United States for many years to come. In contrast, Japan, which has been in a recession since its stock market crashed in 1990, seems to be tentatively coming out of it as of mid-2000. Even though the United States has not had a recession in a decade, one is always possible. By diversifying your portfolio to the growth regions of the world, you can benefit from the observation that corporate earnings are generally highly correlated with national gross domestic product (GDP) growth.

Alternatively, if the United States does not experience a recession and the consumer/capital goods boom continues, foreign suppliers may be a good investment. For example, the French luxury-goods company LVMH (LVMHY) has a lock on Champagne, Cognac, and the Louis Vuitton trademark, among others. LVMH is traded on the Nasdaq in the United States and has considerably higher volatility than the S&P 500 (see Figure 1.3), but it is a truly international company. It remains to be seen whether it has immunity from a general slowdown in the United States.

The opportunity to buy individual foreign stocks allows you to give free rein to your ideas about the way the world works. Diversification is a good thing in its own right, but smart diversification will allow you to pick out the global winners, not just the American ones. If you think the U.S. market will turn down but you want to be invested in stocks, you may choose a higher proportion of foreign stocks for your portfolio. On the other hand, if you think the U.S. market will see significant growth, you may choose a lower proportion of foreign stocks from among those that are less richly priced.

Figure 1.3   LVMH and the S&P 500 (% change)
Data: Reuters DataLink; chart: Metastock.

Mark Mobius, head of the Franklin Templeton Emerging Markets Fund, says in his book, *Passport to Profits* (Warner Books, 1999), that he travels 250 days every year seeking stock bargains. His first rule of investing is that "your best protection is diversification." In all markets, he is looking for "FELT," which stands for markets that are fair, efficient, liquid, and transparent. Mobius also points out that the best profits are to be made after a crisis or market crash, and quotes Sir John Templeton: "If you buy the same securities as other people, you'll get the same results as other people" (p. 43). Think outside the box; be contrarian—but plan for a five-year holding period, he advises, to let your stock choices mature.

CAN YOU AVOID THE TRAP OF "IRRATIONAL EXUBERANCE"?

Foreign stocks are not only an untapped opportunity; they may offer protection from a meltdown in the United States. In December 1996,

Alan Greenspan questioned whether the U.S. stock market was in the grip of "irrational exuberance," a phrase inspired by Yale economist Robert Shiller, whose book with that title was published in May 2000. As of mid-2000, this was yet another complaint, complete with impressive charts and statistics, that the market was overvalued and would crash. Speculation was rife, and speculation is defined as mindless crowd-following. Endless talk of speculative gains can induce normally levelheaded people to succumb to greed and to inject ever more money into the market. As soon as a really big scare comes along, the tight feedback loop will cause an even faster market drop as fear becomes the dominant emotion.

Even if we agree that what existed was a speculative mania that created a full-blown bubble, we don't have to agree that a general market crash would be the only outcome. For the sake of argument, though, let's say that the U.S. market enters a downward trend. Do foreign stocks offer a refuge? Yes; but not on an index basis. A comparison of the Dow Jones World Index Ex-U.S. with the Wilshire 5000 (the broadest U.S. market index) shows that the rest of the world follows the U.S. sentiment lead (see Figure 1.4).

The implication is that to diversify into the international arena, you need to scan the stock universe for individual candidates that match your desired profile, and the first criterion on your profile list should be a negative correlation with the overall U.S. market.

ARE YOU A VALUE INVESTOR OR A MOMENTUM INVESTOR?

The demise in March 2000 of "value investor" Julian Robertson's Tiger Management hedge fund renewed debate about value investing vs. momentum investing. Robertson said he was withdrawing "from an irrational market where earnings and price considerations take a backseat to mouse clicks and momentum." It is a bit frightening when a major investor makes such a statement. How can we expect to succeed as value investors if this famous hedge fund manager was not able to? In 1999 and into early 2000 it seemed as though the only way to succeed was as a momentum investor—the antithesis of value investing.

Figure 1.4   Wilshire 5000 and the Dow Jones World Index Ex-U.S. (% change)
Data: Reuters DataLink; chart: Metastock.

The key to understanding this situation is to understand the value investor's assumptions. First, the value investor assumes that a high-value stock will yield a normal return that is close to the average return over the past x number of years. If the market returns 15 to 20 percent per annum, then a value stock should return 15 to 20 percent per annum. The mistake in clinging to value stocks in 1998–1999 was to miss the simple fact that they faced a new class of competitors for the pool of investment money that was available to the stock market at large. It was a growing pool, but the emergence of the new class reduced the share that could and would be allocated to value stocks.

Some value investors missed the emergence of the new competitors for capital, for two reasons. First, many of the stocks were new. They were real initial public offerings (IPOs), and, by definition, they were excluded from the value investors' universe. No past earnings, no past price performance—no value. And it is true that IPOs are high-risk. Almost 20 percent fail and are no longer around after five years. Only about 30 percent outperform the market after five years.

The second thing the traditional value player probably missed was the importance of the electronic revolution. "Just a fad," many scoffed. When the stock of new or even already established companies took off to the moon, they called it a mania. To price a stock because it offers hope of future earnings is just not the right earnings ratio to use, they believe. And yet, supposedly inflated earnings expectations have in many cases been met, because the electronic revolution is the real thing, on a par with the railroad, the radio, and other major inventions. Fed Chairman Greenspan has likened the effect of the new information and communications technologies to the effect of the telegraph around the time of the Civil War.

The arrival of new-age companies reduced the expected return of old-economy companies. It may not have diminished their intrinsic value, but it did divert capital and the stock market return reasonably to be expected. This drives home the point that expected return is a forecast, not a given that can be taken for granted. Investors can know that a new company has become a value company only after the fact. To detect value while the technological change is taking place requires imagination and a futurist outlook.

Some value investors assumed the electronic revolution to be a fad and may have clung to an outdated idea of what their return should be. They also may have underestimated the risk they were taking in their value stocks. The expected return, based on past average returns, includes periods of loss. They are vital components of the risk measurement process.

Loss may be normal (consistent with the historical pattern), or abnormal (higher than the historical pattern). Investors who hew to the assumption of a long holding period can expect minor, temporary losses from time to time. When those losses become extraordinary—higher than normal—something unexpected is happening. Abnormal losses are the market's way of telling you that you may have made a mistake. "Value" is not fixed forever, and you need to beware a buggy-whip mentality in the age of the automobile.

In the face of an abnormal loss, you have two choices. If you prefer a long holding period (and are sure you don't have a buggy-whip company), then you will have to reduce your expected return. Individual investors can do this, with varying degrees of pain. Professional fund managers have a harder time explaining to their clients that their expectations of gain should now be reduced from past levels because the manager prefers to stick with old-value companies.

Alternatively, when an old-value company disappoints on the downside, you can simply get out. Investment success requires a cold-hearted estimation of expected return—by definition, a number that will happen in the future, whatever its history—and of risk. When either one changes dramatically, you should probably rethink your assumptions. The same thing happens if your Widget Company stock makes 20 percent in one week instead of one year. On the basis of risk and return, the thing to do is "take profit." You have achieved your expected return. More to the point, you have achieved the return that can be expected from this stock, as you yourself determined only a week ago.

This leaves you with at least two problems. The first is a lifestyle problem rather than an investment problem. It takes time and energy to research the next investment that will give you the next 20 percent, and you may prefer to expend that time and energy on other activities. In economists' jargon, you may get less "utility" from researching investments than you get from (say) painting. The second problem is that now you have to reconsider your entire portfolio, not just replacing the one stock that gave you a big loss or a big gain. If a loss, do you now buy a riskier stock with a higher expected return, to try to make up the loss? If it was a gain, do you now buy a less risky stock to protect the gain?

The distinction between "value investing" and "momentum investing" is not a false one, but we have a tendency to attribute to value investments a longer holding period than they may warrant, given rapid changes in the environment. Momentum investments have, in many cases, transformed themselves into value investments because of those same changes. Trading and investing are dynamic processes, and you should be watchful of big-picture developments so that your actual risk and return do not get out of sync with your expected risk and return.

In summing up, new technologies always come along to replace old ones. When these new companies seize the imagination of the public, the market typically bids up their stock prices well beyond the norm, judging by P/E and other conventional measures. Some of the new technology companies are successful and do catch up to outsized earnings estimates, and others fail. The individual investor faces the problem of whether to jump on the bandwagon. There is no single correct answer, since by definition we don't have historical performance to use as a guide. In fact, the emergence of hot new companies will subtract from the historical risk-and-return performance of established companies in ways we cannot foresee and measure. Economics historian Joseph Schumpeter called capitalism a process of creative destruction. This phrase has become very popular—but we tend to neglect the "destruction" part at the same time we celebrate the "creative" part. Contrasts are not always as black-and-white as the buggy whip example; there is also the cruelty of competition. Hardly anyone today remembers the Hudson Automobile Company.

KEEP IN MIND YOUR ULTIMATE GOAL: HIGH RETURN ON YOUR INVESTMENTS

The transformation of the investment environment empowers you to be flexible in your decisions if you are well-organized and clear-thinking. What are you really looking for? You are not looking to trade outside regular U.S. market hours simply because you can; you are looking for buying opportunities. You are not buying Japanese stocks; you are looking for great value in a larger universe. You are not looking for the best three stocks in the tech sector; you are looking to get a specific return. You are not looking to "participate" in biotech; you are looking for securities that will give you a return commensurate with the risk you want to take. You seek a specific return for a specific risk over an unknown holding period regardless of whether the investment vehicle is Cisco (CSCO), soybeans, or Swiss francs. In the August 2000 issue of *Smart Money* magazine, Roger Lowenstein points out that Bill

Miller, of Legg Mason Value Trust, has been a long-term superior performer not because he was a tech investor, but because he saw a bargain. To quote Lowenstein, "The best investments are made when someone sees a bargain. It is that simple." We now have a larger universe in which to seek bargains.

The starting point for investing is not the fundamental or momentum characteristics of a security. It's not market segment, product, management, earnings, or ratios. It's the expected return for a given level of risk, or the expected risk for a given level of return. This doesn't mean you shouldn't learn about these things; you should. But, first think about expected return and its associated risk.

There's a valid reason for this sequence. All we can know for sure is the historical record. When an analyst predicts an extraordinary return, he or she can't tell you the downside risk at the same time because there's no way to know what it is—for you. Risk depends on the holding period. If the expected holding period is five years, the appropriate risk measure is an annual one. If the expected holding period is one week, the measure is the average weekly risk, not annualized. Moreover, if you are using leverage, statistical risk is increased by the amount of the leverage. You need a higher expected return to offset the extra risk of catastrophic loss when you are leveraged.

With new securities that have little or no track record, the best tactic is to impute a risk factor. Common sense is handy. The evolved trader does not accept an estimate of extraordinary future return without also factoring in high risk—which, by definition, dictates that the holding period will be less than forever. This knowledge liberates the trader from all kinds of traditional assumptions and irrelevant information. After all, you cannot be led down the wrong path if you determine the known risks and compute an educated guess of probable risks.

The evolved trader is indifferent between a bundle of securities in East Asia and another bundle from Europe or the United States with the identical risk–return characteristics. If you view the investment process in this light, you become aware of an infinite number of equally valid, high-value portfolios for any single risk–return profile. None of them assumes a holding period of forever.

SUMMING UP

Because 24/7 broadens your world of opportunities it also exposes you to more risk (as we'll see throughout this book). In a 24/7 world it is even more important for you to review how you invest and your choice of investments—to identify your expected return and your holding period ahead of buying a stock. Today investors must hone in on risk. And you have choices—to take on the risk (and the potential reward) yourself by "doing it yourself," or to invest with the pros. Diversification may lessen your risk and increase your rewards—or not. Ultimately, if you keep your eye on the bottom line—a high return on your investments—you will be able to navigate the 24/7 markets more easily.

To find opportunity, you must first understand the basic mechanics of the electronic world available to you, whether U.S.-based or global, and the pros and cons of venturing 24/7 which we'll now examine as we look at the extended hours marketplace and electronic trading.

As the name implies, "24/7 trading" means that your trading need not be confined to regular U.S. market hours. During the hours when the U.S. markets are closed, markets in other parts of the world are working. Even within the United States, Wall Street is closing when workers in San Francisco are walking out the door to grab a late lunch. And Tokyo's population (but probably not its traders) sleeps through the entire regular hours of the New York Stock Exchange, 9:30 A.M. to 4:00 P.M. Eastern time.

Until recently, when companies released earnings and other announcements after the New York close, brokers and other professionals could buy and sell "off the exchange" in response, but this privilege was not available to the general public. With the advent of electronic communication networks (ECNs), trading can be done around the clock, on any day, by private investors.

This chapter describes ECNs—what they are, what they are not, and how they can be utilized in trading U.S. and foreign stocks worldwide. We will also touch on the key issue to successful "around the clock, around the world" trading, electronic or otherwise.

HOW ELECTRONIC COMMUNICATIONS NETWORKS (ECNs) FACILITATE 24/7 TRADING

"The telegraph is ruining our business." This was the lament of James Rothschild in 1851, after the Dover–Calais cable was laid and connected

England with the Continent. He complained that people were working much more, now that "everyone can get the news." They could even open and close a trade on the same day! We've obviously come a long way since the telegraph revolutionized communication in the 1800s. The Internet created the next dramatic revolution in worldwide, real-time, virtually instantaneous communication.

The U.S. stock market is efficient in incorporating new information into prices. Earnings—expected, **whispered,** and actual—are the main focus, but other events make their way into prices, too: mergers, FDA approvals, top management changes, lawsuits, new product launches, and similar developments. (Note that in the United States, companies are legally forbidden to issue earnings estimates, while in Japan and some other countries they are *required* to issue earnings estimates. Whispernumber.com draws its whisper numbers

> ▶ **whisper number**
>
> An estimate of a company's earnings that is talked about, and differs from the written earnings estimates made by professional stock analysts. The consensus earnings estimate from professionals is generally lower than the whisper number.

from sources outside the professional analyst community as well as from inside it, and notes that when the actual number exceeds the whisper number, the stock rises significantly three times out of four. Indirectly related to the whisper number phenomenon is a ruling by the SEC, in the fall of 2000, that companies can no longer discuss the results of operations exclusively with professional analysts in meetings and conference calls without making the information available to the general public at the same time.) Some other countries are not as efficient in disseminating fresh information. Often, they do not see the same immediate response in stock prices because they don't have the breadth and depth of market participation that are available in the United States. Individual investors in foreign stocks therefore have an opportunity to evaluate the news before everybody and his brother appears to jump on it. When the information pertains to a country in which the market happens to be closed at the moment, the individual investor may be able to trade the stock from the United States anyway. This capability is still very limited but is growing.

ECNs started to take over from the telex in 1969, when Instinet (now owned by Reuters) came on the scene. The Nasdaq itself, founded in 1971, is based on its own ECN. (More on the Nasdaq later in this chapter.) The difference today is that individuals have access to ECNs.

It's important to know what an ECN is and what it isn't. An ECN is an automated trading system for equities; it gives brokers the ability to display customers' orders on a screen. Most ECNs simply match buy and sell orders. There is no **market maker** to ensure an "orderly" market (i.e., one without big price gaps) or to guarantee that any particular trade will get done.

> **market maker**
>
> A dealer who consistently makes a firm bid and offer for round lots (amounts generally accepted by market practice) of a security to anyone who has access to the market in which that security is traded.

You may feel that you are trading directly with another individual when you trade on an ECN. Let's say you want to buy a stock. You type in its symbol at an ECN Web site and you look at the list of prices (and the number of shares available at those prices) posted by other individuals. You select the best price and place your order. In this instance, it is a "market order" because you are trading right this instant and you are accepting the market price you have selected. It is a "market price" because the counterparty (the seller) is willing to do the trade this instant. Within seconds, you receive a confirmation that your trade has been done.

The confirmation does not come from the individual who sold the stock to you. It comes from the broker who is sponsoring, or otherwise participating in, the ECN. This is not the kind of transaction that is done on a true auction site (such as eBay), where the site provides the electronic facility but the buyer and seller are taking the risk of dealing with one another. eBay and other auction sites have rules and do monitor transactions against fraud, but if you pay for a product and never receive it, or you receive inferior goods, you do not have recourse to the auctioneer. In trading stocks on an ECN, you have recourse to the broker.

If the broker sends you a confirmation that your trade was done at the price specified, and later the broker finds out that the seller didn't own the stock or didn't own the amount of shares that were supposedly sold, then the broker must make good on your trade. The investment that the ECN companies have made in their back-office infrastructure is directed toward preventing such an occurrence, and "broken trades," as these situations are called, hardly ever occur. If they do, the investor will not necessarily know about them. You are protected from an unscrupulous counterparty by the intermediary, the broker, but do read the fine print in the brokerage contract before you sign an agreement to use a broker's ECN.

One of the benefits of a traditional exchange in the United States is the presence of the market maker—the person designated by the exchange to buy a specific stock in his or her own name if there are no other buyers, or to sell stock from his or her own inventory if there are no other sellers and a customer wants to buy. A market maker is required by the rules of the exchange to buy or sell a stock for a customer if no other buyers or sellers are available. This process favors the individual, who always has a "last resort" buyer or seller, at the expense of the market maker. Both the NYSE and the Nasdaq have appointed market makers.

The purpose of having a market maker is to keep the market "orderly," so that any shortage of buyers or sellers at any moment is not visible to the investing public. Think about why an orderly market is desirable. Suppose that, by pure coincidence, 100 people want to sell stock ABC at 10:00 A.M. on some particular morning. Also, coincidentally, there are no buyers at that moment. Market makers know that other buyers will come along eventually, so they offer to buy the sellers' stock for their own account. Because they are taking a price risk—after all, they may not be able to get rid of this inventory at a profit—they will reduce (slightly) the amount they pay for the stock. This margin protects them if the stock falls.

If the market maker did not exist and if all those sellers could see each others' efforts to sell, they might erroneously conclude that something is wrong with this stock but it hasn't been revealed. This is how a selling panic could begin. When there is a real selling panic, the market makers are still required to be in there buying—against their own interests. For this reason, it may be a good idea to buy a stock immediately after a selling panic. Market makers are motivated sellers; they have too much inventory, and some of it was bought at higher prices than they can get today. They want to take their loss and get on with their other activities.

ECNs may or may not include market makers. A pure ECN is only a matching system, although ECN protocols are changing rapidly. Increasingly, ECNs are forming links with one another and with both Nasdaq and the New York Stock Exchange so that their market makers may be present. In the global ECNs described later in this chapter, investors are always working with market makers and not with just a matching system.

ECNs are not substitutes for traditional brokers—they *are* the traditional brokers, in another guise. For example, Goldman Sachs has invested in three ECNs: Archipelago, OptiMark (designed for big institutional trades), and Primex (an electronic trading system created jointly with Merrill Lynch and Madoff Securities). Island is another ECN (www.island.com). It was founded in 1996 to provide the ability to execute transactions at a low cost, without needing the traditional intermediaries or dealers. Island started representing orders on the Nasdaq system on January 17, 1997, and now has more than 250 subscribing brokerage firms.

Island, Archipelago, Redibook, and other ECNs are registered with the Securities and Exchange Commission under Rule 17a23, and (as far as can be determined) all are also registered members of the National Association of Securities Dealers (NASD) and Securities Investor Protection Corporation (SIPC). Each has major institutional backing. (CNBC has a minority investment in Archipelago and has a representative on its board.) Advertisements suggesting that investors are bypassing the traditional insider broker club are therefore a little misleading; ECNs are *owned* by brokers and *used* by brokers to get trades done and to collect commissions. This observation does not detract from the tremendous advantages of ECNs that accrue to individual investors.

New on the electronic scene (or at least relatively new) are direct-access trading firms that use Internet technology to route orders faster and cheaper because they completely eliminate the broker—buyers and sellers deal directly with each other. Most direct-access firms (Edgetrade.com, Cybercorp) offer traders software (for a fee of between $99 and $180 per month) and then have a per-share or per-trade commission fee (that ranges from $0.02/share to approximately $15 a trade). The technology allows users to enter their own bids, thereby cutting transaction costs substantially. However, the software is technical and seems to be primarily used by a relatively small cadre of active traders—at least at this point. Earlier in 2000, Charles Schwab bought Cybercorp for $500 million. This action would seem to be a vote of confidence for the technology and demand for it in the marketplace.

THE NASDAQ: THE FIRST ELECTRONIC COMMUNICATIONS NETWORK

The Nasdaq is the original ECN, founded in 1971. Its network is the entire trading universe for many stocks. Nasdaq is divided into two tiers. The top tier, the Nasdaq National Market ("Nasdaq NM"), has higher listing standards than the lower tier, the Nasdaq SmallCap Market. The National Market includes some of the largest and best-known companies in the world. The list of 3,832 companies includes Microsoft, Intel, Cisco, and Dell, to name a few. Foreign stocks can also be found on both tiers. Therefore, it's logical for the Nasdaq to take the lead in proposing the model of the future, which will interconnect all the ECNs with exchanges and thus with the Nasdaq's own ECN in various countries. This creates a central information clearinghouse and vastly improves what the academics call "price discovery."

The Nasdaq model of the future is based on a worldwide adoption of its platform, which will then be interconnected. Toward this end, Nasdaq has been making deals around the world at breathtaking speed:

- Nasdaq has an alliance with the UK's TechMark.
- Nasdaq has another alliance with Germany's Neue Markt (the IPO market in Germany).

- Nasdaq has made several deals to associate with European stock exchanges that are in a constant state of change as of this writing in October 2000, as the Frankfurt and London Stock Exchanges make and break alliances. Plans for a London-Frankfurt merger are up in the air and the London Stock Exchange is the subject of an unwelcome merger bid from a company in Sweden. The German Neue Markt announced that it will close its doors, leaving in question the alliance of "new markets" in several countries. Meanwhile, the NYSE has announced a global agreement with ten other exchanges.

- In 1996, Nasdaq took a small stake in Easdaq, a Brussels-based exchange that was supposed to be "the Nasdaq of Europe" but is reportedly ridiculed as "Basdaq" because of the predominance of Belgian companies and Belgian brokers, and a distinct shortage of IPOs.

- Nasdaq formed Nasdaq Japan with the Osaka Exchange and a Japanese high-tech investment company, Softbank. It debuted on June 19, 2000.

- Meanwhile, Nasdaq also set up an alliance with the Hong Kong Stock Exchange.

- A Nasdaq Canada has been agreed to, and (as of this writing) talks are under way between Nasdaq and South Korea and the Johannesburg Exchange in South Africa.

Nobody can predict whether the Nasdaq model will be the winning model worldwide, or even whether there will be a single model. As the first and biggest electronic market, Nasdaq has a stake in participating in all of the ventures. Note that, as of mid-2000, in its overseas ventures, Nasdaq was not maintaining its requirement that a specific member be designated as a market maker in each issue. However, Nasdaq Japan announced that it will switch to a market-making share trading system in autumn 2001 in order to increase public participation.

Investment firms that underwrite IPOs (many of which are publicly traded firms themselves) will probably also play that role even if it is informal and not mandated. As a matter of corporate self-esteem and industry respect, they do not want to be seen consistently mispricing new issues. Ironically, the IPO market worldwide may become safer, from the individual investor's point of view, solely because of the existence of underwriting market makers. The wild price swings that characterize IPOs are inherent and the nature of the beast. In the classic pattern, the holders shift from 80 percent institutional investors to 80 percent individual investors over time. But traders will always be able to exit because the key function of the market maker is to provide liquidity and always to quote the other side of a customer order.

TRADING THE WORLD ELECTRONICALLY

When advisors recommend that you "invest in foreign stocks," they more often than not really mean U.S. mutual funds that invest in foreign stocks (as mentioned in Chapter 1 and discussed in more detail in Chapter 8). Until the beginning of the year 2000, that was the most reasonable way to do foreign investments for virtually all individuals except the very rich.

Trading foreign stocks in their home countries is extraordinarily difficult for average investors. If an American investor walks into a brokerage house in Germany and tries to open an account to trade German stocks, the account will be denied unless the investor can prove residence in Germany. If you call your broker in the United States and say you want to buy a German stock, the broker will try to talk you out of it unless your trade is for a minimum of $10,000 (or $25,000, at some houses). Even if you get the trade done, you will be unhappy with the cost. Foreign brokers often charge 3 to 5 percent of the face amount ($300–$500 for a $10,000 trade). In addition, you will be charged a commission on the U.S. side. You may also get hit with an outrageously marked-up foreign exchange rate, and unexpected charges for clearing and custodial services (which are both cheap and invisible in the United States).

Even professional fund managers have a hard time buying and selling foreign stocks. They have to execute orders through the foreign branches of their brokerage, or their broker's "correspondent broker" in each country. On June 30, 2000, the SEC approved a proposal by the United Kingdom's electronic-based Tradepoint to allow U.S. institutional investors the ability to buy European stocks. Moreover, the available issues are limited to 230 blue-chip European names. Users of the ECN are limited to qualified institutions; it cannot deal with individuals. Tradepoint, which earlier was allowed to offer stocks traded on the London Stock Exchange, is the only European exchange that has been granted this privilege by the SEC. One of the conditions is that Tradepoint's volume on the London Exchange has to stay below 10 percent of total volume. (*The Wall Street Journal* reports that it is less than 1 percent.)

Other exchanges are champing at the bit to tap the American market and offer direct ECN trading. The SEC believes that foreign accounting standards do not measure up to U.S. requirements and has made it difficult for U.S. investors to trade directly on foreign exchanges.

GLOBAL ECNs

So-called "global ECNs" arrived on the scene in January 2000. Because of the SEC's ban on direct trading in foreign securities, these ECNs cannot execute matching trades, as domestic ECNs do. So far, two global ECNs dominate the market, but plans are afoot for many more. As with domestic ECNs, there is a certain amount of fragmentation. Volume for specific companies may be adequate on one ECN but not on another.

International investing has always been popular among high-net-worth individual investors, but is still relatively new to the average investor. According to the NYSE, the non-U.S. component of U.S. investors' equity portfolios is currently around 5 percent. It is expected to double during the next few years.

The big international banks and brokers seem, at least initially, to have underappreciated the average investor's appetite for foreign securities. The first two global ECNs (intltrader.com and globeshare.com) are relatively new and independent companies. E*Trade and other broker-ages are now forming alliances and joint ventures with local stock market brokers around the world. The other top names in domestic U.S. securities (such as Merrill Lynch, Salomon Smith Barney, and Schwab) operate separately in individual countries around the world and claim that they will be ready soon. Instinet, an institutional broker, has access to 40 markets worldwide. Separately, it is launching a service for the retail investor in the fourth quarter of 2000. Instinet has not yet announced whether the retail service will include foreign stocks traded on their home exchanges.

Trading Rules and Costs of Global ECNs

There is no guarantee at intltrader.com or globeshare.com that investors will find a counterparty at a price they like, although neither is an auction or matching-only ECN, like most domestic ECNs. Instead, intltrader.com claims to "make a market" in foreign issues, and globe-share.com is linked with actual local brokers in their home countries. Globeshare.com's price quotes are time-delayed at least 15 minutes. Both claim that trading is available 24 hours a day, but quotes are real-time only during U.S. trading hours on intltrader.com. After regular hours, investors are essentially on Instinet, the largest global network. On both systems, investors can place market and limit orders, but not stops. Cost is a drawback on globeshare.com. It passes on local clearing and custodial fees, which can be hefty, as well as stamp taxes. An ordinary trade can cost $250 and up—an acceptable price for a longer holding period if a giant gain is realized, but not practical for short-term trading or day-trading. Intltrader.com charges a flat $29.95 per trade.

Research on Global ECNs

Researching a country and researching a sector or company in that country can be complex and time-consuming. As of the writing of this book, intltrader.com has more research than globeshare.com, and includes the following information:

- Country "spotlights."

- Comparisons of foreign companies with their U.S. equivalents.

- News on cross-border mergers.

- Links to news and analysis at established sites such as Bridge and Zacks.

- Company profiles (available to members only).

Be careful about taking everything you read on all sites as statements of fact. For example, at the very start of the intltrader.com tour, the site says that international investing provides a hedge against a fall in the U.S. dollar—an odd statement, given that you take no currency risk when you invest in your home currency. You do take a risk investing in a foreign currency (see Appendix B for a primer on foreign exchange). Also, the site has a risk/return "robot" that uses historical risk, return, and currency factors to estimate the proportion of a portfolio to put in various foreign investments. The currency component uses the price of currencies as valued against precious metals, which supposedly always retain their intrinsic value. Most professional metals traders would disagree with this approach and would say that you should estimate future foreign currency returns only in your home currency.

Globeshare.com offers brokerage house research from the home countries of the companies. You have to register to get information, including price quotes and research. Most information is available only to people who open trading accounts. Foreign brokerage research reports can be quite different from U.S. brokerage research reports. Not only can you deduce quite a lot about the business environment in the country, but you can get a feel for the factors that are considered to contribute to "value." Note that foreign brokerage research reports should be read with a critical eye. In many cases, the broker is also the underwriter or otherwise may have a position in the security. Foreign accounting rules may be a mystery, too. Be aware that U.S. transparency and accountability rules and guidelines do not exist in many countries, and an auditor's statement in the annual report attests to compliance with local rules, not U.S. standards, even if the auditor is a big U.S. accounting firm. Every country has an accounting standards board or association so theoretically it is possible to obtain and compare the standards. As a practical matter, this kind of evaluation and analysis would be a massive undertaking.

The trading capability is confusing. Some countries' stocks can be traded only in "real time" (when their exchanges are open). In some other countries, you can trade only during U.S. market hours, even if the country is halfway around the world and its market is closed during regular U.S. trading hours. This means that a market maker is in the background, and that is good news for an individual trader because it means liquidity is never zero, as it can be on a matching ECN. To highlight the confused state of affairs, you can trade in French securities only when French markets are open, and you can trade in German shares only during regular U.S. market hours. Globeshare says that these conditions are evolving all the time and, by year-end 2000, it will be closer to true 24/7 trading in 50 countries. (See Tables 2.1 and 2.2 for trading availability at the time of this writing.)

TABLE 2.1
GLOBESHARE REAL–TIME TRADING

Argentina	Hong Kong	Thailand
Belgium	Netherlands	Turkey
EASDAQ	Peru	United States
France	Portugal	Uruguay
Greece	Spain	

TABLE 2.2
GLOBESHARE TRADING DURING REGULAR
U.S. MARKET HOURS

Australia	Ireland	Mexico
Canada	Israel	Switzerland
Germany	Japan	United Kingdom

Foreign IPOs Not Available to U.S. Investors

In a segment on CNBC or in financial magazine articles, you have probably seen descriptions of the wonderful "new markets" in Europe and Japan. In Europe, new markets were formed in Germany, France, The Netherlands, Belgium, and Italy. They joined together in an alliance in 1999, and new markets in Denmark, Sweden, and elsewhere are expected to join. Go to www.euronm.com for a tour, a list of brokers, market statistics, and links to each site in English. These new markets are electronic markets on the Nasdaq model and are designed for IPOs. The rules governing the issues and trading in them are very clear. They are posted under "regulation" on each site. The euronm.com site has news, prices and price history, company information and analysis, charts, and a host of useful information, as do the individual sites. Figure 2.1 shows a price index overview of the Neue Markt.

These exciting new markets have, upon occasion, outperformed the U.S. markets, but there is a drawback for U.S. investors: Foreign IPOs have to go through a lockdown period mandated by the SEC before they can be sold to U.S. residents, and then they have to list on a U.S. exchange (normally, Nasdaq). Your broker will not help you buy a foreign "new market" stock, and will tell you that these stocks are simply not available to U.S. residents. Meanwhile, overseas brokers will not open an account for U.S. residents to trade on the new markets, either. (We

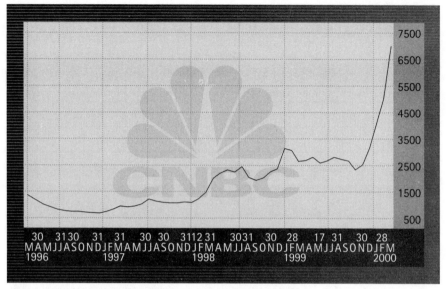

Figure 2.1   Neue Markt All Share Price Index Overview

Source: www.euronm.com; chart: MetaStock.

sent out ten requests for account-opening forms and did not receive a single reply over the course of 90 days. We asked intltrader.com and globeshare.com whether "new market" issues are available to U.S. residents, and were told both "yes" and "no" by each site at different times.)

What's Next in Global ECNs

ECNs that deal in their home country or region abound overseas. In fact, the United States may be considered somewhat lagging in this respect, although it has the potential to catch up quickly because of the size of the investor pool. The Web sites of most national exchanges list the brokers that are licensed to deal in those countries.

Because the SEC prohibits foreign brokers from soliciting U.S. residents' accounts, foreign brokers do not advertise their ECN capabilities in the United States or on U.S.-content financial Web sites. To get their names, you have to conduct research on foreign-content sites. Here are a few:

- www.europeaninvestor.com is linked to broker sites in 30 countries.
- www.blueskyinc.com evaluates brokers, banks, insurance companies, and other financial institutions in many countries.
- www.asiadragons.com is a general-purpose site that will lead you to broker sites in Asia.
- www.irasia offers material on brokers in Hong Kong, Singapore, and Taiwan, and other content of interest. A Schwab Hong Kong link offers research on Asian ADRs, including China and Thailand, for example.
- The top financial newspaper in Japan, the *Nihon Keizai Shimbun* (www.nni.nikkei.co.jp), offers a comprehensive "Asia Web Guide."
- www.economatica.com, which covers Latin America, has plans to start or associate itself with an ECN in the United States at some point in the future.

Most of the big U.S. banks and brokers—including Bank of America Securities, American Express, and Citicorp—offer research and services on foreign stocks. In most cases, you have to be a customer or at least register at the site to see research. So far, however, you cannot open a "foreign" brokerage account unless you are an overseas resident, and only a limited number of foreign stocks are made available on the ECNs managed by these banks and brokers. If you try to apply for a brokerage account at a non-U.S. firm in London, Frankfurt, or Tokyo, you will meet with reluctance to open the account, although technically it is not illegal for U.S. residents to have such an account, nor illegal in most locations for the brokers to open an account for you.

KEY ADVANTAGES OF ECNs

The first advantage of ECNs is that no preferential treatment is given to any trader. The biggest institution or the richest individual investor is treated the same way that the smallest investor is treated when trading on an ECN. Orders are matched by the computer according to the sequence of their arrival. Nobody can jump the queue.

The second advantage of ECNs is that they allow you to see the highest bid (if you are a seller) and the lowest offer (if you are a buyer). In the past, brokers posted the lowest bid and the highest offer at their own discretion. Now, on most ECNs, you can see the "order book" and judge for yourself the balance of supply and demand for a particular stock. This makes you a price setter instead of a price taker, and it narrows the gap between you and the professionals. The top three ECNs (by volume traded) are Island (www.isld.com), Archipelago (www.tradearca.com), and Redibook (www.redibook.com). Type in the symbol of a stock you are following, and you can see all the bids and offers for that stock, including, in some cases, the bids and offers posted on competing ECNs. You can actually post your own bid or offer only on the ECN that your online broker uses.

A third advantage of ECNs is that when relevant news comes out during regular trading hours, you can get virtually instant execution. Speed counts if you are day-trading or need a fast turnover or are sensitive to specific price levels. When news comes out during extended hours, you can get it on CNBC, or the Internet, at the same time as the professionals. If you are prepared to slot the new information into a knowledge base, you may be able to use it profitably.

There are many good examples of the profit potential of extended-hours trading on ECNs. Earnings announcements often provide opportunities because interpreting what earnings mean for the future trend of a stock can be tricky. For example, on July 11, 2000, Yahoo! opened at 9:30 A.M. gap down (i.e., substantially below the 4:00 P.M. close the previous day). (See Figure 2.2.) The open was $104.90, down from $110 the day before. During the day, ahead of the earnings announcement, it rose a bit and closed at $105.50. After the closing bell, earnings were released. They were favorable, so traders in the extended-hours market started to buy the stock. By the time the market officially opened at 9:30 A.M. the next day (July 12), the stock was at $120.50. Technically, any trading after the closing bell is attributed to the next day's trading, so the opening gap didn't really happen at the opening. It had taken place the night before and early that morning, before the 9:30 A.M. opening bell.

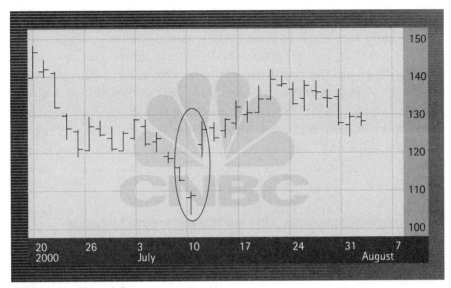

Figure 2.2   Yahoo! Gap

Data: Reuters DataLink; chart: Metastock.

If you were an investor who wanted to buy the stock but were not using an extended-hours ECN, you would have had to accept the official opening price of $120.50. Those using ECNs before the open (the night or morning before) would have gotten the stock as cheaply as $105.50—a $15 saving per share. As Timothy Vick writes, in *Wall Street on Sale: How to Beat the Market as a Value Investor,* you want to buy your stocks when they are "on sale"—that is, temporarily under-valued by the market. Some observers believe that stock prices in general will exhibit more such gaps in the future than in the past because of extended-hours trading on ECNs. This conclusion implies that if you are an active trader, you must get into the swing of extended-hours trading or you will be passing up golden opportunities (or paying higher prices than you need to). Of course, there are many challenges to extended-hours trading, especially liquidity, which we'll discuss in Chapter 3.

One thing goes without saying: you have to know what to do with the information. For example, an extended-hours announcement of earnings above expectations does not necessarily result in a price rise.

The extended-hours market has, upon occasion, moved the price of a stock inordinately, only to have traders, in the regular trading session, give the extended-hours participants a comeuppance. This response is thought to be at least partly a function of chat rooms, where enthusiasts post overly optimistic or overly pessimistic remarks. Unless you choose to specialize in heavily chatted issues—a strategy in its own right—keep in mind that when participating in chat rooms, you need to "consider the source" (which, by the very nature of chat rooms, is difficult to do because, on the Internet, anyone can be, do, or say almost anything, and it is difficult to verify their claims).

24/7 TRADING MEANS LESS REGULATORY OVERSIGHT AND MORE INDIVIDUAL RESPONSIBILITY

There's more to equity investing and trading than the mechanics of trade execution. Brokerage firms and the exchanges themselves are, to a great extent, self-regulating, although they receive considerable prodding from the Securities and Exchange Commission (SEC) upon occasion. Brokers must be licensed, and the license requires knowledge of all the rules and customs of the market as well as an understanding of business ethics.

A visit to the SEC Web site (www.sec.gov) is instructive. In the center of the homepage is the motto: "We are the investor's advocate," a quote from former SEC Commissioner and Supreme Court Justice William O. Douglas. The SEC serves as a watchdog for the public interest against fraud, malfeasance, and outright theft. It has a Division of Enforcement, but anyone who has ever had a dispute with a broker knows that the broker is usually highly motivated to resolve the conflict long before it gets to the level of a complaint to the SEC.

You may think that the transparency of ECN trading (where, in most instances, you can see the order book) would result in making anachronisms of the broker associations and even the SEC. But regulation is still desirable, if only to prevent big organizations with deep pockets from exercising their market power at the expense of the individual. The repeal of NYSE Rule 390 in December 1999 is a case in point. This rule prohibited member brokers from trading stocks listed on the NYSE before 1979 anywhere but on the floor of the exchange. It applied only to stocks listed after April 1979 and thus became of limited effectiveness, although, at the time the rule was repealed, it did apply to 46 percent of NYSE volume (if only 23 percent of NYSE listings).

It is a misconception that Rule 390 required members to send all orders to the floor. They could send orders to any market, including ECNs, or to any exchange of which they were a member, as long as the member firms did not trade on the other side of those orders or represent both sides of the trade. The point or purpose of Rule 390 was to protect the individual investor from brokers. To some degree, its repeal makes individuals responsible for their own protection, which consists of checking the bid and offer in more than one place. ECNs make it easy to see whether a broker is giving an accurate market price over the telephone (the old-fashioned way of trading). The broker and the exchange are no longer the single authoritative source of information on the price. According to the press, the rule was repealed due to pressure from the SEC led by Arthur Levitt, who seemed to be concerned about anticompetitive practices. Other rules exist to prevent "self-dealing," "front-running," and "ramping" (a British term that means artificially running up a stock's price either by spreading false rumors—that is, pump-and-dump—or displaying higher and higher bids that may not actually exist). In a purely electronic marketplace, such activities are harder to get away with, but not impossible.

Investor Protection with Global ECNs: More SEC Rules and NASD Regulations

The SEC regulates brokers, and the securities themselves, through pile upon pile of strict rules. For example, the SEC requires that brokers in the United States advise clients only on securities that are appropriate for their income and sophistication level.

The "penny stock rule" is one such requirement. The term *penny stock* refers to low-priced (below $5) speculative securities of very small companies. Penny stocks trade in the OTC Bulletin Board or the "pink sheets." A broker has to get the customer's signature on a risk disclosure document, reveal his or her compensation for the trade, reprice it monthly, and so on. The SEC Web site (www.sec.gov) has a long list of disciplinary actions that have been taken against brokers dealing in penny stocks, and advises customers to read its *Compliance Guide to the Registration and Regulation of Brokers and Dealers*. The SEC also offers *Microcap Stocks—A Guide for Investors*.

As of June 2000, a new NASD rule requires that all Bulletin Board issuers, including foreign issuers, file financial reports with the SEC. Before then, investors would have a hard time getting even such basic information as a company's annual report, if the company was not in the mood to send it by mail. The NASD also recently won approval from the SEC to halt trading in Bulletin Board securities under certain conditions. For instance, if a Bulletin Board stock is foreign, and regulators in its home country suspend trading in the issue, then NASD officials can simultaneously halt trading in the United States.

Theoretically, a penny stock registered in a foreign country and made available on a global ECN could be pumped and dumped by locals taking advantage of less knowledgeable foreigners. This is outside the regulatory jurisdiction of the SEC, which normally would keep an eagle eye out for such abusive practices. The online SEC booklet, *How to Invest in International Stocks,* states that American citizens are free to invest in foreign stocks if they can find a broker to do it for them, but foreign brokers are prohibited from soliciting investments in the United States. This is a catch-22. While it protects individual investors against international scams, the SEC's blanket rule against foreign brokers deprives honest foreign brokers of American business and denies American investors international opportunities. Thus, there is no infrastructure of foreign brokers in the United States, and few domestic institutions are comfortable with offering foreign securities. Global ECNs have rushed to fill the vacuum.

Global ECNs address the investor protection issue via the U.S. registration of the global broker and its clearinghouse. The two global ECNs we discussed earlier, www.intltrader.com and www.globeshare.com, are fully registered and licensed in the United States, and the trades, as with domestic trades, are insured by the SIPC. Ultimately, the legal contract underlying a foreign stock trade, as evidenced by the trade confirmation, falls to the clearinghouse, which has the responsibility, under U.S. law, to maintain its relationship with the foreign clearinghouse and custodian in such a way that the beneficial owner of the securities is properly protected. For example, Intltrader.com does not offer Indian securities because it doesn't like the level of back-office clearing and custodial performance. Separately, some newspaper articles have pointed out that pump-and-dump is common in the Indian equivalent of penny stocks.

Market Making, Fragmentation, and the Central Limit Order Book (CLOB)

The Stockholm and Sydney Stock Exchanges were the first exchanges to "demutualize"—that is, become regular stock-issuing companies. The London Stock Exchange, the NYSE, and Nasdaq are all following suit (with futures exchanges right behind them). Meanwhile, ECNs are applying to become registered "exchanges." When the exchanges become for-profit companies, what happens to their self-regulatory status?

As noted earlier, one of the features of established exchanges is market making, which confers a benefit on individual investors; it can also, however, put the market maker in the privileged position of using the information on deal flow to his or her own advantage. Only a few years ago, Nasdaq was forced by the SEC to adopt strict order-handling rules to prevent price fixing by its members. One consequence was Nasdaq's obligation to display and execute customer limit orders (i.e., to sell above or buy below a set limit) when a price is better than the one the market maker is offering. This allows market makers' own customers to compete with them, and the predictable effects are a narrowing of the bid-offer spread and reduction of market makers' profit. Nasdaq's customers, of course, include the ECNs, which are generally only matching systems. Nasdaq claims to embrace ECNs, but the fact remains that they have siphoned off some 30 percent of the Nasdaq's deal flow and thus reduced both the Nasdaq's liquidity and the liquidity of the equity trading system overall.

One of the chief worries of the SEC is that the proliferation of ECNs is fragmenting the market so that liquidity on any one of them does not satisfy the condition of fairness in pricing. Both the NYSE and Nasdaq are committed to "making a market," that is, always providing the other side of a customer order. One alternative to the market-maker system is a central limit order book (CLOB), which does not yet exist anywhere. Universal smart routing is another alternative currently being used. We'll get to it in a minute.

A CLOB would show all the bids and offers of each stock individually, not just the ones entered on a particular ECN (including the Nasdaq, which, as noted, is an ECN in its own right). A CLOB would, in other words, consolidate all the bids and offers. This would be the fairest and most efficient procedure. It would show buyers the very lowest prices and sellers the very highest prices in the market at the moment, not just the prices posted on the ECN used by the broker where the individual customer has his or her account. In short, the market is somewhat fragmented by the absence of a CLOB. Planning for a CLOB has been proposed and is supported by Frank Zarb, the President of Nasdaq, and by other exchanges and industry leaders.

When the conventional exchanges find it inconvenient and unprofitable to make a market and they have become for-profit companies, the efficiency of electronic trading may become of less significance than the loss of orderly deal flow—or so fear some regulators. It is interesting that Fed Chairman Greenspan believes fragmentation is only a temporary phenomenon in a truly free and competitive market. So far, the ECNs themselves, whose major shareholders are big financial institutions, are willing to slug it out and let the best one win.

THE DRAWBACKS OF ELECTRONIC COMMUNICATION NETWORKS

The advantages of ECNs are that they are efficient and fast, and they confer on the average individual investor (as well as the big institution) the ability to respond to news outside of the exchanges' regular hours. They do have several disadvantages, however.

The major drawback is the need to check prices on several ECNs to ensure the best price. Each ECN is a marketplace unto itself, in the absence of a CLOB. Lack of liquidity and the resulting horror stories are well documented in the mainstream press, especially on occasions when an important news release inspired off-hours traders to anticipate, wrongly, a big price move in regular hours. There is no shortage of instructive stories on investors' getting it wrong because they made a poor market call during extended-hours trading. These mistakes, though, are really no different from the mistakes that investors make when they call a broker to place an order.

A second disadvantage is the fact that ECNs make it easier to trade online, in extended hours, and, therefore easier to make "simple" mistakes that can actually be extremely expensive. Mechanical errors—buying when you mean to sell, or doubling or tripling the order because you are unsure whether your message got through—these are simply errors and have nothing to do with the mode of execution *per se*. With ECNs, you make mistakes more quickly and more cheaply. Instead of a misunderstood order by your broker, you make typos or hit the send button before you intended. Caution, however, will render these types of errors preventable.

A third disadvantage of ECNs is that they are not efficient with respect to the order types they will accept and their window of opportunity.

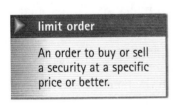

limit order

An order to buy or sell a security at a specific price or better.

At this writing, some ECNs do not have **limit orders** and some do not have stop orders (or offer only limited application of stop orders). Global ECNs do not have stop orders at all. (We discuss the importance of stop loss orders in several places in this book and in Appendix A.) It is important to note here that many professional traders swear by them. In the absence of a stop loss order capability, you have only one way to protect your new position: Watch the market. This can be inconvenient, to say the least. It also arouses, in some investors, an obsessive attention to the market, as though the act of having executed a trade online has tied them to their computer screen. People talk about "addiction" to online trading, and "compulsive" behavior that is only a gnat's eyelash from compulsive gambling. A lesser form of the same phenomenon is the false impression that because the ECN empowers investors to act decisively, they also have the ability to make good decisions. The addition of the stop loss order would go a long way toward ameliorating some of these problems.

The window of opportunity to trade generally opens at 8:00 A.M. and closes somewhere between 8:00 and 10:00 P.M. Eastern Standard Time. If you are watching prices and events in the Far East, Middle East, or Europe, you still have to wait to act upon whatever blinding insight occurs to you—unless you are separately linked to ECNs in one of those areas or have become linked to each of them via a global ECN. In short, you may end up owning several accounts, each for a specialized purpose, which will increase your bookkeeping and portfolio management time. Individual investors are getting greater capabilities at a lower cost but, at least in this setting-up period, less total efficiency.

YOU'RE ON YOUR OWN, SO BE WARY OF STOCK PRICE MANIPULATION

Regulatory and supervisory agencies are in turmoil over how and to what extent to protect individual investors as the brokerage landscape transforms itself. As you trade during extended hours and contemplate investing in foreign securities, keep an eye peeled not only for liquidity in each market, but also for other investor protections. Stock price manipulation—including pumping and dumping—is not easy to detect in the absence of a central limit order book. With the increasing popularity of message boards and chat rooms, those with a vested interest can (and do) contribute to the run-up in stock prices. The SEC has already clamped down on some individuals.

Cutting out the intermediary is a great cost-saving idea, but it's not yet applicable to all stocks everywhere. For example, about 38 percent of all Nasdaq trades occurred over ECNs in the fourth quarter of 1999, but hardly any occurred on the NYSE. This is partly a function of liquidity. "Smart routing" is one new technology being used by Schwab. It surveys all the available price quotes for a particular stock from various ECNs before directing a customer's order to the best one. This is a proprietary solution to the problem of not having a CLOB.

Efficient routing may be in the best interests of the customer, but not the broker. In a 1999 study of 29 online brokerage firms, the SEC found that 17 of these firms improperly emphasized "payment for order flow" (the online brokerage is paid one or two cents a share for its orders). The SEC also found that most of these brokers routed orders to market centers where the execution quality (defined as the percentage of trading orders that were improved) was well below industry averages. As we know, those pennies add up.

SUMMING UP

The emerging 24/7 capability offers the opportunity to become systematic in your thinking, if only in self-defense when facing an overwhelming oversupply of information. As Mark Mobius laments, even after extensive research, including his fact-gathering trips, emerging markets can still throw up obstacles to successful investing, including issues that are routinely taken for granted in developed markets, such as something as simple as whether the securities are actually registered with the country's exchange. Like the peripatetic Jim Rogers, once George Soros' partner and author of *Investment Biker* (Adams Media, 1995), Mobius likes the top-down approach—first find a country or region with the right kind of investing environment, and then find the most promising sectors and companies. The "right kind of investing environment" is not necessarily neat and tidy; to get extraordinary returns, you may have to take risks you would not normally want to take, and you have to live with a higher degree of uncertainty and ambiguity than you would accept in purely domestic investing. It's hard work and the inevitable occasional losses may be larger, too.

Now that you know more about ECNs and the difficulties investors face (both U.S.-based and global), the next thing you need to think about is *liquidity*. All through this book, you will see references to liquidity. It is the single most important attribute of any market. Chapter 3 discusses it in detail.

LIQUIDITY 24/7

In this chapter, we are not measuring the size of the expected return of an investment or its volatility, but rather the expected return variables specific to international investing and extended hours trading. The most important of these variables is liquidity. Liquidity in financial markets is equivalent to location in real estate—a determining factor of price at all times, but *the* determining factor in an emergency. This chapter explains the importance of liquidity, which you should understand and keep in mind at all times when trading. After stock selection itself, it is the key to preserving capital.

WHY LIQUIDITY IS CRITICAL TO 24/7 TRADING

In a nutshell, *liquidity* is the ability to buy or sell a specific security at any time. It depends on the presence of market makers who will always make a bid and an offer on the security in question. Some exchanges have official "market makers" who are specialists, but, as discussed in Chapter 2, we may also deem a market maker to be any party who will make a bid or an offer if the price is right. Thus, market makers may be the floor specialists, institutions that make a market in the stock, or the general public. In short, a liquid market is one that has lots of buyers and sellers.

You may have heard of a situation where "there was no market." You hear of some fabulous stock, including the ever-elusive IPOs. You want to buy, but there are no offers. For example, when the new Japanese IPO "Mothers" market opened in early 2000, this is what happened with the first stocks listed—there were no sellers for weeks on end. The purpose of a market is price discovery through the actions of buyers *and* sellers; you have to have both. In the 1987 crash, the opposite situation developed; sellers couldn't find a buyer as prices fell. Firms were buying their own stocks to avoid losing face vis-à-vis competitors, but don't count on that happening when you're buying stocks—especially when you're buying in a 24/7 environment.

As we discussed in Chapter 2, in the United States, the ultimate market maker is the specialist. One of the reasons for the lasting success of the New York Stock Exchange is its system of floor specialists. They are required to make a market in their stocks, even at the risk of terrible losses. By definition, a market maker always faces the possibility of being stiffed. When you visit the Web sites of major world stock exchanges, you may not immediately find out whether they employ the floor specialist system. For example, the Australian Stock Exchange is the twelfth largest exchange in the world, yet its Web site does not address that question. However, it does address the regulatory and supervisory functions of the exchange, as well as the responsibility of the 80 participating brokers to keep the market fair, orderly, competitive, and efficient.

"Orderly" is the operative word. It means there is always some liquidity, thereby preventing frequent large price gaps. Every security and every market has price gaps once in a while, in the wake of an announcement or special event, but an orderly market doesn't have them often.

In some cases, liquidity will be provided by the underwriting broker, even long after the initial or secondary issue, or by large institutional holders of the stock in question. Such support is enlightened self-interest. As discussed previously, no underwriter or big institution wants to be associated with securities that crash and burn. The underwriter may be suspected of mispricing if new issues display such a pattern, and big institutions do not like to appear to have been bamboozled. On occasion, large brokerage houses are suspected of banding together to provide market support as a form of crash protection. In April 2000, a *New York Post* writer wondered whether a "plunge protection team" consisting of Morgan Stanley, Goldman Sachs, and other big brokerage houses may have been big buyers for their own accounts when the U.S. stock market took a tumble, as was suggested by a *Washington Post* writer about an earlier decline in February 1997 (www.nypost.com/business/2250.htm). If so, this would be enlightened self-interest, not only to avoid having to make good on trade guarantees on suddenly acquired positions from insolvent traders, but also to prevent a bear market, which discourages participation in equities and sends investors to cash and bonds.

We sometimes hear that a government agency in a foreign country has intervened in that country's stock market. This can take different forms. In Japan, for example, "Kampo" is a government agency that manages pension funds, including those invested in stocks. It has been a buyer at delicate moments, and the Japanese government has confirmed the appropriateness, in its view, of providing such support. In other countries, government intervention may consist of halting trading even in the absence of exchange rules that would have done the same thing. This has happened in Russia a number of times. As a practical matter, most exchanges have adopted rules about the conditions under which trading will be halted in particular issues. When trading is halted, of course, you have no liquidity at all.

You can sometimes see liquidity biased in one direction or another. For example, in the spring of 2000, brokers and institutional investors in Greece were reported, by the Reuters newswire, as having protested a speech by a campaigning politician: They drove down the Athens General Index. The next day, when their favored candidate was speaking, they pushed the index up.

LOOK AT THE WEB SITE OF THE COUNTRY'S STOCK EXCHANGE

The first thing to do, when you are selecting a foreign stock market, is to visit the Web site of the national stock exchange. Links to practically every foreign exchange are provided at www.intltrader.com and www.intrax.ch/stockexchanges.htm. Don't just skim, either. As discussed in Chapter 2, you can't assume that the same investor protections enjoyed in the United States are in place in other countries. Look for the specific corner of the Web sites labeled "investor complaints," "arbitration procedures," and the like (an example of this is provided in Chapter 6).

One item to look for is membership in the international association of stock exchanges, the International Federation of Stock Exchanges (FIBV) (www.fibv.com). The name is French and the organization is located in Paris, but the association is international in scope and the Web site is in English.

Keep in mind, though, that membership in the FIBV is not a seal of approval, nor is lack of membership a condemnation, but membership does connote that regulatory authority and responsibility is being taken. Here's a quick overview of world membership in the FIBV:

- Every major world stock exchange is a member.
- The "Affiliated and Correspondent" section includes both the Nigerian Stock Exchange and the Pacific Exchange in San Francisco.
- The "Corresponding Emerging" section includes the Siberian, Kazakhstan, and Zagreb Stock Exchanges, and the Bourse de Casablanca.
- The Hong Kong Stock Exchange is a full member; the Shanghai Exchange is not yet a correspondent or affiliate.

FIBV's goals are to provide standardized data, encourage harmonization of supervision, and regularize clearance and settlement.

The FIBV Web site is useful for information such as market holidays and how many days it takes to settle a trade; more important, it includes data. Its giant Excel spreadsheets offer the following information, among many other factors:

- National stock index performance.
- The importance of the stock market in the economy [as a percentage of gross domestic product (GDP)].

- New capital raised in the most recent year.
- Market capitalization.
- Share turnover.
- The market capitalization of the top ten companies.
- Average price/earnings (P/E) ratio.

Warning: The giant spreadsheets are a challenge to print unless you are an experienced Excel user.

Most of these statistics can be used to draw inferences about market liquidity, and the FIBV Web site (www.fibv.com) is an authoritative source of this information. Share turnover is the most direct statistic because it measures the volume traded. Right away, we hit a snag because some exchanges report turnover using the Trading System View (where only trades on "the system," or on the floor itself, are counted); other exchanges use the Regulatory Environment View (which counts all trades under the regulatory supervision of the exchange). The Trading System View would therefore exclude electronic trading, and the Regulatory Environment View would include it (in places that have electronic trading). The two versions of turnover are therefore not comparable. Nevertheless, some comparisons are interesting, as Table 3.1 shows.

It stands to reason that, as a trader, you will want to choose countries that have rising stock trading volumes. Rising trading volumes suggest that more people are interested in that country's stocks, either domestically or from abroad. If the interest is domestic, it generally means incomes and savings are rising—the amount of investable funds is growing. Stock prices can rise only if more money is flowing into the stock market. If the interest is foreign, it means international investors have identified opportunities in the country. Either way, rising volumes are a desirable characteristic. In Table 3.1, Greece is a standout, with 1998–1999 growth of 228.4 percent. Stock market investing has captured the imagination of the populace, or foreigners see extraordinary opportunities in Greece. Conversely, volume fell in Argentina, probably due to a recession during that period. People "dissaved"; they liquidated their stock market holdings to get money for everyday living. Alternatively, there could have been an outflow from stocks to other assets, such as bonds, or a foreign outflow may have occurred.

TABLE 3.1
SHARE TURNOVER
Selected Countries ($US Millions)

Exchange/Country	Value of Share Trading, 1999 (in Millions of Dollars)	Percentage Change, 1998–1999
United States (NYSE)	$8,945,205.2	22.2%
Mexico	35,172.3	12.8
Argentina	11,874.8	−54.4
Germany	1,551,467.4	4.0
Greece	189,280	228.4
Finland	109,901.6	79.8
Malaysia	42,431.3	58.1
Australia	198,195.1	23.1
Japan	1,675,640.6	123.2

Source: www.fibv.com.

Other clues to liquidity are the depth and breadth of participation in the domestic stock market among a country's institutions and citizenry. (See Table 3.2.) Here, we are on slippery ground; data simply do not exist for most countries. We need to be careful when we use stock market importance as a percentage of GDP. It's possible that only a handful of institutions or individuals dominate the market. The statistics make interesting reading, though. The FIBV Web site shows the numbers for year-end 1998 and 1999. An update in *The Economist* (May 27, 2000) shows that, as of April 28, 2000, Finland had the most valuable stock market in the world, with more than three times its annual GDP. Switzerland, The Netherlands, and the United Kingdom all have a higher stock market valuation as a percentage of GDP than the

TABLE 3.2
STOCK MARKET CAPITALIZATION AS A PERCENTAGE OF GDP
Selected Countries, 1998

Country	Stock Market Capitalization as a Percentage of GDP
United States	148.6%
Mexico	22.1
Argentina	15.7
Germany	50.9
Greece	66.4
Finland	121.6
Malaysia	95.2
Australia	86.7
Japan	65.7

Source: www.fibv.com.

United States, but this does not necessarily mean that those markets are more liquid.

In the case of Finland, a single stock dominates the market: Nokia, which has the biggest market cap of all the stocks in Europe (at the moment). This brings up the issue of market domination by a few stocks. The FIBV Web site shows concentration; see Table 3.3 for a sample.

A high concentration of market cap in a few names means that these are the names in your prospective universe if you want to be sure of sufficient market liquidity to buy at a fair price and sell, anytime you choose, at a fair price. Sometimes the universe of such stocks is shockingly low—your choices are limited to only a few names. In Australia, for example, the top ten companies account for 45.5 percent of the

TABLE 3.3
CONCENTRATION OF MARKET CAP IN TOP TEN STOCKS
Selected Countries, 1999

Country	Top Ten Stocks' Capitalization as a Percentage of Total Market Cap
United States (NYSE)	22.7%
Mexico	54.1
Argentina (Buenos Aires)	76.3
Germany (Deutsche Börse)	53.5
Greece	34.1
Finland	87.4
Malaysia	35.3
Australia	45.5
Japan (Tokyo Stock Exchange)	29.5

Source: www.fibv.com.

total market cap of the exchange, compared to 22.7 percent at the New York Stock Exchange.

INSTITUTIONAL OWNERSHIP— WHO OWNS THE STOCK?

Another technique for determining liquidity is to go to the Web site of each company and check the extent of its institutional ownership. Some companies report the information and some do not. As a rule of thumb, you want stocks to have at least some institutional ownership because it proves that the company is worthy of professional attention and not a shell (having no real business operations) or a fraud. If a company's business is sufficiently good to warrant institutional ownership, it usually means that the institution has performed "due diligence." It has verified that the financial statements have been audited by a reputable auditor and were found to be accurate and acceptable, and other measures. In most cases, the institution will visit the company and literally check such items as how big and appropriate the premises are, whether the number of employees is as reported, and, sometimes, whether the inventory and work-in-progress are consistent with the financial statements. Institutional investors are usually working under rules and regulations that impose on them a "fiduciary responsibility" to make "prudent" investments on behalf of those who have entrusted their money to the institution.

In the United States, the United Kingdom, Europe, and Japan, institutions that accept money from the public for investment purposes—and advisors who recommend investments—are regulated by government agencies (in some cases, by more than one). In other countries, such institutions may not be as closely scrutinized or regulated. Therefore, foreign institutional ownership of a stock is not an ironclad guarantee that the institution has done all its homework or that it has drawn the right conclusion. In countries where "crony capitalism" has been identified as a problem (more on this in Chapter 6), institutional ownership of a company's stock is not necessarily evidence that fair and objective due diligence has been conducted. For example, in some countries, crony capitalism is considered standard operating procedure. Banks may have made loans to their investment subsidiaries or affiliates who then invested in the company you are researching. Sometimes you can discover these cozy relationships by checking the last names of the principals of the company, the bank, and the investment affiliate. When they are all the same, you may have to consider what this institutional ownership means. Institutional ownership in the United States, for instance, tends to imply that professionals have performed objective due diligence. Where crony capitalism is found, this may not be the case.

On the other side of the same coin, you may want to spend the effort to find out which institutions do the best research. William O'Neil, in *How to Make Money in Stocks* (McGraw-Hill, 1988), says it could pay off to check the investment returns of the institutions that have a stake in the company you are researching. If they have high returns compared to other institutions, there is a chance that your company was also subject to the same high standards for producing future stock gains. O'Neil calls it the "quality of sponsorship."

How much institutional ownership are you looking for? This is a subjective judgment. You want institutional ownership to provide (1) some measure of assurance that a professional has researched the firm in detail and found it acceptable, and (2) buying support when you want to sell. Different advisors choose different numbers. You can get guidance on this subject by reading interviews of advisors and managers in the financial press, such as *Barron's*. Ten percent is usually considered the bare minimum, but, obviously, one size does not fit all. If you are looking at a large company whose stock is among the top ten in market capitalization in a country and it has only 10 percent institutional ownership, you would want to ask yourself why it is so small. Similarly, a new company—and especially an IPO—will have practically no institutional sponsorship (except its underwriter) until it has built a performance track record for a year or more. You may be getting in on the ground floor of the next big winner—ahead of the institutions—by eschewing institutional ownership altogether.

But be aware that you can have too much institutional ownership. Again, how much is too much is a matter of personal judgment. You may think it is favorable when institutions own 75 percent or more of a stock, since it shows they all like it, but stop and think what will happen to the price if the company reports bad earnings or some other negative factor comes along. All the institutions may go into "sell" mode simultaneously, and you will be the victim of oversupply of the stock. O'Neil says that when a stock is widely owned by institutions, it has already been bought up to its potential high price. In his words, "The heart is already out of the watermelon."

The extent of institutional ownership has another effect. Most fund managers are judged, by their bosses and by the marketplace, on the basis of benchmarks. The benchmarks are usually those provided by Morgan Stanley Capital International, which uses a market capitalization basis to create the country and regional benchmark indices. In some cases, the stocks in the indices are so monopolized by institutions that they are not really available for trading by the general public—the "effective float" is far less than the notional float. The minute a new stock is added to the country or regional index (because its market cap has grown), index-tracking funds rush in to add it to their own list. Conversely, when a company is pushed off the list, the institutions rush for the exit. This can have pleasant or unpleasant side effects on the holdings of smaller investors. Morgan Stanley Capital International has announced that it is reconsidering how to modify market capitalization to put an end to these effects. Meanwhile, be aware that if you buy a major stock in a foreign country that is included by virtue of its market cap in one of the Morgan Stanley Capital International indices, it may be subject to one of these effects. (The same thing is true of any stock that belongs to any well-followed index, of course. Indices are recalculated from time to time, just as the Dow was reconstituted in the fall of 1999. When the Nikkei 225 in Japan was reconstituted in May 2000, the new stocks being added were more expensive than the stocks being removed from the index. This had the mechanical effect of pushing the entire index down, because institutional investors had to sell some stocks to raise cash to be able to buy the new index entrants.)

INSIDE OWNERSHIP—WHAT IT MAY MEAN

Inside ownership is another factor you should evaluate. You may have to calculate inside ownership of foreign stocks by mining the footnotes of the annual report. For U.S. and European stocks, the information is usually available at finance Web sites such as cnbc.com, yahoo!, and others. If the information is not readily available but the annual report contains the information, it's easy enough to add up the number of shares owned by the top executives and divide by the total number of shares outstanding to get the percentage of inside ownership.

Inside ownership, like institutional sponsorship, is a two-edged sword. A little inside ownership is good; it shows that the people who know the company best believe that it is a good investment among the universe of investments. Too much inside ownership is bad for an individual investor because it suggests that the stock will have low liquidity when he or she wants to sell—i.e., the pool of investors interested in the stock is small, and if you want to sell, maybe they do too, for the same reason.

Inside ownership has to be evaluated differently for foreign stocks than for U.S. stocks. The chief reason is that, in the United States, we have a "shareholder culture," promoted with the greatest publicity by the California state pension fund (known as CALPERS), but also by other big institutional investors. They attend shareholder meetings and demand changes in the management of companies that will result in higher shareholder value (aka a rise in the stock). One such demand, for example, is that boards of directors have a higher proportion of nonemployee outsiders. The purpose of this demand is to stop or prevent collusion by board members in decisions that are not in the shareholders' best interests. The shareholder culture explicitly recognizes that shareholders are a constituency of the company whose interests are not the same as the interests of management, employees ("labor"), clients, suppliers, or other interested parties.

In the United States, ownership of a single share entitles the shareholder to attend the annual meeting and to ask questions or propose changes. Upon occasion, shareholder "gadflies" have managed to cause change in corporate management. In other countries, this is not the norm. Several years ago, for example, a big American investor bought stock in Japanese companies specifically to be able to attend their annual meetings and request changes in corporate governance. He wasn't allowed in the auditorium. In fact, during the late 1990s, companies were accused of hiring gangsters to keep shareholders out of annual meetings in Japan. This became a scandal and cause célèbre in Japan, with some companies claiming they were the victims of the gangsters.

Japan and some other countries, such as Germany, are now in the process of reducing or eliminating cross shareholdings that operate to the detriment of the individual shareholder. In both Japan and Germany, banks are major shareholders in industrial companies. In some cases, customers and suppliers are shareholders, too. This has resulted in a confusing tangle of interests. It can be hard to know whether any particular corporate decision is made because of authentic strategic or cost considerations, or because of these shareholder relationships. Among Japanese companies, Sony has been in the forefront of reorganizing itself and shedding cross shareholdings to give it more of a U.S.-style shareholder culture.

How can an investor determine who is an "insider" and who is not, when looking at foreign companies? In emerging markets in particular, insiders usually consist of the original entrepreneur and his or her family, which may be an extended family. Entrepreneurs often take their companies public in order to substitute outside equity cash for bank debt—without having any intention of giving power or influence to outside investors through the mechanism of annual shareholder meetings or in any other way, such as a takeover. This is not unique to foreign companies, of course; it is a pattern in family-held companies everywhere. Examples revealed in years past include companies in Latin America (Venezuela and Chile) and in southeast Asia. In Malaysia, for instance, a 1970s law required that "native" Malaysians (as opposed to Malaysians of Chinese descent or foreigners) be represented in the ownership and management of every publicly traded company. This was an effort to open up companies closely held by the Chinese merchant elite, and has controversial repercussions even today.

Keep in mind that closely held companies are common outside the United States. In many cases, a company will list on its national exchange as a matter of pride and prestige, and it will care little or nothing about the external price of the stock. In such closely held companies, the insiders get their return from salaries, expense accounts, and dividends rather than from share value as a management performance criterion or from options. For this reason, you need to *read the annual report carefully* to find out whether there is more than one class of shares—one for the insiders with its own dividend rate, and another for the public with a different dividend rate. Although you don't usually buy stocks only to collect dividends, the presence of two classes of shares will show you whether the company is discriminating against outside investors. This is one factor that well-regulated and supervised exchanges focus on, because it addresses the perception and reality of fairness.

There are really two issues here. The first is whether there is discrimination against all outside shareholders to the benefit of the insiders.

Some famous lawsuits have dragged on for many years on this issue. Shareholders believe they have or should have rights against the prerogatives of the founding family, and the founding family wants to give up as little control over management decisions as possible. An existing or potential lawsuit between outside and inside shareholders does not necessarily imply that the stock will be affected, but it's logical that some investors will shy away from any company engaged in any lawsuit because lawsuits drain energy and resources from the core business.

The second issue is whether there is discrimination against foreigners. Many countries have such laws and rules, written and unwritten. Within Europe, for example, the French have been accused of making their banks unavailable to acquisition by foreigners. The People's Republic of China has two classes of stock, one available to Chinese only and one available to foreigners only. This is due to a complex situation arising from the confluence of capital controls, a fixed exchange rate, and efforts to prevent foreign stock participation from overwhelming the nascent domestic participation in stock markets. Nevertheless, the net effect is still one of discrimination against foreign investors. This doesn't mean that there are not wonderful stocks for foreigners to buy in China. It does mean that the ownership of such stocks is purely foreign, and thus possibly "hot," that is, ready to run for the exits in the event of an adverse change in the environment, such as war with Taiwan or a major natural disaster. Note that such a view is not held by everyone. Foreign institutions in particular may not be in any hurry to dispose of their stock holdings even if a war or a natural disaster occurred. They may wish to retain a proportional holding in China to meet standard regional index benchmarks, or simply to avoid missing growth opportunities as a long-term strategic decision.

ASSESSING INSIDER TRADING

After liquidity, the next issue you want to ask the local broker about is insider trading. Keep in mind that, in many countries, it is not illegal. You cannot get this information from the national exchange Web sites or from any other single source that we have found. Insider trading can be found even in well-supervised markets. For example, the Paris Bourse has been investigating a purported case of insider trading by major institutions in the shares of Eurotunnel in 1994, according to a feature article in *The Economist* (May 27, 2000). The institutions are accused of selling vast amounts of shares just after a meeting with Eurotunnel officials and just before a secondary offering.

Insider trading is a touchy subject. In the United States, insiders are required to report purchases and sales of the stocks of the companies they work for (www.insiderscores.com). Some traders swear by the information and others note that insiders, like anyone else, need to sell stock to pay for college tuition, weddings, and other life events; thus, their transactions do not necessarily imply anything about the current stock price. In some countries, insiders may be required to report their transactions to the regulatory authority but the information is not made available to the public; in others, they may not be required to report at all. We were unable to find systematic information on insider trading in other countries. It has to be researched on a case-by-case basis, although it seems that foreign countries are becoming more sensitive to the issue. Germany, for example, was criticized for allowing insider trading and passed regulations against it in the late 1990s. Every once in a while, *The Wall Street Journal, Financial Times,* or *The Economist* carries a story on insider trading in a particular country. These are excellent research resources. *The Wall Street Journal* (www.interactive.wsj.com) and *The Economist* (www.economist.com) carry a subscription cost. The *Financial Times* Web site is free but you must register (www.ft.com).

A face-to-face question put to a broker in his or her office may elicit an interesting response, or it may not. You probably wouldn't want to go to the expense of a foreign trip merely to ask that one question, but rather to get the feel of the place.

Another way to detect the existence of insider trading, or of leaks of inside information, is to look at charts. When you see an upward trend suddenly start to reverse on rising volume and then crash on release of some important piece of news, you can deduce that there was a leak, to be charitable. A consistent pattern in the same security, immediately ahead of announcements, is usually a pretty good tip-off. On the other hand, it's possible that many people simply wanted to get out ahead of the announcement. You may never be able to verify insider trading or leaks. Once you know that such a pattern exists, however, forewarned is forearmed.

USING CHARTS TO DEMONSTRATE LIQUIDITY

When there is ample liquidity in a market, the representative index will show infrequent gaps. A gap is a difference between yesterday's closing price and today's opening price. Generally, a stock will open pretty much where it closed unless fresh news, such as announced earnings or earnings warnings, came out after the close. The news usually comes from the company itself, but sometimes news from one company will affect the shares of all the other companies in the same business or sector. For example, on July 26, 2000, when Finnish telecom giant Nokia (NOK) gave an earnings warning for the upcoming quarter, its shares gapped down tremendously (see Figure 3.1) and so did other companies in the telecom sector, regardless of their countries of origin.

Nokia is widely held, but having lots of gaps in an index or a specific stock usually sends a warning that the investing crowd is too small and there may be a concentration in market sentiment, where the whole (limited) crowd sways one way or the other. It can be difficult to know the breadth of ownership in any single stock. As noted previously, you can generally find out what proportion of the total "float" (shares outstanding) is owned by institutions. For U.S. stocks, you can also find the "short interest," that is, how many shares have been sold short. (To sell short is to sell a stock you do not own in anticipation of buying it back later when it is less expensive. You expect the stock to fall in price. Technically, you are borrowing the stock from the broker temporarily, to be able to sell it.) The liquidity issue pertaining to short sales is that when a stock does not decline as expected by the short-sellers, they are racking up paper losses. When those paper losses become large, they abandon the short sale, which means buying the stock—causing it to rise higher. In domino fashion, several more short-sellers will then

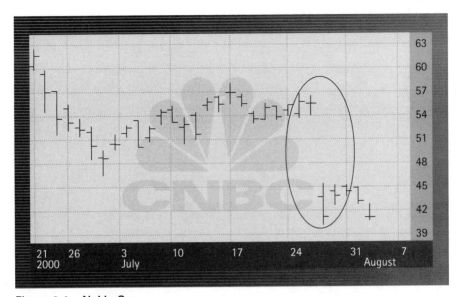

Figure 3.1   Nokia Gap

Data: Reuters DataLink; chart: Metastock.

"cover" their short positions by buying the stock. Suddenly, the stock experiences an upward surge in price. This "crowd behavior" temporarily swamps any sellers who coincidentally chose that same period of time to sell. In fact, long-term holders of a stock are sometimes accused of buying more of the stock than they really want, precisely so that they can force short-sellers out of the market and get that upward surge in the price. This is an example of high but one-sided liquidity.

When you study a chart of a national market index, you are usually looking at the history of major economic and political events in the country, too. You can see the six-year election cycle in the Mexican Bolsa Index, for example, in Figure 3.2. Mexico holds elections every six years. 1994 was a typical year in which stock prices fell, before the July election. This may have indicated a flight out of stocks and into other Mexican assets, or it may have been a flight from all Mexican assets to foreign assets. In the July 2000 elections, the Mexican index did not fall as much as in 1994.

You should check gaps in charts of individual stocks, too. In addition, when you are evaluating the liquidity of any single security, a

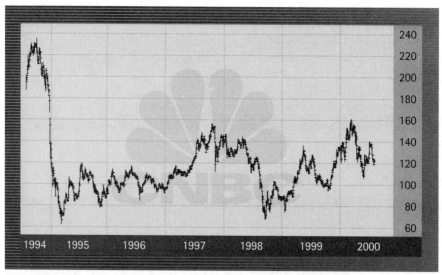

Figure 3.2   Mexican Bolsa Index
Data: Reuters DataLink; chart: Metastock.

useful indicator is the average bid–offer spread (discussed in Chapter 2). This information is seldom available for foreign stocks today, but that will change as global integration occurs. For example, suppose the bid–offer spread usually averages three currency units, and suddenly you notice that it is now ten units, or twenty. If the price of the last reported trade is higher, the widening of the bid–offer spread means that buyers are chasing increasingly reluctant sellers. If the last few trades are at lower prices, sellers are dumping into an increasingly price-picky crowd of buyers. The shorter your expected holding period, the more important it is to study the bid–offer spread.

VISIT THE FLOOR OF THE FOREIGN STOCK EXCHANGE

Last on the liquidity list is a visit to the floor of the foreign stock exchange. This is not always practical, of course, and may be expensive.

But if you like foreign travel, why not visit the countries you may want to invest in?

Every exchange we contacted offers a tour, with tour guides who are more or less competent in English and other major languages. The tour guides are, of course, cheerleaders for their exchanges, and their pronouncements have to be taken with a grain of salt. As witnessed first-hand by many professionals and reported in the *Far Eastern Economic Review,* sometimes you see charming anomalies, such as a state-of-the-art electronic board that isn't used and an old-fashioned chalk board that is updated minute-by-minute; or computers and electronic calculators sitting idle while the brokers perform their calculations on an abacus (Bahrain, Istanbul). You may hear no phones ring and see no trades go by in an hour (Kuwait), or you may see trading so active and frantic that pushing, shoving, and occasional fist-fights break out (Hong Kong, Taiwan).

Visiting the floor of a foreign exchange is fun but offers limited information value. If you are going to travel to the country, better information comes from calling on a few local brokers, including the offices of U.S. brokers in foreign cities.

The presence of a U.S., European, or Japanese brokerage in a foreign market is itself a suggestion (albeit not proof) that this is a stock market with sufficient liquidity, not to mention at least moderately modern back offices and commercial laws and customs that protect private investors. This information is available at almost every national stock exchange Web site.

For example, if you go to the National Stock Exchange of India site (www.nseindia.com), you'll find 82 brokers, including Merrill Lynch and Hoare Govett (a UK firm). On the Bombay Stock Exchange site (www.bseindia.com), however, the "member" page is unavailable. You shouldn't draw any conclusion from that. A letter to the Web master will get you the list. It would be helpful to know that Bombay (now called Mumbai in India) is the commercial and financial center of India, and thus the members of the national stock exchange are likely to be members of the Bombay exchange, too.

If you can travel to the home country of interesting stocks, be sure to ask about all of the following:

- Market concentration.
- Degree of institutional holding and insider ownership.
- Availability of IPOs to the public.
- Other liquidity-focused questions, such as whether insider trading is permitted or forbidden.
- The efficacy of the investor complaint process. Somewhat counterintuitively, you actually want to see investor complaints being litigated and arbitrated. Keep in mind, though, that just because no one ever complains, it may not be because the investing environment is fraud- and error-free. Instead, individuals may lack confidence in the conflict-resolution process.

THE CORRELATION BETWEEN THE FOREIGN STOCK AND ITS HOME STOCK EXCHANGE

When you buy an individual foreign stock, you are not buying the country or its main index, but rather a specific **discounted future cash flow** and other **earnings** characteristics that should determine the price. All the same, you need to know the degree of correlation of your individual stock to the overall index. For example, in the case of L.M. Ericsson, a Swedish electronics and telecommunications firm, to buy Ericsson is to buy "the Swedish market." As described in Chapter 8, the iShare Sweden is an instrument that follows the Morgan Stanley Capital International index for Sweden, which is close (but not identical) to the primary stock index, the Affardsvarden. They are very highly correlated, as is visible in Figure 3.3. Similarly, to buy the Finnish company Nokia is to

> **discounted future cash flow**
>
> The known or estimated cash flow from a security that is expected to be received in the future and is discounted at the current interest rate on its value today.

> **earnings**
>
> The cash a security returns to an investor; earnings can take the form of dividends, interest, or appreciation (an increase in the value of the security).

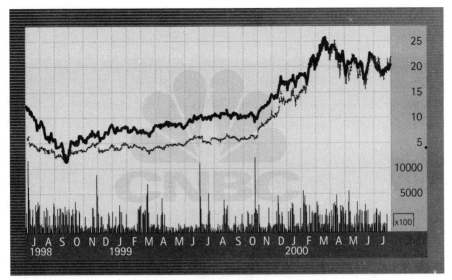

Figure 3.3   iShare Sweden (Heavy Line) and LM Ericsson

Data: Reuters DataLink; chart: Metastock.

buy the Helsinki Stock Exchange (Figure 3.4). The correlation is almost perfect.

The converse is true, too. To buy another stock on the Helsinki Stock Exchange is to become vulnerable to the fate of Nokia. The metaphor that "a rising tide raises all ships" is not entirely accurate. A crummy company will not necessarily follow if Nokia soars, but you take a risk on any Finnish stock, at least in the short run, if Nokia falls.

Therefore, you have to make a decision. Do you want a stock that follows the national index or is somewhat independent of it? The trade-off, not surprisingly, is between liquidity and correlation with the overall national index. The case of Nokia and the Finnish HEX is an extreme one, but it is generally true that the more liquid the stock, the bigger it is and therefore the bigger its slice of the national index.

You will not find "correlation with the national index" as a standard feature on any site. If you want to know this information, you have to develop it yourself. A quick-and-dirty way is to print out a chart of the stock and a same-size chart of the index, overlay them, and hold

Figure 3.4   Nokia (Heavy Line) and Helsinki General Index (HEX)
Data: Reuters DataLink; chart: Metastock.

them up to a window. Don't laugh. This grade-school technique works well enough, if the correlation is high. When the lines overlay one another without much discrepancy, your stock pick is highly correlated with the national index. If there are substantial variations or if you are seeking a noncorrelated stock, then you have to download the data into Excel or another spreadsheet program, and perform the correlation function. If you do it for multiple time frames as well as over the entire data series (you should have at least three years' worth of data), this exercise takes about one hour per security.

SUMMING UP

Liquidity is the most important criterion you need to research. You need to find out about the liquidity of the market in general and the liquidity of individual stocks. The purpose of making sure you have adequate liquidity is to be able to meet what many experts believe is the first rule of investing: Preserve your capital. In the United States, getting information about liquidity is relatively easy. In some foreign countries, you may have to work harder to develop the information, but it will be worth it if you are able to avoid investing in situations where liquidity vanishes just when you want to exit the position.

Before we explore researching specific stocks, we need to tackle the subject of assessing your risk level. Stock research depends on knowing what your risk is and where a stock fits in your portfolio.

CHAPTER 4

RISK 24/7

Before we research specific stocks, which we'll get to in Chapter 5, we need to assess the current level of risk in our overall portfolio and in our individual stocks, and gauge how it will affect our future investment decisions. This chapter reviews several resources that are available for evaluating the risk level of a portfolio. Some target individual investors. Others were traditionally available only to professional investors but can now be used by individuals as well. This chapter also describes the key options and potential trade-offs of each. It concludes with a discussion of how to assess the potential risk of your portfolio over a defined period of time.

BUILDING A PORTFOLIO

The first issue to consider is how deeply you need to research a stock. If you are an experienced momentum trader and you have proven technical tools, live real-time prices, and a holding period of only a day or two, your concern is whether fresh news will suffice to make your trade profitable. If your holding period is longer than intraday, then it's only prudent to perform research to try to get the biggest bang for your buck.

Assuming you are not day-trading your entire portfolio every day, the second issue to consider is how to integrate a new security into your overall portfolio to get an estimation of the overall risk and return. There are basically two ways to build a portfolio: from the bottom up and from the top down. Let's look at each approach.

Most people build a portfolio from the bottom up. They add and delete stocks according to fresh inspiration, news, and research. Later, they endure exasperation when a stock fails to deliver the high returns they hoped for. It's a natural process of accretion as they acquire more savings with which to buy stocks. It would be very hard to sell everything and stand back to figure out the optimum portfolio from the top down. And yet that is exactly what you might want to do, at least in your imagination, as you contemplate the emerging 24/7 environment.

The top-down exercise starts with an intuitive understanding of how much risk you have to take in order to meet your financial goals. Let's say you want to double your money over the next two years. To achieve that, you would need a rate of return of 36 percent per annum. (Use the "rule of 72s." Divide the number of years that you want to invest into 72. The result is the rate of return required to double the starting sum, using annual compounding. The rule of 72s is credited to Albert Einstein, who called compound interest "the greatest mathematical discovery of all time.") Somewhere in the world today, there is a combination of securities and trading strategies that, together, will return 36 percent per annum with the least amount of combined risk. You may not be wild about some of the securities that you would need in such a portfolio, but, theoretically, the portfolio is possible.

The challenge is that the portfolio theory on which today's optimization models are built takes a long-term view. Asset allocation models might not be ideal for the shorter-term, active trader, but reviewing them is excellent practice for training your mind in the all-important matter of the risk–return trade-off.

ESTIMATING RISK: IT'S OKAY TO BE UNCERTAIN, BUT NOT TO IGNORE RISK

When people buy stocks, all too often their focus tends to be on the potential *gain,* with little or no discussion of *risk* except perhaps to acknowledge that a new business is "risky" or a new technology is "very risky." If any one word has come to dominate the airwaves and print space, that word is *risk.* It is certainly central to any discussion of investing and trading but, more often than not, it is used promiscuously.

Risk is not a vague idea that every person is free to interpret according to his or her own semantic fancy. In statistics, risk is *described* by the distribution of possible outcomes, the "probability distribution," and *measured* by a unit called **standard deviation**. The textbook example is to measure the height of all the people in a room. The range of possible outcomes is (let's say) from 4'11" to 6'6". The height of most of the people measured will cluster around the average, 5'9". A smaller number of people will be distributed in the range 5'2" to 5'7" and in the range 5'11" to 6'2". The smallest number of people will be distributed at the extreme ends (4'11" to 5'2" and 6'2" to 6'6"). When you graph height on the horizontal axis and the number of people in each height category on the vertical axis, you get a probability distribution curve that is shaped like a bell (see Figure 6.2, p. 148, for an example of a bell curve). The average or mean is in the center and the less-often-observed heights are off on each side, near the edge of the bell. These outer edges are called "tails."

> **standard deviation**
>
> A unit of measure of variability away from the average of a price series. A high standard deviation means the price varies far from the average. A low standard deviation means that the price stays near the average.

Scientists, engineers, and financial professionals use probability distributions all the time. Your electric utility knows the average use of electricity for every hour of the day in exactly this form. Customers tend to use less electricity at 3:00 A.M. than they do at 3:00 P.M. For every set of discrete events, there is a "norm" and there are occurrences that are rare ("in the tail") but nevertheless do occur. In financial terms, if you invest in a security that has returned 10 percent per annum over 20 years, that is its norm, and it is the most likely outcome you will get. Let's say that during the year you invest in it, that security returns 20 percent, an outcome that was less likely but did occur. But the new most probable outcome for the upcoming year is still 10 percent, not 20 percent. You were the lucky recipient of a return that was abnormally distributed during that particular year. The 20 percent return was "in the tail." It can be a fatal error to assume that statistically abnormal returns will continue. It is more probable that the statistically normal return will occur.

This is why Nobel prize winner William Sharpe says, in his book *Portfolio Theory and Capital Markets:*

> Portfolio theory cannot directly help those for whom probability distributions are fuzzy. The extent of such "fuzziness" has been termed the *degree of ignorance.* A decision maker has two alternatives. He can act as if some distribution is relevant; portfolio theory can then be utilized directly. Or, he can refuse to do so; the theory is then of no use. To summarize, portfolio theory assumes that investors are uncertain, but not ignorant. (p. 26)

What this means is that every security and class of security has its own normal distribution, and, accordingly, its own most likely, less likely, and least likely outcomes. These are not questions of opinion, guesses, or wishes. They are historical facts, organized in such a way as to be directly relevant to your decisions. You will be a better investor if you acknowledge that these distributions exist and you have a clear understanding of their meaning.

A "naïve" trader is one who expects a favorable return from a chosen stock without having the slightest idea of whether that return is probable—or, if probable, to what extent. The naïve investor doesn't know the difference between what is colloquially known as a dead cert and a long shot. It goes without saying that, in stocks, nothing is a dead cert. The closest we can come is the most likely outcome, or the mean. This seems too obvious to mention, but you can probably recall situations in which someone has said, "It gained 50 percent last year and will do it again this year"—without mentioning that, for the previous 19 years, it gained only 10 percent per annum. This reveals a fuzzy understanding of what the probability distribution is actually showing.

HOW TO ESTIMATE RISK

Professional and evolved individual traders know that *they must estimate the risk of every trade,* even if the estimate has a high degree of uncertainty. Moreover, the risk has to be reestimated repeatedly because changes are inevitable. Critical to choosing a risk-estimation technique is knowing the expected holding period. It is important to compare like with like—a stock to be held for a week should be assessed on the basis of weekly data, a stock held for a month with monthly data, and so on. Additionally, it is risky to base risk estimations on broad categories of asset class when the specific security in which you are investing has its own risk characteristics. For example, Nokia is an ADR, but you would not use the ADR Index to calculate its future riskiness when you can directly estimate Nokia's riskiness.

The Concept of Risk Is Popular

At the beginning of the twenty-first century, portfolio theory and its offspring have trickled down into public consciousness. Financial TV and the Internet deserve the credit for breaking the dam. Yet, the "math" is still pretty fuzzy to most people.

The industry of financial advisory firms, brokerages, and the like performs an important educational function when it not only informs consumers about new products but educates them about what they can and should demand of suppliers. No one would deny that the United States today is obsessed with the subject of risk. You can't turn on all-news radio without hearing about "asset allocation." In the past, terms like asset allocation and probability distributions were the province of Wall Street rocket scientists called quantitative analysts (or financial engineers). Today, they are rolling off the tongues of ordinary investors who are as concerned about risk as financial institutions.

The investment industry has recently started to offer information on probability distributions, although that somewhat daunting term is not usually employed. In some ads and on some Web sites, it is

> **asset allocation**
>
> The mathematical process by which a capital sum is divided among a fixed universe of different investment vehicles (classes of stocks, stocks and bonds, etc.) according to estimations of their expected return, risk as measured by standard deviation, and degree of correlation, with the goal of maximizing the total return and minimizing the total risk of the entire portfolio going forward in time.

common to name the highest high and the lowest low over the evaluation period, with the standard deviation and other risk criteria clearly stated.

But forget about the math for a second. Explained most simply, asset allocation involves choosing the percentage of the type of asset "eggs" you want to hold in your basket to generate returns based on your risk appetite. Let's look at how this is done.

Case Study: An Exercise in Asset Allocation

Let's review an asset allocation exercise and examine why assets are allocated as they are and what it would mean for a portfolio. We'll give the investor investible assets of $500,000 and rebalance his portfolio in April 2000. We start with current allocation versus a target allocation for the amount of capital assumed, as shown in Table 4.1. In dollar terms, the percentages are shown in Table 4.2.

We want to ask two questions about the reallocation: why were these specific "target" recommendations made, and did it work either to reduce risk or raise return? Let's start by assuming that the DJIA

TABLE 4.1
CURRENT ASSET ALLOCATION (PERCENTAGE)

Asset Class	Current	Target	Difference
Large company	72%	35%	(37%)
Small company	8	20	12
International	6	21	15
Fixed income	12	20	8
Cash or equivalent	2	5	3

TABLE 4.2
CURRENT ASSET ALLOCATION (IN DOLLARS)

Asset Class	Current	Target	Difference
Large company	$360,000	$175,000	$(185,000)
Small company	40,000	100,000	60,000
International	30,000	105,000	75,000
Fixed income	60,000	100,000	40,000
Cash or equivalent	10,000	25,000	15,000

represents the large company asset class, the Russell 2000 represents small companies, and the Dow Jones World Index Ex-U.S. represents international. Now let's look at some assumptions.

The first assumption is that there is a better allocation among asset classes for the investor *in the environment* as of April 2000. Instead of having 14 percent in bonds and cash, he should have 25 percent. Where does this idea come from? After all, as of year-end 1999, the U.S. stock market was enjoying its tenth year of above-average appreciation. To take money out of the stock market would be to miss the opportunity of more of the same. Or would it?

The answer is very clear to the professional market statistician— volatility in the first quarter of 2000 had risen to a very high level. When we say volatility, we mean that the daily high-low range was widening, the daily open-close range was widening, and the close on any single day varied by a large amount from the close x number of days ago, whether x is 3, 5, 10, or a higher number like 21 (the average number of days in a trading month) or 250 (the average number of days in a trading year). To a statistical analyst, it doesn't matter whether the variation is a gain or a loss. Variability has no plus or minus sign.

Statisticians assume that the higher the variability, the higher the potential gain or loss.

There's a simple way for the average investor to gauge this variability. Look at the size of the bars on any chart, such as in Figure 4.1. Forget direction and look only at the bars themselves. In a bar, the high is the top, the low is the bottom, and the open is designated by a little horizontal line to the left and the close is the little horizontal line to the right.

Observing that the bars were becoming abnormally large compared to their size in prior periods is sufficient for the average investor to deduce that the risk of being invested in stocks was becoming higher. The reallocation advice to decrease exposure to stocks and to protect savings by holding more bonds and cash is intuitively obvious. Notice that this has nothing to do with whether stocks are valued correctly or whether they are rising or falling. It is statistics, pure and simple.

The second assumption—hold fewer large caps and more small caps—is based on the same kind of analysis. Large cap variability (whether measured by the high-low range, the open-close range, or the

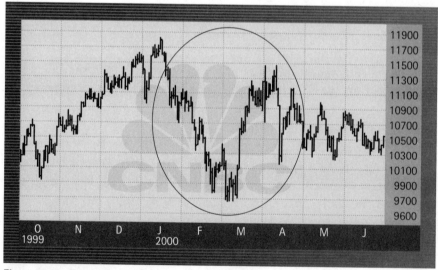

Figure 4.1   Dow Jones Industrial Average (DJIA)
Data: Reuters DataLink; chart: Metastock.

daily closing vs. the closing *x* periods ago) was trending higher than the variability of small caps at the time (April 2000).

Finally, the third recommendation, which was to increase the proportion of foreign stocks, is sound advice. Figure 4.2 gets down to brass tacks and displays the 21-day standard deviation of the S&P 500 on the same chart with the standard deviation of the Dow Jones World Index Ex-U.S. The standard deviation is a measure of **variability**, here over 21 days. Notice that the standard deviation doesn't imply anything about the actual *rate* of return, only the *variability* of the return. Figure 4.3 shows the same indices in regular price terms. It looks like the World Index is shadowing the S&P quite closely; in other words, they are positively correlated.

> **variability**
>
> The degree by which prices differ from the average price over a specific time period. Variability can be measured in percentage terms or, more commonly, in the statistical measurement unit called standard deviation.

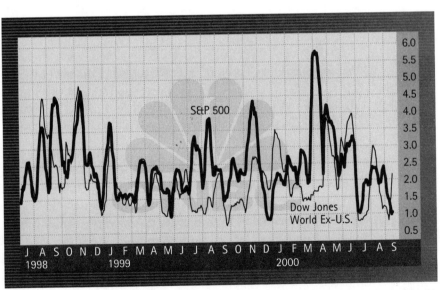

Figure 4.2   A 21–Day Standard Deviation of the S&P 500 and Dow Jones World Index Ex–U.S.

Data: Reuters DataLink; chart: Metastock.

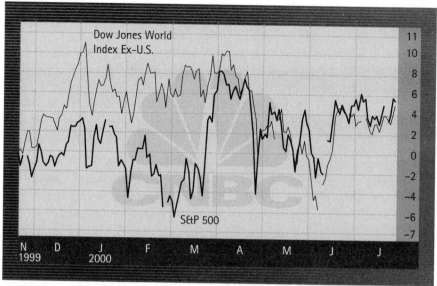

Figure 4.3   The S&P 500 and the Dow Jones World Index Ex–U.S.
(Percentage Change)

Data: Reuters DataLink; chart: Metastock.

In fact, the correlation coefficient is 0.77 percent, meaning that a rise in the S&P 500 will most likely be met by a rise in the World Index, and a fall in the S&P 500 will be almost matched by a fall in the World Index. (A correlation of 1.0 implies that two price benchmarks track perfectly. A figure of 0.0 implies that there isn't any measurable relationship between price movements. A negative correlation of −1.0 implies that there is an offsetting tracking relationship between the two benchmarks.) However, reallocating to international stocks over the longer run should have the effect of protecting the total portfolio. If U.S. stocks fall, foreign stocks may fall, too, *but they should fall by less.* The reallocation in this case seems to be a defensive move, that is, a way to stay invested in stocks while taking less risk in the stocks chosen.

Now we need to see whether the reallocation was effective a few months later, in August 2000. From January 3, to April 17, 2000, the Dow Jones Industrial Average had fallen from 11,357.50 to 10,582.50, or 6.82 percent. The Nasdaq had fallen 14.2 percent, and the Russell 2000 had fallen 7.5 percent—big moves in a short time. There was a certain amount of panic in the air. By August 17, the Dow and the Nasdaq were up from April but still below the January 3 level, but the Russell had gained 4 percent from January and 12.5 percent from April. The gains for each index between April and August 17 are shown in parentheses in Table 4.3.

The result of the recommended rebalancing is fruitful. Raising the proportion of capital allocated to small company stocks was a good idea—the Russell 2000 gained 12.5 percent over the period, almost three times the 4.47 percent gained in the Dow—but international stocks underperformed both of the other categories, so that reallocating from big stocks to international stocks resulted in a net $177 opportunity loss overall from the exercise.

But, it was still the right thing to do. First, some capital was taken off the stock market table entirely, by removing $55,000 from stocks

TABLE 4.3
EFFECT OF REBALANCING THE PORTFOLIO
April 17–August 17, 2000

Asset Class	Gain/Loss on Current	Gain/Loss on Target	Gain/Loss from Rebalancing Portfolio
Large company (DJIA: +4.47%)	$16,092.00	$ 7,822.50	$(8,269.50)
Small company (Russell 2000: +12.5%)	5,000.00	12,500.00	7,500.00
International (Dow Jones World Index Ex-U.S.: +0.79%)	237.00	829.50	592.50
Total	$27,329.00	$27,152.00	$ (177.00)

and putting it into bonds and cash. Money is not at risk of stock market volatility if it is not invested in the stock market. That may seem too obvious to mention, but surprisingly, people sometimes forget that you take less risk the more you are out of the market. This observation supports portfolio rebalancing. The additional bond and cash holdings would have generated a return of about $976 in the target portfolio (assuming a 6 percent per annum rate of return), offsetting the stock market opportunity loss. Now we are really ahead on a net basis.

Secondly and more importantly, the target portfolio is taking less risk than the original portfolio. The standard deviation, which measures how widely dispersed prices are from the mean, is very low for the Dow Jones World Index Ex-U.S., only 6.31 over the entire period from January 3 to August 17, 2000. The Russell 2000 is five times more variable, and the DJIA is over ten times more variable than the Russell 2000. Therefore, it would appear that the safest stock index is the DJ World Ex-U.S., in terms of the probability of a big swing against the entry price. The riskiest, for this period, was the Dow. The investor who rebalanced using this allocation model made a minor gain (from interest on the bonds and cash) and reduced risk substantially, and this was a valuable benefit.

In a nutshell, rebalancing the portfolio reduced risk at a time when fear of loss was widespread. Over a longer-term horizon, it is beneficial. The challenge with asset allocation models is that they are limiting for the shorter-term trader.

"IN THE LONG RUN, WE ARE ALL DEAD"

Asset allocation models used by investment advisors use very long-term statistical information to build the ideal portfolio for you. The central idea is that returns in an asset class will revert to the historical mean—eventually. If one segment of the stock market—the Nasdaq, for example—returned 87 percent in 1999, that is a statistical abnormality. Be prepared to see it relapse to the norm.

The idea that stocks are the best asset class for the long haul has a long history. Virtually every book on stock investing has a chart or a table showing that the returns from stock investing far surpass the returns from investing in any other asset class.

One of the seminal books on the subject is Jeremy Siegel's *Stocks for the Long Run* (now in its second edition). Siegel says, up front: "Even such calamitous events as the Great 1929 Stock Crash did not negate the superiority of stocks as long-term investments." This is in the context of nearly two centuries of data comparing stocks, bonds, Treasury bills, and gold. As Table 4.4 indicates, the average real rate of return (*real* meaning the return after inflation), for the period from 1802 to 1997, is 7 percent for stocks and less than 3 percent for bonds. Therefore, one dollar invested in stocks in 1800 would have returned $7.47 million by 1997, whereas the same dollar invested in bonds would have yielded only $10,744. (Gold would have got you a measly $11.17.)

TABLE 4.4
ANNUAL STOCK AND BOND RETURNS, 1802–1997

	Stocks	Bonds
1802–1997	7.0	2.9
Post-World War II Periods:		
1948–1997	7.5	0.5
1966–1981	−0.4	−0.2
1966–1997	6.0	1.4
1982–1997	12.8	2.9

Source: Jeremy J. Siegel, *Stocks for the Long Run,* 2nd ed. (McGraw-Hill, 1998), pp. 13, 15.

Siegel, a professor of finance at the Wharton School of Business, acknowledges that nobody lives for 195 years. As economist John Maynard Keynes wryly observed, "In the long run, we are all dead." (Keynes made his fortune speculating in commodities.) Therefore, using a reasonable assumption of a 30-year investing life, buying at the market peak in 1929 would have yielded $565 on a $100 investment, compared to a mere $141 in bonds. Better yet, a 30-year holding period in stocks has only two-thirds the risk (measured by standard deviation) as the risk attached to bonds or bills. In fact, the longer you hold a stock, the faster its standard deviation falls (i.e., the more you are protected from a nasty shock).

The challenge with the long-run view, particularly for 24/7 traders, is that the short-term returns may be very different. For instance, a person who started a first job on January 2, 1987, and invested in a fund tracking the S&P 500 on June 1, would have had a 14.7 percent *loss* by year-end. In contrast, a plain-vanilla CD would have yielded a positive return.

Many other stand-alone losing periods, some of which lasted years, are embedded in the long-term statistics. For example, the S&P 500 fell 43 percent from December 1972 to September 1974. To those who lost, it's cold comfort to know that hanging on long enough would have returned the original capital and a bit more. They may have had to cash out of the market to pay for an event in life, like a college education or a wedding or retirement. Stocks are the best investment only if you never have a sudden need for capital.

The traditional, standard asset allocation or portfolio diversification models used by many banks and brokers assume that investors will accept the average historical return as the expected return and also that the risk horizon is forever—that is, the investors will use a buy-and-hold strategy and rebalance their portfolios no more than once a year. This strategy is perfectly reasonable for hands-off, passive investors, but it is not consistent with the goals of most active investors. The average holding period for NYSE stocks is 18 months. For Nasdaq stocks, it is five months.

The traditional, standard asset allocation and portfolio diversification exercises may not be relevant to your holding period, but it is still worthwhile to spend the time needed to become familiar with the techniques widely available today. As we saw, they provide useful practice in thinking about risk.

Resources That Help You Evaluate Your Portfolio

Today's investors have access to numerous resources for tracking investment portfolios and conducting research. In fact, so much information is available through the Web that the uninitiated can become easily dazed and confused. Let's look at the pros and cons of some of the available asset allocation resources.

AmericanExpress.com Of the big financial institutions offering real portfolio evaluation, www.americanexpress.com has an "Equity Portfolio Evaluator" that will give you an overview. As a general rule, portfolio evaluation sites will let you include foreign equities only if they are in ADR form or incorporated in a fund. These are all strategic allocation exercises for the long term and a buy-and-hold approach.

Quicken.com This site has an asset allocation program that analyzes a given portfolio in terms of composition by asset class—large cap, small cap, international stocks, bonds, money market. If there are mutual funds in the portfolio, these are broken down as well, based on asset data provided by Value Line Inc. Depending on the portfolio's composition, the program suggests a portfolio that offers similar historical returns. The assertion is that you can achieve the same level of return, but with less risk, by using a different combination of asset classes. Note that the measure of risk used is the standard deviation of historical returns by asset class, not by specific investments.

Quicken.com also has a mutual fund search and stock selector: Drop-down menus are available to help you identify funds or stocks that fit your investment criteria. You can select from a list of 33 variables, use preset criteria that are based on popular investing strategies, or use a combination of both. This category can be used in conjunction with their asset allocation feature to define (or redefine) the portfolio.

Financialengines.com   This site is co-produced by William Sharpe, a Nobel prize winner for his work on portfolio analysis and asset allocation (mentioned earlier in this chapter). It encompasses your entire portfolio of trading accounts and retirement accounts, your income tax rates, and your income sources, and tells you the likelihood of reaching your financial goals. The initial analysis is free, but further advice on how to improve your returns is not. (The fee is $14.95 per quarter for advice on one tax-deferred account, or $49.95 per quarter for all your tax-deferred accounts.)

You define your personal situation, including your salary and the features of your 401(k). Then you set your retirement income goal and input the details of your investment portfolio(s). Given these inputs, the program simulates economic scenarios to determine how your investments might perform in the future. The result is expressed as an average percentage that represents your chance of reaching your investment goal. Best-case, worst-case, and median projections of the value of your investments at retirement are also presented.

Because the advice focuses on tax-deferred accounts, you don't have the option to list individual equities as alternative investments. This is a vehicle for rebalancing funds only.

After you perform a portfolio balancing exercise, you can check back into the Financial Engines Web site to determine how the forecast has changed after a period of high market volatility (the first half of 2000, for example). If you are not satisfied with this outcome, you can adjust the acceptable risk parameters. The program will then recalculate your forecast and adjust your portfolio allocation. Unfortunately for the 24/7 trader, there was no way to "force" the program to add foreign funds to the portfolio.

Morningstar's ClearFuture (www.morningstar.com)   Morningstar's ClearFuture recommended adding foreign funds to the same asset mix. ClearFuture is a premium service available on Morningstar for $10 per month. Using a portfolio specification identical to the one used on Financial Engines, the two services agreed on 75 percent of their advice. ClearFuture actually recommended adding two foreign mutual funds to the portfolio. That decision was driven, to a large

extent, by ClearFuture's overall stock portfolio guidelines, which are stated in terms of percentage allocations per asset class. Specifically, 15 percent of its "ideal" stock portfolio is allocated to international stocks. In its notes, Morningstar refers to the differing views on foreign stocks, and states that it considers 15 percent sufficient to diversify the portfolio while remaining reasonable to a majority of investors.

To summarize, with the three main asset allocation sites for individual investors researched in detail, we could not add return to an existing portfolio by diversifying into individual international stocks. So, how do the professionals do it?

Evaluating Portfolio Risk: The Resources Used by Professional Investors

Software for professional financial planners includes offerings from Wilson Associates International (www.wilsonintl.com) and Ibbotson Associates (www.ibbotson.com). Both sites have useful information on the asset allocation process.

Like financial planning tools available on the Internet, these offline programs require inputs such as your personal data (age, income, filing status, tax bracket, funding for children's education needs, and so on), your investment goals, and your current portfolio holdings. If you hire a professional financial planner to perform this work for you, the professional will probably be using one of these two programs.

> **efficient frontier**
>
> The single line that connects securities graphed according to risk on the horizontal axis and return on the vertical axis. It shows the highest return with the lowest risk. No other graphed line can produce a higher return without also incurring higher risk.

Based on the inputs, the optimization process produces graphs of the current portfolio's risk/return and asset style. The outcome of the analysis is also illustrated vis-à-vis the **efficient frontier**. The efficient frontier is a graphic depiction of the trade-off between risk and return. It also identifies the best combination of risk and return, given a specific collection of securities in the statistical universe. You can then adjust your risk–reward profile from your starting position. A portfolio recommendation can be defined by selecting specific securities (stocks, bonds, mutual funds, or cash) within the prescribed asset classifications.

Both Wilson and Ibbotson provide databases that allow you to select from the asset classes recommended by the model. These databases are updated on a regular basis. The desired time horizon can be adjusted over a variety of periods, starting from one year. You can use your own asset data in addition to, or in lieu of, the data sets provided. For example, Reuters data (from the Web-based Reuters Data Link) can be downloaded into an Excel spreadsheet and imported into the software.

With respect to global investments, both programs do take them into account in their optimization analyses and include them in their optimal mix. In both programs, rate of return and standard deviation data are available on asset classes, defined by foreign indices. However, in the security selection process (when defining a "recommended" portfolio), the software can pull up only ADRs and foreign/global mutual funds that are listed in the United States. If you wish to include foreign stocks in your portfolio recommendation, you will need to import data that the program can use.

If you are statistics-literate, you could build your own system with off-the-shelf software. CrystalBall (www.decisioneering.com) is an affordable planning/projecting software used by major multinational corporations for a wide range of scenario-testing functions. It can be customized to perform asset allocation and portfolio diversification according to your estimates and using your data. The company also provides education and training in statistical methods. The software is available in several different versions of varying sophistication and difficulty, and is used by some financial planners. You would need to select a raw data source to feed the program. Reuters DataLink (www.reutersdatalink.com), Compuserve (www.compuserve.com), and S&P Comstock (www.spcomstock.com) contain all U.S. and Canadian stocks and mutual funds, and virtually every foreign stock index. The cost for Reuters is a couple hundred dollars per year. Reuters says it will be adding foreign stocks starting near year-end 2000. The basic version of CrystalBall starts at $300.

As you might expect, the cost of most of the professional programs is very steep (as much as several thousands of dollars per year) and may be prohibitive for the average investor. But at least we now know how the professional gets his or her information.

Getting raw historical data on foreign stocks is a virtually impossible task for the average investor—at the moment. The major vendors restrict distribution to institutions, and the cost is prohibitive (a minimum of $10,000 a year at Interactive Data Corporation, for example). The *Financial Times* Web site (www.ft.com) shows the most recent five days' data. The charts (by BigCharts) are based on considerably more data, but do not provide the original numbers that the graph lines represent. Many stock exchanges, however, have historical data. (More on foreign data in Chapter 5.)

The prospect of doing asset allocation and portfolio diversification yourself is daunting. But help is at hand, through a different approach.

ASSESSING THE VALUE AT RISK (VaR) OF YOUR PORTFOLIO

Value at risk (VaR) is an estimate of the potential loss a portfolio can incur over a specified time period, and the probability of that happening. It is most frequently communicated in snappy declarative sentences, such as "We don't expect losses to exceed 5 percent of a portfolio's market value in more than one out of the next 36 quarters." As a risk metric, it is very useful because it probabilistically measures financial risk in terms of possible dollar loss or adverse returns, and can do so consistently across different types of portfolios or among different securities within the same asset class. VaR models were first used by Wall Street financial institutions (JP Morgan and Bankers Trust are often considered the first) as a largely dependable way to quantify possible daily financial exposures to trading desks and at a firmwide risk level across a number of trading desks in many markets. It was a proactive way to measure risk daily on an ongoing basis, rather than statistically, because of the limitations of portfolio theory. VaR has become a probability-based metric for quantifying the

> ### value at risk (VaR)
>
> VaR is a statistical risk measure used extensively for measuring the market risk of portfolios of assets. Most succinctly, it is the amount of money that a portfolio is expected not to lose *more than,* in a probabilistic sense, over a specified time interval. If you said your 1-day, 99 percent VaR was $X or Y percent, this means you would expect a loss less than $X or Y percent 99 days out of 100. Other time horizon and confidence levels may be expressed. If you said your $1 million portfolio had a 1-month, 95 percent VaR of $50,000, that would mean the portfolio would be expected to lose less than $50,000 95 months out of 100 in a probabilistic sense.

market risk of assets and portfolios that has become an industry standard. More and more professional money managers have begun to add it to their risk measurement toolkits, and it can also now be used by individual investors.

It is important to remember that the probability and corresponding loss amount expressed by VaR are not associated with any particular event. Instead, *all* events are encompassed by the model chosen. VaR is not the *maximum* potential loss. What VaR expresses is the chance that an investor will cross the loss level threshold specified; the actual loss can be much higher than VaR indicates.

VaR has to be specifically configured, and certain decisions have to be made:

- *Time horizon.* This will depend on the objectives of your portfolio and the liquidity of your portfolio holdings.

- *Confidence interval.* This is the amount of time (expressed as a percentage) during which you do not wish to lose more than the VaR amount.

- *Data series.* You must decide whether to use historical data, implied data, or other data for your calculations, and how much data you need or wish to consider. Historical data are typically used because implied data are not readily available. The issue of outliers (abnormal results "in the tail") needs to be carefully considered because excluding special events such as the 1987 U.S. stock market crash, the 1997 Asian crisis, and the crisis in Russia could result in very different VaRs.

One way to solve this issue is by using **exponential weighting**. Recent data are then given more weight, which allows the VaR model to react more quickly to changing market events.

> **exponential weighting**
>
> Weighting current prices in a price series more heavily than past prices, thereby giving greater importance to current data. Usually, the greatest weight is given to the most recent prices. Exponential weighting is in contrast to arithmetic averaging, which gives every price in the series equal weight so that past data are as important to the average as current data.

- *Relevant risk factors.* For the VaR model to be computationally manageable, trade-offs are necessary between theoretical accuracy and operational practicality. For example, using actual historical prices for each and every portfolio holding may not be operationally possible. Instead, securities can be categorized into asset classes, or mapped to industries, risk factors, indices, and so on.

Table 4.5 shows a hypothetical portfolio consisting of two mutual funds: a growth fund and a technology fund.

The technology fund's absolute VaR of −12.7 percent, compared to the growth fund's −6.7 percent, confirms the technology fund's inherently riskier nature. If you discover this amount of concentration, you can reduce the overall risk of your portfolio by rebalancing the fund mix. This would be a good idea if a portfolio (or a fund) with a high VaR does not live up to expectations of high returns.

Within each fund, we can also see the risk profile of individual securities. For instance, in Table 4.5, note that Citigroup's absolute VaR of −12.9 percent translates into a marginal VaR of only −29.3 percent (marginal VaR is a measurement of how much risk a single asset is contributing to a larger portfolio; lower marginal risk indicates better diversification), which is much less than that of other holdings, even though Citigroup is the third largest position within this fund. This reflects Citigroup's negative correlation with the other securities held.

TABLE 4.5
APPLICATIONS OF VaR IN PORTFOLIO MANAGEMENT

Account	Security	Position	Price	Market Value	VaR	Absolute VaR[1]	Marginal VaR[2]	Marginal VaR %
Combined portfolio				$407,300	$(43,820)	−10.7%		
Growth				83,897	(5,643)	−6.7	$(2,710)	−48.0%
	AT&T	350	49.56	17,281	(2,022)	−11.7	(1,175)	−58.0
	Cisco	100	132.19	13,218	(1,621)	−12.2	(1,074)	−66.2
	Citigroup	274	51.81	14,196	(1,833)	−12.9	(538)	−29.3
	Compaq	100	24.94	2,512	(515)	−20.5	(287)	−55.8
	General Motors	25	76.06	1,913	(194)	−10.1	24	12.4
	Home Depot	225	57.50	12,937	(1,266)	−9.7	(680)	−53.7
	Johnson & Johnson	75	72.00	5,400	(433)	−8.0	(166)	−38.4
	Microsoft	100	89.38	8,937	(1,063)	−11.8	(596)	−56.0
Technology				323,403	(41,110)	−12.7	(38,177)	−92.8
	Amgen	−600	68.19	(40,912)	(7,053)	17.2	446	6.3
	Broadcom	300	197.38	59,212	(9,977)	−16.8	(3,905)	−39.1
	Ebay	700	143.38	100,362	(33,238)	−33.1	(19,060)	−57.3
	Immunex	300	197.44	59,231	(10,345)	−17.4	(1,706)	−16.4
	JDS Uniphase	200	263.63	52,775	(9,196)	−17.4	(3,831)	−41.6
	Nokia	200	211.36	40,759	(5,596)	−13.7	(843)	−15.0
	Qualcom	400	142.44	56,975	(9,524)	−16.7	(1,599)	−16.7
	Vertical Net	−100	220.00	(22,000)	(13,532)	61.5	1,407	10.3

[1] Represents the total amount of risk for a specific portfolio or position in isolation. The higher the VaR percent, the higher the risk.
[2] Indicates how much risk an individual asset is contributing to the overall portfolio. Lower marginal risk as a percentage of VaR indicates better diversification within the overall portfolio.

Source: www.measurisk.com.

VaR is a universally used risk management tool but is usually supplemented by professionals and investment firms by subjecting a portfolio to stress tests to see how it will perform in various worst-case scenarios. (A stress test is a test whereby you see how well a portfolio performs in various scenarios.) As an example, if interest rates rise by 1 percent, 2 percent, and 5 percent, the 1 percent increase may not have a terribly negative effect, but the 5 percent jump could have a disproportional effect.

In short, at the institutional and professional levels, risk modeling programs are constantly evolving. Entire magazines (such as *Risk* magazine) and seminars and conferences are devoted to this thorny subject.

Making VaR Analysis Easier for Individual Investors

Because value-at-risk software from specialist companies is expensive, it is typically used by banks, professional trading companies, portfolio managers, and corporate treasuries. However, for $29.99, individual investors can obtain a VaR analysis of their portfolio (up to 50 securities) from www.measurisk.com. Measurisk.com is a joint venture among Morgan Stanley Dean Witter, Bank of Bermuda, Bermuda-based insurer–reinsurer XL Capital, and Micro Modelling, a New York-based consultancy. To learn more about VaR and risk management in general, a free training course, *Exploring Risk*, is available at www.riskmetrics.

In May 2000, Risk Metrics launched a new statistical tool named "RiskGrades," for each stock or stock index—an easier-to-use variation of VaR. Like VaR, a RiskGrade is dynamic and adjusts to current market conditions, so it can be consulted daily. It is a standardized measure of volatility calculated on a scale of zero to 1,000 (actually, higher numbers are possible), where 100 corresponds to the average RiskGrade of major equity market indices during normal market conditions from 1995 to 1999. Cash has a RiskGrade of zero. If a Brazilian stock has a RiskGrade of, say, 300, compared to a bond fund with a RiskGrade of 50, the Brazilian stock would be six times riskier than the bond fund.

The RiskGrade system is J.P. Morgan's tool for evaluating its own portfolio of ever-changing assets, and the technique is now used by many financial institutions around the world. The methodology is clearly explained in a 61-page primer available at www.riskgrades.com. It will also be accessible through Morgan OnLine, FTyourmoney.com, sharepeople.com, worldlyinvestor.com, and LionShares.com, and the company says it plans to announce additional partnerships with online brokers and financial portals in the future.

RiskGrades has a lot of virtues. It acknowledges that the volatility of a security must be judged in terms of its currency. An owner of Nokia in Finland, who has the euro as a home currency, will see a different RiskGrade than will an owner of Nokia in the United States or Canada. For the Finnish investor, the euro is a riskless component.

Another benefit is that the RiskGrade volatility is calculated using an exponentially weighted moving average that gives a larger weight to more recent data. As explained earlier in this chapter, this is a critical improvement over simply using the 10-year average employed in most exercises. Because the risk rises as shocks occur and are reflected in prices, traders have the ability to predict extremes as they are happening. The risk recedes exponentially when the effect of the shock on prices falls away. For example, investments in Asian equities or funds are not permanently tarred with the brush of the 1997 crisis. (We'll see an example in Chapter 6.)

The concept of "scaled volatility" takes a little getting used to. A RiskGrade of 100 is set to represent a volatility of 20 percent. If a security has a RiskGrade of 200, you would expect it to be twice as volatile as the benchmark. RiskGrades comes up with this scaling process by taking the market-cap weighted average volatility during the period from January 1995 to December 1999 as a representative group of indices, and noting that it comes to 20 percent. The list is fair, the volatility is based on 151 days of rolling data, and the measure is further refined as to how fast volatility brings on **decays.** Table 4.6 shows the group and its weights, as presented on riskgrades.com after a price shock.

> **decay**
>
> The tendency of a price series statistic—such as its mean, median, or standard deviation—to decline after a one-time price shock; also, the effect of a declining cost of financing as a maturity date approaches.

TABLE 4.6
VOLATILITY OF EQUITY INDICES

Index Ticker	Country	Market-Cap Weight (%) Europe	Asia/Pacific	Americas	Annualized Volatility (%)
AEX	Netherlands	2.4			40.52
All ordinaries	Australia		1.3		13.06
ASIN	Singapore		0.6		21.32
BEL20	Belgium	1.0			15.49
CAC40	France	3.9			19.80
DAX	Germany	4.3			21.10
FTSE100	UK	9.4			15.31
HangSeng	Hong Kong		1.4		30.96
HEX	Finland	0.6			26.48
IBEX	Spain	1.4			20.72
IPC	Mexico			0.4	30.08
KOSPI200	Korea		0.5		34.76
Merval	Argentina			0.5	37.10
MIB	Italy	2.2			23.65
Nasdaq	United States			10.3	28.11
NIKKEI225	Japan		9.7		22.54
OMX	Sweden	1.1			21.09
NYSE	United States			43.1	13.89
SMI	Switzerland	2.1			18.40
TSE100	Canada			2.2	14.80
TWII	Taiwan		1.0		23.99
Total		29.0			18.85

Source: RiskMetrics Group, www.riskgrades.com.

The usefulness of RiskGrades comes into play when you try out a new security in an existing portfolio. You can immediately see its effect on the riskiness of the total portfolio. First, you "grade your portfolio" with a module that lets you input your current holdings and evaluate them against various benchmarks of your choosing. Then you add and subtract securities in the "what if" module to see how different securities might affect the total. Finally, you get a "risk ranking" of the items in your portfolio, whereupon you may feel inclined to go back to "what if." You can also see the historical riskiness of individual securities. For example, Sony has a RiskGrade of 235 in Japan, where the average RiskGrade is 239. In Japan, the universe of stocks has RiskGrades ranging from a minimum of 16 to a maximum of 3,936. In the United States, where Sony trades as an ADR, the RiskGrade is 228 against an average RiskGrade of 286 and a maximum RiskGrade of 3,278. For a U.S.-based user of this feature, the minimum RiskGrade is zero.

Throughout the process, you do not have to estimate anything. You do not have to specify your age, income, tax bracket, or other personal information. This avoids the normative judgments inherent in most allocation exercises (such as an assumption that older people should take less risk). RiskMetrics just gives you the statistics. If you want a portfolio that is 100 times riskier than the S&P 500, that's your choice.

The number of selections for playing "what if" is limited to country indices and individual stocks and funds in the United States, along with a short list of countries—France, Germany, Italy, Japan, Spain, and the United Kingdom. This list should be expanded over time. For now, if you want to experiment with stocks from South Africa, Thailand, or Ecuador, you have to find something on the existing list that is comparable to your candidate with respect to its riskiness. Such an estimation process is fraught with statistical pitfalls, although you could try matching up your stock's standard deviation (or beta) with the standard deviation of a company on the RiskGrades list. (This is relatively easy with Excel.)

SUMMING UP

Assessing risk is never easy—for institutions or individuals. New technologies and market demand have brought tools once available only to the professional to the individual. These risk management techniques will not eliminate loss but they can go a long way toward helping us reduce our risk of loss.

Now that you know how to assess your risk (or at least where to go to get help), you can get down to the business of researching specific stocks. This raises the question of how to find good stocks in the first place. Among several tools that can help you identify potential investments are stock screening and scanning, which we'll now turn to.

Venturing

Around

the

World

| CHAPTER 5 | FINDING STOCKS |
| | 24/7 |

There are essentially two ways to research stocks: read research reports, the press, mine Web sites, examine annual reports, and the like; and (or) use "programs" that allow you to scan and screen the universe of stocks based on fundamental, statistical, or technical criteria. The 24/7 trader will have to become a proficient researcher in either case.

This chapter suggests sources of stock information; provides guidance on researching foreign stocks in Europe, Asia, and Latin America in particular; and presents several methodologies for selecting stocks.

SCREENING STOCKS

As an investment tool, stock screening is at least as old as the computer, but until the Internet became available to individual investors, stock screening was mostly the domain of the professional investment community. Now, Web sites that screen for stocks abound. At these sites, individual investors set up a number of criteria they are looking for in stocks, and the screening service then searches for stocks that match those criteria. At a minimum, the criteria usually include (but are by no means limited to):

- Price characteristics.
- Company statistics (asset size, number of employees).
- Financial performance (fundamentals).
- Technical characteristics.
- Industry grouping.

Screening services are usually part of a larger financial information Web site, and the screening component may be hidden among all the "bells and whistles."

Any screening service has to bring together price data (from one vendor or another), fundamental data (from another vendor), and, if there is also a technical analysis feature, charting capability (from yet another vendor). Another category of useful information is a "statistical" category that covers information on **insider trading,** institutional ownership, and analysts' recommendations. These, too, come from a separate source. In some cases, the assembly of all these different information modules is seamless and you will be unaware of the machinery putting it together in the background.

You will have to examine several screening sites and services to find the one(s) you like. Throughout this chapter you will be referred to sources that some individual investors and professionals have found useful. Keep in mind that new services pop up frequently. But first, let's take a look at how scanning and screening work.

> **insider trading**
>
> Trading done by people with information that is not available publicly but will influence the price of a security. An insider is anyone who has the information in advance of its being made public. This category includes company executives, lawyers, secretaries, printers, journalists, or outside analysts. Insider trading is illegal in the United States.

KEEP IN MIND THAT THERE ARE ENDLESS COMBINATIONS OF SCREENING CRITERIA

It pays to practice with screening utilities because there are literally thousands of stocks and hundreds of criteria to choose from, and the combinations and permutations of the criteria are endless. If you are familiar with scanning and screening, do keep in mind that what works in the United States may not work in foreign markets.

For example, a few years ago, James O'Shaughnessy, author of the best-selling and highly acclaimed book *What Works on Wall Street,* performed in-depth analysis of the factors that deliver consistent market-beating returns. He carefully dissected the performance of companies over a 44-year period, 1950 to 1994, and he quantified the extra return to be gained from selecting stocks that have low ratios of price/earnings, price/cash flow, price/book, and price/sales (as partially indicated in Table 5.1). A surprising outcome was the efficacy of the

TABLE 5.1
THE RELATIONSHIP BETWEEN RATIOS AND RETURNS

	Annual Return, 1952–1994
All stocks	14.6%
50 stocks with lowest price/book (P/B) ratios	17.5
50 stocks with highest P/B ratios	11.9
50 stocks with lowest price/cash flow (P/CF) ratios	17.1
50 stocks with highest P/CF ratios	10.8
50 stocks with lowest price/sales (P/S) ratios	18.9
50 stocks with highest P/S ratios	8.2

Source: James P. O'Shaughnessy, *What Works on Wall Street* (New York: McGraw-Hill, 1997), quoted in Timothy P. Vick, *Wall Street on Sale* (New York: McGraw-Hill, 1999), p. 29. Reproduced with permission of The McGraw-Hill Companies.

price/sales ratio in raising returns above the average, which is great news for analyzing U.S. stocks. But when this factor is mentioned to Japanese analysts, they are puzzled. In the Japanese environment, the way to judge sales is by market share; stock price has little to do with company sales. So keep in mind that factors that apply to U.S. securities may not apply to foreign securities.

Learning to use stock screens will be indispensable when more extensive foreign stock screening becomes available. Previously, foreign stock picking has been done almost exclusively by professionals at mutual funds and the like. With the exception of a few experts such as Mark Mobius, very little has been publicly disclosed about what "works" overseas. And what works in Germany, for instance, may not work in, say, Argentina or Turkey. Some countries don't mind a lot of debt, and some countries do. The only way to identify the factors that are valued by domestic institutional investors is to read their research reports. Help is at hand through services such as Multex. (They have screening capabilities for U.S. stocks with 700 criteria and indicate that they will have foreign stock screening by year-end 2000.) StockWiz also offers a screening service and the raw data that investors can feed into their own programs, at a very low price ($9.95/month). StockWiz also provides the ability to back-test technical indicators. Its screening service, for instance, links you to professional research reports on the securities that emerge from your personal screening exercise. Some of these are free and some are pay-per-view. StockWiz is another site that links to report sites.

Sample Screening Using Market Statistics

One of the basic tools in the technical analysis pantheon of models is the **relative comparative strength indicator** (see Appendix A for an in-depth discussion of technical analysis and offline charting

> **relative comparative strength indicator**
>
> A statistic that measures the degree of correlation between one security and another, or one security and the index to which it belongs.

programs). Just as **beta** measures the riskiness of an individual stock against its class (represented by the index), relative comparative strength measures the individual stock's gain or loss against the index's gain or loss over a particular time period. A rising tide doesn't lift all ships equally, and a falling tide doesn't lower all ships equally. Different sectors respond to fresh news differently. For example, bank stocks and construction industry stocks are both interest-rate-sensitive, but in opposite ways. When the interest rate environment points to rising rates, bank stocks usually rise and construction stocks usually fall. The overall index usually falls, too. The rising bank stocks would have rising relative comparative strength vis-à-vis the index, and the construction stocks would have falling relative strength compared to the index.

> **beta**
>
> A coefficient measuring a stock's relative volatility, which is the degree to which it will rise or fall relative to a benchmark such as the Standard & Poor's 500 Stock Index.

Barron's conducted a technical screening exercise on the Nasdaq and Nasdaq stocks, which serves as a model on what to do and why to do it. *Barron's* used data and screening software supplied by FactSet Research Systems (www.factset.com), which does not sell to individual investors. (Individual investors can, however, replicate this exercise at most of the scanning sites mentioned in this chapter.) The *Barron's* article (June 19, 2000) noted that the Nasdaq rose 90 percent between October 15, 1999, and March 10, 2000, but then fell 37 percent between March 10 and May 23, 2000, before resuming an upward direction.

The first goal of the screening exercise was to find the individual Nasdaq stocks that rose more than the Nasdaq when the Nasdaq was rising. Excluding ADRs at the outset, *Barron's* found that 1,046 stocks—or nearly one-third of the Nasdaq universe—outperformed the Nasdaq.

The second goal was to find the Nasdaq stocks that fell less than the Nasdaq, when it fell during the second period. The screen netted 285 stocks. Refining further, the next screen was for stocks that outperformed the Nasdaq from May 23 to June 12, 2000 (a very short period of time). The count here was 109 companies. Then companies with less than $350 million market caps were winnowed, leaving 59 companies. The article, which lists the 59 companies, warns that this was a technical screen, not a fundamental one. Because some undesirable fundamentals can easily be lurking within it, the list should be viewed as just a starting point for researching these stocks, and not a final destination.

If we go beyond where the article ends and apply risk-averse ideas about the price/earnings ratio (P/E; the only fundamental statistic given in the article), right away we can eliminate some of the names. For example, 14 companies have no 12-month trailing P/E, presumably because they do not have earnings. That leaves 45 companies. Another 15 have P/Es over 100. (In fact, one has a P/E of 889.3.) That leaves 30 names. Eliminating the companies with P/Es over 20 leaves only three, with industry descriptions of "memory devices," "digital signal processing," and "regional banks."

You may not like those industries, or you may reason that the two high-tech industry names "should" have a higher P/E and, in effect, the market is undervaluing these specific names vis-à-vis the industry, and must have a reason for it. We can deduce that the market has less faith in the future earning power of these particular names than it has in others in the same industry, but we won't know for sure unless we dig a little deeper into analysts' reports or original research. Still, if you are looking for relative strength compared to the index, following this exercise is how you get it.

Sample Screening Exercise Using Fundamental Criteria

To learn the process, we used the Multex site to drill down to the stocks that met certain criteria. We selected several criteria, such as inside ownership and debt/equity. There are hundreds of variables to choose from, and you could spend days on end doing this. Table 5.2 lists the criteria and illustrates the drill-down process.

Clicking on the four names we derived, one was a utility and one was an online seller of music paraphernalia to teenagers. Neither was of

TABLE 5.2 SAMPLE SCREENING	
Criterion	Matches
Listed on Nasdaq	4,761
Beta > 1	1,219
Beta < 3	1,187
Institutional ownership > 40%	426
Inside ownership > 20%	325
Sales growth current qtr/year-ago qtr > 15%	223
Net income growth current qtr/year-ago qtr > 15%	117
Quick ratio > 2	60
Debt/equity < 0.50	57
Price/sales > 10	26
Price/book > 2	24
Price/earnings < 20	4

interest, but the other two, we decided, were worth investigating. We could have avoided the utility and the paraphernalia companies by specifying "industry" up-front. We could also have derived an entirely different list by specifying that the company's numbers had to be better than the industry average in various categories. We achieved the objective of turning an unmanageable number of stocks (4,761) into two worth researching. This exercise illustrates the value of screening, which offers a more sophisticated methodology for finding new stocks than hearing or reading about them randomly. The essence of screening is its systematic approach, and that helps to promote an objective point of view.

Using Data-Mining Software for Really, Really Advanced Stock Screening

The application of search engine technology to financial market analysis reaches an advanced stage with something called the Profile Analyzer, from Performance Trading Technologies (www.ptti.com). With "data mining," you can research the probability of specific outcomes under varying market conditions, as determined by price data, fundamental information, economic indicators, technical studies, and market-moving news items. The Profile Analyzer is used by sophisticated traders and by professional analysts and money managers. It costs $975/month, obviously quite expensive for individual investors, but it is good to know what the pros use.

The Profile Analyzer does not cover individual stocks, but it delivers information on bond, currency, and index futures, including the major foreign stock and bond indices. As a sample, you can ask: How often has the S&P index been down more than 25 points by 10:00 A.M. and how much additional downside can be expected later in the day? What are the probabilities of the S&P being higher the next day? Certain economic releases are Events (with a capital E) that consistently trigger the same or similar responses in various markets.

The program allows you to estimate the risk–reward probabilities (before you do a trade), set stops and profit targets, and test what-if scenarios. You can ask very complex questions that combine fundamental and technical components. Scenario rehearsal is an alternative to forecasting. You are essentially asking: What did the market do the last time this happened? The statistical answer can give you an edge.

SCREENING FOREIGN STOCKS

Most of the scanning and screening tools available on the Internet for free or at very low cost are for U.S. and Canadian stocks. Many (though not all) also include ADRs and iShares. Web sites for screening stocks in Europe, Asia, and Latin America are also available.

In the United States, we are accustomed to getting price quotes and other information for free, including historical prices that can be downladed to a PC. While there are many Web sites that give free price quotes for foreign stocks, not every country and security is covered at every one, and so you need to assemble a list of the free sites that cater to your list of securities. Of the global information companies, two leaders in the industry are Reuters and Bloomberg. At both their Web sites you get limited quotes and information. At Reuters.com, for example, there is a short list of foreign exchanges (Hong Kong is represented, but not Tokyo). Company news and data are also limited, although you can draw a chart with up to five years of data. No historical data are available directly at the site. Similarly, bloomberg.com carries quotes from a selected list of foreign stock exchanges, top financial news, and some stock market updates. The Bloomberg site does not contain historical data, although, again, you can see a chart.

To get the entire Reuters database, including live quotes (which include Nasdaq Level II), news, historical data, analysis, and some predefined technical analysis, you need to subscribe to ReutersPlus (www.reutersplus.com). This entails a one-time fee of $150 and $295/month, plus exchange fees for the exchanges you specify. Bloomberg's professional service is a non-Internet service, and it carries all the live quotes on all the markets (stocks, bonds, and commodities), plus breaking news, analysis, charting, and historical data. As you might guess from the designation "professional," this is an expensive service at $1400/month.

Another stock screening and data information service used by professional fund managers is PiranhaWEB, offered by Primark (www.primark.com), a Thomson Financial Company. Primark makes the service available to individual investors, but does not publish a fixed menu of prices. Individuals specify what they want, and prices are set on a case-by-case basis. You can get a free trial, though. Depending on how many companies and countries you want to explore, the price can vary from under $100 per month to several hundred dollars. PiranhaWEB uses price and other data from an associated Primark company, I/B/E/S International (www.ibes.com), which has a database on 18,000 companies in 60 countries. Price quotes and a vast array of other company information, including earnings estimates, are offered according to the number of companies you plan to follow (so you need to know your universe of stocks first). The "global" package covers 25 U.S. and international companies for

$49.95; the "premium global" covers 150 U.S. and international companies for $249.95 per month.

Screening Stocks in Europe

One Web site that covers Europe is www.stockpoint.com. It covers stocks in the United Kingdom, Germany, France, the Netherlands, and Italy, as well as the United States and Canada. The screening process has five easy steps:

1. Pick a top criterion such as "growth and value," "high dividend," or "low price to book value."
2. Pick an industry from a long list.
3. Research the price data (percentage change over 4, 13, or 52 weeks) and risk data (beta, current ratio, insider shares, percentage of inside ownership).
4. Choose your target-size company, as measured by its market capitalization, number of employees, and shares outstanding.
5. Choose an option from among those on the Revenue and Earnings screen: revenue per share, book value per share, earnings per share, revenue growth rate, EPS growth rate, P/E ratio, price/book ratio, and dividend yield.

The process is not as sophisticated as at U.S.-only sites, and you will have to have some idea of the minimum and maximum numbers you are looking for. You can then ward off getting a list with a hundred names of possible stocks.

Investtech, at www.investtech.com, tracks stocks and funds in the Nordic countries, Germany, the Netherlands, and a few other countries.

Screening Stocks in Asia

If you're looking for stocks in Asia, you might want to check out www.nni.nikkei.co.jp. Here, the screening process is technical and is based on advanced pattern recognition. Five patterns are available, and you get 10 charts for each of the patterns; however, the patterns are limited to 65 days of trading history. This is the Web site of *Nihon*

Keizai Shimbun, a financial newspaper that has strong search capability once you have found the names of the companies you want to research. The annual cost is $69. By year-end 2000, multex.com will be introducing its version for Japanese stocks.

Screening Stocks in Latin America

Another foreign stock screening site that is used by professionals and covers Latin America is www.economatica, which was founded in 1986 and went online in November 1999. It covers seven countries: Argentina, Brazil, Chile, Colombia, Peru, Mexico, and Venezuela. Among its U.S. clients are several major U.S. institutions: Bear Stearns, Salomon Smith Barney, Morgan Stanley, J.P. Morgan, Goldman Sachs, Merrill Lynch, Lehman Brothers, Fidelity, Scudder-Stevens & Clark, Prudential, and Chase. This is where fund managers are getting their information. Clients also include the major banks and brokers within each country covered, as well as major European institutions: Santander, UBS–SBC, ING–Barings, Deutsche Morgan Grenfell, Société General, ABN–AMRO, Kleinwort–Benson, Robert Fleming, and Pictet.

The Economatica system consists of screening software that has to be installed on a PC and cannot be accessed online, as well as data that are updated at the end of the day (i.e., no intraday data are listed). The system is very expensive for individuals ($700/month) but Economatica delivers data to other services, such as Yahoo!, and to www.starmedia .com, a site that requires reading Spanish or Portuguese. Another place to find information is snapshot.economatica.com (no www), a service that will be integrated into the economatica site by year-end 2000. Snapshot has information on 1,000 of the largest Latin-American companies, and 200 U.S. companies that are cross-listed there:

Country	Companies
Argentina	80
Brazil	340
Chile	160
Colombia	50
Mexico	160
Peru	120
Venezuela	50

The cross-listings are interesting to anyone who might want to try to **arbitrage** between markets. This activity could be either geographic arbitrage (Brazil, on a different continent, starts two hours ahead of New York) or time-zone arbitrage (New York starts two hours ahead of Mexico because it is in a different North American time zone). In Argentina, Microsoft, Oracle, and Sun Microsystems are listed, along with Applied Materials, Amgen, Citigroup, and Dell. Argentina's currency, the peso, is pegged to the U.S. dollar, so there is no **currency risk** in such an exercise. (See Appendix B for an in-depth discussion of currency risk and arbitrage.) Volume is a bit low compared to the Nasdaq and the Big Board, however.

> **arbitrage**
>
> The simultaneous or near-simultaneous purchase and sale of the same security in different markets at different prices, to produce a profit.

> **currency risk**
>
> The risk associated with the fluctuation in a price when the currency is not the investor's home or base currency.

For example, Microsoft traded only 164,360 shares in Argentina on June 16, 2000, whereas it routinely trades in the millions of shares in the United States.

The information on the economatica site is well organized. Visitors can see a snapshot of trading activity and other information, including the beta calculated against the local stock index, and the stock's correlation with the index. For example, Microsoft has an 18-month beta of 0.07 against the Argentine Merval index, an 18-month correlation of 0.05, and a 21-day volatility of 0.89. The low beta means that Microsoft, as traded in Argentina, is very low risk (compared to the risk of the index), is not correlated with the index, and demonstrates low volatility (i.e., the price does not vary greatly from day to day). All information can be seen in local currency or dollar terms. The site also offers technical analysis charts, charts showing the stock versus the index, and, for the domestic companies, all the major financial statement information for three years (P/E, price/sales, and price/book ratios; EPS, dividend yield, market cap, gross margin, net margin, debt, and so on).

In many instances, you will see how stocks that are ADRs in the United States trade in their home countries. For example, Telefonos de Mexico ("Telmex") has been traded on the NYSE since 1991. It is a large-cap stock that is actively traded both in Mexico and the United States. A lower ending price in Mexico, which closes after New York, might interest a short-seller at the New York open. The Mexican peso is not pegged to the U.S. dollar. If you see that the Mexican index is on a falling trend and the beta of Telmex is 1.04 (it should fall further than the index), and the peso is falling, too, a short sale of Telmex could give you a double-dip gain; one on the stock and one on the currency. ADRs are denominated in U.S. dollars, but the underlying stock is, of course, denominated in pesos, and the New York price will reflect that, if the peso falls during the trading day.

METHODOLOGIES FOR SELECTING STOCKS

There are as many stock-picking strategies and methods as there are stock pickers. Successful strategies depend on so much—market conditions, sectors, liquidity, just to name a few. Moreover, what works for one investor may not work for another. Strategies are highly personal and involve a certain comfort level. If you are uncomfortable with technical trading strategies, then those sorts of methodologies would not be appropriate for you any more than a purely fundamental strategy would be for a market technician.

In a 24/7 world where the opportunities (and challenges) open to the investor are great, it is sensible to review some of the strategies to see what has worked. Combined with study of foreign market conditions and analyst reports, the investor should then be able to venture 24/7 with some selection tools.

While we do not endorse any particular strategy, it is worth reviewing a couple to see the kinds of selection criteria that the investor may want to include in the analysis and research. For instance, William O'Neil, author of *How to Make Money in Stocks* and founder of

Investor's Business Daily, follows a style of stock selection he calls CANSLIM. O'Neil contends that "price patterns taken from successful stocks in the past few years should definitely be used as models or precedents for future selection of successful stocks" (*How to Make Money in Stocks,* Second Edition, p. 161). The acronym is made up of the first letter of each of the seven factors he examines to seek the best return. His seven factors are:

1. *Current quarterly earnings per share* should be up significantly—at least 20 percent, and higher in bull markets—from the same quarter in the previous year. Three out of four of the top 500 stocks from 1953 to 1993 showed earnings increases averaging more than 70 percent in the most recent quarter, compared to that quarter a year earlier. Earnings surprises are good, too, but watch out for window dressing and be sure to use a log scale (which shows that a 10 percent gain on $10 is proportionately higher and more meaningful than a 10 percent gain on $100). Earnings (actual, expected, and whispered) can be found at zacks.com, firstcall.com, siliconinvestor.com, and thewhispernumber.com (also stockz.net and whisperearnings.com).

2. *Annual earnings should be increasing each year* over the past five years and should have a growth rate of at least 25 percent per year. Consistency is important, and so is not believing the "growth" labels applied by the press or by analysts. The P/E ratio can be a trap. Top-performing stocks between 1953 and 1985 had P/Es of 20, compared to 15 for the Dow Industrials. When companies are "emerging," it's OK for the P/E to be very high.

3. *News.* Stocks about to break out often have new management or new products, or they have just hit new price highs. This is one of the hardest lessons to learn in trading. New highs do not mean the stock has to fall (that's a gambler's fallacy). In fact, new highs probably mean more new highs. Bloomberg.com has a feature that identifies news that broke after-hours and may affect prices the next day. Stockhouse.com will send you, via e-mail, all the news items it collects on your list of companies.

4.   *Supply and demand is a key factor in price,* but it has to be understood in the widest Economics 101 sense. Start with stocks that have less than 25 million shares outstanding; historically, these have been the best bets. Then watch for splits and buybacks (which you can track via buybackletter.com). On the demand side, look at charts that include volume (see bigcharts.com).

5.   *Leaders in an industry are the best investment.* A stock should have a relative price strength better than 70, which means it is outperforming 70 percent of the stocks on the S&P 500. (Note that this is the same as *relative comparative strength,* mentioned above.) motleyfool.com has an article in the Workshop section called "Thirty Years of Great Returns," which shows that the idea is sound. A newsletter that is based on the relative strength concept is thechartist.com, ranked among the top newsletters by Hulbert. You can sign up for a free 30-day trial, but you must register and give a credit card number "to avoid interruption of service" (and the site does not tell you the cost). Separately, another screening service is at investools.com, which has a "William O'Neil winners screen," among nine preset screens. The free trial is 30 days; the price is then $9.95/month. Analysts' recommendations cost an additional $5.95 to $24.95/month.

6.   *Institutional sponsorship* means that there should be some ownership by at least a few mutual funds, pension funds, and investment advisors. When institutional ownership is very high, though, you are at risk of the stock's being dumped all at once. The quality of the institution counts, too. You can check institutional ownership at many sites, including multex.com and lionshares.com, among many other sites.

7.   *Market direction is important.* Holding on through thick and thin, with the idea that you are a "long-term value investor," can be profit-draining. Markets do rise and fall on sentiment, and markets do crash. You should watch trends and remain open and flexible to the idea of market timing. Technical

analysis provides big-picture guidance, as do market sentiment guides. Pitbull.com has a "crash index" and lowrisk.com has a lot of material on history and on relationships to watch out for.

Similarly, another stock selection system is MAGNET developed by Jordon Kimmel (and from his book *MAGNET Investing: Build a Portfolio from Picking Winning Stocks Using Your Home Computer* and endorsed by Sam Stovall of Standard & Poor's). MAGNET is similar to CANSLIM as some of the criteria are quantifiable and others are subjective: For example:

- M stands for outstanding *management and momentum.*
- A stands for *acceleration* of earnings, revenues, and margins.
- G is the *growth rate,* which must be higher than the current valuation is giving it credit for.
- N stands for *new product* (or new management).
- E represents the *emerging market or product* that creates the growth opportunity.
- T is for *timing,* which must be right, and leads us back to technical analysis.

And, finally, at www.validea.com, you can screen stocks according to the strategies used by such successful investors as Peter Lynch, Benjamin Graham, Motley Fool, David Dremen, Martin Zewig, Kenneth Fisher, James O'Shaughnessy, and others. You can select the "guru" of your choice and scan for the stocks that get a "pass" according to the guru's criteria. You can also select stocks and see which and how many guru tests they pass. Under each criterion is a note as to whether the stock passes and if not, why not.

Guidelines for evaluating foreign stocks have not yet been written. There is no book or even a set of periodical articles equivalent to the O'Shaughnessy book on "what works" in foreign markets. This research almost certainly does exist—in the hands of institutional investors, including mutual funds, hedge funds, pension fund managers, and others. Public interest in diversification into foreign markets is relatively recent and just taking off in the new millennium. Within the next five years, books on the subject will probably start appearing.

Note the plural, books. What works in Thailand may not be what works in Finland. Every country or region may deserve its own book. As noted, some countries (such as Japan) are more tolerant of debt than are analysts in the United States. The American obsession with the price/earnings ratio is not shared equally by stock market participants elsewhere. The legal environment is different—for example, monopolies, oligopolies, and cartels are routinely accepted in some countries, giving the companies involved a competitive advantage that won't necessarily shown up in U.S.-style ratios. Most foreign companies have a higher dividend pay-out ratio than in the United States, where investors prefer companies to plough earnings back into growth. Differences abound.

The United States has a vast amount of publicly available and free information on stock selection, including stock screening, because public participation in the stock market is so deep in the United States. Over 40 percent of households own stocks, whereas the proportion in Japan, for example, is only about 5 percent. Therefore, we don't have books written for an American audience on how to analyze Japanese stocks; there is very little written in Japanese on how to analyze Japanese stocks, either. Accordingly, foreign stock scanning and screening Web sites are only now starting to appear. An exhaustive search of many countries' Web sites failed to turn up screening utilities outside of the English-speaking countries and Europe, even in places like Hong Kong (where there is a wide following of the local stock market). Yahoo!Finance, which offers a screening service for U.S. and Canadian stocks, does not offer it elsewhere in the world, as far as we can tell. It's hard to know—the local sites are written in the country's language.

Therefore, guidance on selecting international funds is welcome. The "island principle" is described in *Getting Started in Global Investing,* by Robert Kreitler (Wiley, 2000). It refers to our tendency to view the U.S. market as an island and the rest of the world as one "place," when in fact the rest of the world offers multiple markets. You can take advantage of the risk-reducing and/or return-enhancing opportunities of these markets by acknowledging that the benefits of international diversification depend on low correlation of individual markets with the U.S. market. Kreitler reproduces the Morgan Stanley Capital International country correlation matrix. It shouldn't surprise you to learn that the MSCI index for Canada has a 73 percent correlation with the U.S. stock market, but you may be surprised by which countries have the lowest correlations—Japan (28 percent), Italy (26 percent), and Austria (17 percent). *Low correlation is what makes diversification work to reduce risk or enhance return.* As we'll discuss in the next chapter, diversification also helps investors resist panic if one or another market suddenly becomes volatile, and to stick to long-term investment programs instead of jumping around unsystematically. Accordingly, investors can put a higher proportion of total capital in stocks because the diversified stock portfolio is less risky than a one-country stock portfolio. Kreitler encourages diversification in the form of global mutual funds, which give investors access to the top professional managers even if they have only a modest sum to invest. He describes how to evaluate and select a fund manager, and offers a detailed list of the questions to ask—and what to do with the information after you learn how to get it, including revising the initial portfolio.

PUTTING ALL YOUR RESEARCH TOGETHER

Researching stocks is very similar to a journalist researching a story. Following a lead is OK, provided you do further research before acting on the lead. If you build a portfolio of ill-researched stocks, you will almost certainly end up with a hodgepodge of risk-and-return characteristics that do not constitute a well-ordered and optimal portfolio. The alternative is to conduct research from the top down, on a fundamental, technical, and/or statistical basis.

The virtue of the scanning/screening process is that you quickly become attuned to the mix of fundamental and technical factors that, together, make a winning stock. *The purpose of investing is to make money.* Any tool that works is welcome.

Acceptance of this point of view is helpful when you deal in foreign stocks. Fundamental screening is still very limited, except in Latin America and some European countries. You can obtain raw historical data for use in technical analysis screening, and then research the companies one-by-one in the conventional way. Another idea is to collect leads from analysts on television, in magazine and newspaper articles, or at Web sites, and then apply fundamental research and technical screening. Upon discovering a valid new stock, you can also see whether it fits into your portfolio by taking it out for a ride at riskgrades.com (covered in Chapter 4).

SUMMING UP

It seems almost mundane to say that the Internet has opened up a whole new world of stock research to the individual investor. But the fact is that investors now have a plethora of tools to choose from. The challenge is to adapt these tools to the 24/7 environment where data is still limited. But this appears to be changing rapidly and when the kind of foreign stock data comparable to U.S. data becomes available screening and scanning technology will help us more easily identify profit opportunities.

Now you have an idea of what stocks you might be interested in (or at least how to find them), you need to select the ones that are right for your portfolio. Chapter 6 discusses diversification and explains how you might evaluate the stocks that will fit best in your portfolio.

WHY GO 24/7?

CNBC

Now that you know more about how to find stocks in the 24/7 world, as well as how to screen them to ensure that they fit into your portfolio and are aligned with your targeted risk level, this chapter explains more about *why* you should want to invest around the clock and around the world. It explains the benefits of diversification by investing in foreign stocks, and it demystifies the subject of portfolio theory.

DIVERSIFICATION REDUCES RISK

We often hear or read that "diversification reduces risk," but we seldom get an explanation of exactly why this is so. Everyone intuitively understands the adage: "Don't put all your eggs in one basket." But the theory behind this concept is a bit more complicated. Essentially, modern portfolio theory (on which the idea that diversification reduces risk is based) makes assumptions about the future based on past data. Many investors think that all they need to do is input some information (i.e., their own assumptions about the future, based on past data) and a model portfolio will miraculously appear. They then expect that this portfolio will suddenly and mysteriously replace their 100 shares of IBM with 123 shares of Japan's Hitachi and 56 shares of Finland's Nokia. Alas, it's not that simple.

Whether you hire a financial advisor to rebalance your portfolio, buy expensive software to do it yourself, or use one of the sites available on the Internet, you should have a basic understanding of the diversification principle and process. The logic is easy to understand, but the math can be daunting. We'll try to explain it here.

Portfolio theory states that, for any given level of return, there are securities outside your existing portfolio that can make it "more efficient"—that is, lower its risk. Moreover, for any given level of risk, there are securities outside your existing portfolio that can raise its return. Often, you can do both things—lower risk *and* raise return. This occurs when you add to the portfolio some securities that have **noncorrelated** returns with the securities already there. The output of the portfolio model program is a list of optimum portfolios that lie on the "efficient frontier." You can choose the trade-off of risk and return that suits you, but your choices are limited to the list of optimum portfolios. The minute you change the composition of the portfolio by adding or subtracting a component, you have to perform the exercise all over again.

> **noncorrelated**
>
> A descriptive term for two securities whose price behavior is not linked by market conditions. When one security's price goes up, the other may go up, go down, or not move at all.

A lot depends on how you define the universe of "securities" outside your portfolio. "Security" is a generic word for any financial asset that has some market liquidity and can be bought and sold on a physical exchange or in cyberspace. Thus, "security" encompasses all stocks, bonds, and derivative instruments, foreign and domestic. When you define the universe of securities this way, you can easily imagine that an infinite number of combinations and permutations of securities can be assembled to improve your trading and investing results. In fact, by just using equities but expanding the category to include foreign equities, you can construct an infinite number of equally efficient portfolios that contain *no* U.S. equities.

It would be wonderful to have a giant spreadsheet menu of securities on which Column A contained a list of all the securities with low risk/low return, Column B had all securities of moderate risk/moderate return, and so on, with the final column reserved for extraordinarily high risk/extraordinarily high return. You could mix and match from the different columns, ask a portfolio optimization program to devise multiple portfolio scenarios of equally desirable securities, and then research each one to drill down the specific securities you want to hold.

For example, the extraordinarily high risk/high return column might include Russian stocks, oil futures, Israeli CDs, Tanzanian bonds, and U.S. **bulletin board stocks.** The program would tell you that you are indifferent as to which of these to buy. It would also advise you on the exact dollar proportion of your total portfolio that should be put in the category so that you can boost your expected *return* without, at the same time, raising your *risk*.

> **bulletin board stocks**
>
> Stocks that are not listed on a recognized exchange and can be bought and sold only by qualified investors—those defined by the SEC as being rich and sophisticated.

Unfortunately, such a menu does not exist. In fact, all of the academic work on diversification uses broad *classes of securities*—either indices or index-tracking mutual funds—rather than *individual securities*. Most store-bought and online portfolio programs do, too. This does not reflect any defect in portfolio theory; rather, it reveals the unhappy fact that one of the needed inputs is the correlation between and among securities. Diversification is effective—it either reduces risk for a given level of return or raises return for a given level of risk—chiefly because of the noncorrelation of some securities with others. Determining the degree of correlation between a pair of securities is not prohibitively difficult, but maintaining and updating a matrix of correlations among many securities is a computational nightmare.

For example, for many years, the managed futures industry used the noncorrelation of futures with equities and bonds as a major selling point. Their thinking was: To diversify your portfolio by adding some proportion of managed futures would increase the return on your portfolio without increasing your risk by much (if at all), even though futures generally incorporate higher risk due to the use of leverage. Now that global opportunities are expanding, foreign securities are filling the space once occupied by managed futures. This is understandable; it's a lot easier to think about owning a Japanese stock outright than to think about owning a managed futures fund that is shorting soybeans.

Consider the Qualitative Risks of International Diversification

Today, two conventional wisdoms are competing on the subject of international diversification. One camp insists that the benefits of global diversification have been proven beyond a shadow of doubt. According to proponents of this theory, if you fail to diversify internationally, you may be missing golden opportunities.

The other camp concedes the virtues of diversification but thinks that the additional *qualitative* risks of investing in foreign securities—that is, risks that do not show up in the statistics—outweigh the potential returns. This view is magnified when the foreign security is from an emerging market where the realities are: less information generally about the company and its business environment, unclear accounting standards, and perhaps unacceptably low investor protection against stock manipulation and other dangers (and we've already dicussed the challenges of researching securities in foreign markets). "Enhancing shareholder value," a top priority in the United States, is only slowly making its way out into the rest of the world. Portfolio theory does not take these qualitative issues into account.

PAST IS PROLOGUE

"Expected return" is the linchpin of all asset allocation modeling and risk management practices. Actually, there are three components of asset allocation and portfolio diversification exercises:

1. Expected return.
2. The volatility of returns.
3. The correlation of returns (explained later in this chapter).

Like a beam of light originating on Earth and landing on Mars, a small difference at the starting point can end up as a huge difference by the time it reaches the end point. If the beam of light is a laser beam that travels in a straight line instead of a widening cone, any error at the starting point results in a completely unintended and wrong destination.

So it is with estimations of the three key components of portfolio theory. Small errors of estimation can be transformed into incorrect conclusions through the power of compounding. Recent advances in computing promise to give us a cone at the end point, or a range of optimum outcomes within which the "correct" answer will reside. For the moment, however, we need to keep in mind that we are working with a mathematically linear computation process.

Portfolio theory is the umbrella that encompasses the use of **probability theory** to measure risk and return. One application is asset allocation (which we discussed in Chapter 4), which works on the assumption of two classes of securities, one risk-free and one risky. Another application, "portfolio diversification," works with securities having differing degrees of risk or the same degree of risk but different

> **probability theory**
>
> A set of ideas that define the mathematical likelihood of different outcomes, given a specific set of conditions. Also used in gambling and quantum physics.

and sometimes noncorrelated returns. Another offshoot of portfolio theory is beta, which was defined in Chapter 5 and will be discussed in detail later in this chapter: For now, all you need to know about beta is that it is the relative risk of an individual stock, compared to the class of stocks to which it belongs, such as the Nasdaq. A stock with a beta of 1 is exactly as risky as the whole class. A beta of 2 is double the riskiness, and a beta of 0.5 is half the riskiness.

How Asset Allocation Works

For asset allocation, we start with a portfolio of two securities. One is riskless with a certain return, and one carries risk with an uncertain future return. To estimate future return, we use past return and its variability. We want to know what combination of the two assets will give us the most "efficient" portfolio—that is, the highest possible return with the lowest possible risk. For example, the general rule today is that a portfolio of 30 to 40 percent bonds (certain return) and 60 to 70 percent stocks (uncertain return) is efficient. Note that fund managers who announce such allocation shifts do not state exactly what historical data led them to arrive at the new balance, or for how long the portfolio allocation will be valid. When Abby Joseph Cohen announces that she is reducing her mix of stocks and bonds from a 70–30 allocation to a 65–35 allocation, you do not know the statistical basis of her decision, but you can be sure that a great deal of computational effort went into it.

Modern portfolio theory holds that the risk and return of a portfolio are different from the risk and return of its component asset classes. In other words, you can't just add up the proportionally weighted returns on the two classes and average them. The geometric mean of a portfolio (calculated using the sum of square roots) always exceeds the weighted sum of the component geometric means. You don't have to understand the mathematics; just be aware that it is not simple arithmetic (like averaging).

The optimum blend of stocks and bonds (or even stocks and different stocks) is calculated according to ideas first put forth in 1952 by a financial economist named Harry Markowitz (and later expanded by William Sharpe in a book that has recently been reissued: *Portfolio Theory and Capital Markets*). The central concept is that the return on every security displays a measurable variability from its **mean** value. Variability, or **variance,** is measured by the standard deviation, a statistical unit that is then manipulated to produce an annualized risk factor in percentage terms.

> **mean**
>
> An arithmetic average derived by dividing the sum of a series of prices by the number of prices.

> **variance**
>
> The extent of price movements away from a mean.

To illustrate the risk factor, let's say you have Security A and Security B, and each has an annual average return of 10 percent. On this information alone, you could not choose between the two securities. But Figure 6.1 shows that your Security A has an obviously greater variability around its mean than does Security B. If you were the unlucky buyer of Security A when it was at a high point, and you had to liquidate the investment for some personal reason when it was at a low point, it would have been a bad assumption to project the 10 percent historical return as the expected return without

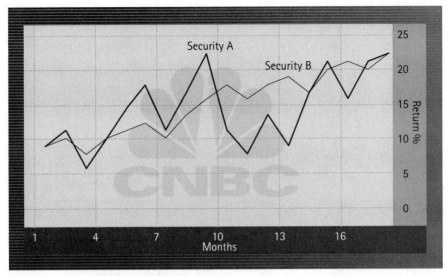

Figure 6.1   Variability in Two Securities

also calculating the potential loss. You would need to see the risk-adjusted return in order to make an informed decision.

Another way of illustrating risk is to show the distribution of possible outcomes around the mean. The resulting chart (see Figure 6.2) is a normal bell-shaped curve. The mean is in the center, the most probable outcomes are clustered around it, and the remotely possible outcomes are in the two tails. Note the two axes: We are measuring return (in percentage terms) on the horizontal axis, and the frequency of the different outcomes on the vertical axis. The highest frequency is right in the middle; most of the outcomes will occur at or near the center of the graph. The outcomes shown in the tails occur less frequently. The wider the distribution of returns (i.e., the longer the tails), the higher the risk.

AVOID THE GAMBLER'S FALLACY

Basing *expected* return on *past* return is tricky. The historical return on U.S. stocks was 15.5 percent during the period from 1980 to 1998. The

	-40	-30	-20	-10	0	10	20	30	40	50	60	
												20
						1996	1999					19
						1988	1998					18
						1986	1997					17
				1994		1983	1989					16
				1987		1982	1985					15
				1984		1980	1976					14
				1977	1993	1979	1975					13
				1970	1992	1972	1967					12
			1990	1960	1978	1971	1961					11
			1981	1953	1968	1965	1955					10
			1969	1948	1956	1964	1950					9
			1966	1947	1942	1963	1949	1995				8
			1962	1940	1939	1959	1943	1991				7
			1957	1923	1934	1952	1925	1945				6
			1941	1918	1932	1951	1922	1938				5
	1974	1973	1929	1916	1919	1944	1921	1936	1958			4
	1937	1946	1920	1914	1912	1926	1905	1935	1928			3
	1931	1930	1910	1913	1911	1909	1904	1927	1915	1954		2
	1907	1917	1903	1906	1902	1901	1900	1924	1908	1933		1
	-40	-30	-20	-10	0	10	20	30	40	50	60	

Figure 6.2   Histogram of U.S. Real Equity Returns (percent per annum)

Source: Data provided by Elroy Dimson, Paul Marsh, and Mike Staunton, authors of *The Millennium Book: A Century of Investment Returns* (ABN Amro and London Business School, 2000).

accompanying annualized standard deviation was 15.3 percent. We can multiply our capital stake to get, in the upcoming year, an expected rate of return of the same 15.5 percent plus or minus 15.3 percent. Let's say that, in the following year, we get the maximum likely return—30.8 percent.

What is the likely return in the year after that? The new historical average return is fractionally higher for the new 19-year period because of the addition of one more year of data, but the standard deviation is actually about the same. Therefore, our projection for expected return for the upcoming year is still about 15.5 percent plus or minus 15.3 percent. In short, we got lucky. We had two consecutive years in which returns were less probable than the mean return, but we knew they were possible. They were in the tail of the normal distribution curve describing the frequency of outcomes. It is true that, over time, the mean may shift to a higher rate, but it would take many years for the 30.8 percent return to become the normal mean return. This is a simple fact of life arising from the averaging function. Meanwhile, the frequency distribution of returns will shift even more slowly because of the way it is calculated. (If you are interested in the financial math, see www.motleyfool.com for further educational material.)

Curmudgeons who complain that today's young whippersnappers have never seen a bear market are referring to the statistical improbability of getting returns in the positive tail every year. They are perfectly correct, too. The mean—the most likely outcome—changes very slowly, and the variation around the mean changes more slowly still. It is not true, however, that next year we are likely to be in the other tail—the losing one. Instead, the most probable rate of return will still be 15.5 percent, and the standard deviation will still be 15.3 percent (unless it turns out to be an unusually wild year). Going into a new year, we have no more reason to expect a bad extreme outcome than we do to expect a good extreme outcome—at least, not on a statistical basis.

For example, let's say you are gambling on a coin toss. The probability of heads and tails is equal, 50 percent. If you are betting on heads and have a run of luck in which 50 tosses give you heads, many people will think that the probability that the next toss will result in tails is higher now. But the probability of heads is still 50 percent. To think that your luck will change in the face of statistical logic is to fall victim to the gambler's fallacy—that recent outcomes influence the next outcomes. In a true game of chance like coin tossing, they do not.

The stock market is not a true game of chance. Recent outcomes do influence current and upcoming outcomes. A string of losses (representing outcomes in the tail) will influence the loss-taking investors. For example, they may exit the market altogether—a move that would reduce liquidity and thus raise the volatility of the market for those remaining. On the other hand, a string of abnormally large gains (representing outcomes in the other tail) influences those who made the gains—who may now allocate more of their total equity stake to the winning security or market—as well as others who want to emulate the winner.

This is how manias get started. Those in the grip of the mania project the immediate past return into the future as their expected return (greed), instead of projecting the mean average return over a longer historical period and with its associated probability of loss. If they did that, there would be more fear.

Table 6.1 shows that, over time, people have become accustomed to the idea that stock market returns are on a rising trend. In some cases, they may feel entitled to ever-increasing stock market returns. This can be a dangerous assumption; they need to consider the normal variability of returns, too.

THE VOLATILITY OF THE EXPECTED RETURN

Analysts use historical volatility to calculate probable outcomes in the future. For example, if you have a security that is currently trading at $100 and its historical volatility is 10 percent, there is a 66 percent probability that the actual future outcome will be somewhere between $90 (worst case) and $110 (best case). The 66 percent probability comes from using a one-standard-deviation measure. The two-standard-deviations version would raise to 99 percent the probability of knowing the range of outcomes.

Notice that we assume a symmetrical range of outcomes. This is not realistic, because many securities are skewed for long periods of time to the upside or the downside. A more serious issue is where the 10 percent number comes from. We can take data over one-day intervals, one-week intervals, one-month intervals, quarterly intervals, or annual intervals. Each choice results in a different standard deviation, which, in turn, will result in a different annualized percentage risk factor. Which interval is the "correct" interval?

The answer is another question: What's the holding period? If you are analyzing a security's riskiness with the intention of holding it for years, monthly returns going back five or ten years are appropriate. If you plan to hold the security for a short period of time—say, 60 days—you would want to use multiple 60-day periods, and you needn't go back so far, because it is *recent* volatility that interests you (assuming that recent volatility is more relevant than long-past volatility for the immediate future).

This is an absolutely critical point. Most calculations performed by asset allocation programs (including those you can do yourself, online)

TABLE 6.1
RISING EXPECTATIONS

Dow Jones Industrial Average: Gains per Decade

Decade	Begin	End	Percent of Change
1900s	$ 66.08	$ 99.05	49.89%
1910s	99.05	107.23	8.26
1920s	107.23	248.48	131.73
1930s	248.48	150.24	−39.54
1940s	150.24	200.13	33.21
1950s	200.13	679.36	239.46
1960s	679.36	800.36	17.81
1970s	800.36	838.74	4.80
1980s	838.74	2,753.20	228.25
1990s	2,753.20	11,224.70	307.70
Nasdaq Gains per Decade			
1970s*	$ 100.00	$ 151.14	51.14%
1980s	151.14	454.82	200.93
1990s	454.82	3,620.24	659.27

*Note that Nasdaq began in 1971.
Source: The Wall Street Journal, December 13, 1999.

use a fixed-period standard deviation, usually based on monthly returns. Therefore, a swing trader who holds positions for three to five days would not find the annualized standard deviation, based on monthly data, to be at all useful in determining when to take profit and when to stop a loss. In addition, the fixed-period risk factor, used by most advisors and funds to describe their riskiness, is usually based on annualized monthly or quarterly returns. This is why switching your money between funds of equal riskiness—even if you could do it without transaction costs and taxes—is usually a no-win short-term strategy *unless* you have some specific reason to suppose that, in the upcoming period, the expected return on one fund will tend to land in the tail.

Relative Volatility

Theoretically, you could use the historical return and variance of any pair of securities to come up with the optimum blend of the two that would be the most efficient in producing the highest return with the least risk. But because there are tens of thousands of securities, this would be a monumental calculation task. Worse, you would have to perform the calculations many times, for each pair of securities, according to the time frame of the expected holding period. This is not practical, so financial economists came up with a different concept: measuring the riskiness of one security against a basket of securities.

Thus was born the idea of beta, which measures the risk of a *particular* stock in terms of the risk of the *class* to which it belongs. By definition, the class is the index that includes it, such as the Dow, the S&P 500, the Nasdaq, or subsets of those indices, such as the Nasdaq 100. The broadest and most inclusive index is the Wilshire 5000, which includes about 7,400 U.S.-domiciled company stocks that have any trading activity to speak of. Bulletin-board and foreign-domiciled stocks are excluded. Usually, beta is calculated on a smaller universe than the Wilshire 5000.

The beta for a class is always set at 1.00. For example, if you buy a stock with a beta of less than 1.00—say, 0.75—your stock will probably have only 75 percent of the risk (and 75 percent of the return) of the index to which it belongs. A stock with a beta of 2.00 has double the risk and likely return of the index—and of a mutual fund linked one-to-one with that index. This is why some people say they will never buy an index-linked mutual fund. They feel that they are taking all the risk of the index, but, because of fees, they are always getting less than the associated return.

Many stocks belong to more than one index. For example, a Nasdaq-traded stock may also be an S&P 500 stock. On some Web sites, you cannot choose which index will be used to calculate the beta of your stock. For example, because the Nasdaq is a more volatile index than the S&P 500, a Nasdaq stock's beta will be lower when compared to the Nasdaq than when compared to the S&P 500 (or the Wilshire 5000).

The beta value of a security can change. A stock may have a high beta early in its life, after its IPO. At this stage, the price is gyrating. Institutional investors sell off to individual investors, and the perception of the value of the company is undergoing continuous revision. But a more sedate beta may evolve as the company reaches maturity.

The beta of a particular company can also fall if it is stabilizing while the rest of the market is becoming more volatile. This happened in the first quarter of 2000, when the Nasdaq became extraordinarily volatile but many companies had steady and even falling betas. Beta is therefore a fixed number only for a snapshot in time.

If you buy a stock with a beta *less* than 1.00, you expect your risk to be less than the risk of the market at large (exemplified by an index-following fund, for example). On the other hand, if you buy a stock with a beta *greater* than 1.00, you expect to take more risk *and* to get a higher return. Most people own more than one stock, of course, and each stock has a different beta. It is mathematically incorrect to add up the betas, even if they are weighted proportionately, in an effort to arrive at some *average* beta for the combined portfolio. For example, if you bought, in equal amounts, one stock with a beta of 0.50 and another with a beta of 1.5, the combined risk of your portfolio is not 1.00. *Beta applies only to individual stocks, not to portfolios.* To arrive at the riskiness of a portfolio, you have to use the fancier math of portfolio theory.

AN INFINITY OF CHOICES: EVALUATING THE CORRELATION OF THE STOCKS IN YOUR PORTFOLIO

Returning to our two-securities model (one riskless and one risky), we can combine the proportions in hundreds of ways—5 percent risk-free and 95 percent risky; 10 percent risk-free and 90 percent risky; and so on. The blend that should, mathematically, result in the highest return for the least risk is calculated by using geometric means. Discussions of **mean variance optimization** abound in the academic literature and on the Internet. One site that offers more information on this topic is www.effisols.com.

> **mean variance optimization**
>
> A form of optimization that uses a geometric mean. See optimization on page 156.

Risk and return are not the whole story, though. In the model that uses only a risk-free and a risky asset, the return on each one is independent of the other. Yet in real-life modeling, we are usually looking at securities whose returns are not entirely independent. We therefore want to find out how correlated they are.

Statistically, correlation is expressed by a number that ranges from +1 (positively correlated) to −1 (inversely correlated). For example:

- Two securities that are perfectly correlated would have a correlation of +1 and would move in lockstep. A 10 percent move in one would be mirrored perfectly by a 10 percent move in the other, *both up and down.*

- Two securities that are inversely correlated would have a correlation coefficient of −1. A 10 percent rise in one would be matched by a 10 percent fall in the other, and vice versa.

It's important to note that some securities are positively correlated when one is falling, say the U.S. stock market and the dollar, but not correlated when one is rising. We often note that a bad day for the Dow may be labeled as a key factor in dragging down the dollar that day, but on days when the stock market rises, the dollar does not get a commensurate boost. Asymmetric correlations over varying time periods are the very devil to work with, even for professional statisticians.

If we combine two risky securities to get the best portfolio balance, we want the returns on the two securities to be uncorrelated or to be inversely correlated. If they are not correlated at all, we may have a period when they both go up or they both go down. If they are truly uncorrelated, this is just the luck of the draw in the time period under examination.

Perfect inverse correlation is better. When the return on one goes up, the return on the other goes down proportionately. Some hedge funds and some mutual funds use this technique, called "pairs trading." The challenge, of course, is that returns are not static and neither is the correlation coefficient. Pairs trading is elegant in theory, but it has to be managed with great care to avoid getting a zero return when one rises and the other falls by the exact same amount.

Suppose your portfolio has two securities that have equal rates of return, are of equal riskiness, and are, say, 25 percent negatively correlated. A $1 rise in the first security will be accompanied by a 25-cent fall in the second one. The goal of the optimum portfolio calculation is to tell you what proportion of each security you should hold in your portfolio to ensure the highest return with the lowest risk. As you might expect, a 75 percent allocation to the first security and a 25 percent allocation to the second one is not the answer.

YOU NEED A MATHEMATICIAN

> **quadratic programming**
>
> A mathematical procedure in which expected return, risk, and correlation are used as inputs to generate an optimum portfolio.

Portfolio optimization requires **quadratic programming.** This is a complex mathematical process. Each of the three components of the optimum portfolio—expected return, risk, and correlation—is subject to assumption and calculation errors that can render the hypothetical optimum portfolio less than optimum in practice.

> **optimization**
>
> The mathematical modeling process by which a set of portfolios is identified from a specific universe of securities; the set represents the portfolios that are the most efficient, that is, each one has the highest return for the risk taken. The optimum sets are displayed graphically on an "efficient frontier," a line that defines the risk-return trade-off. The investor can choose a portfolio with higher risk to get higher return, or lower risk with lower associated return. All other portfolios are inferior, that is, they take more risk than is necessary to get the same return as an efficient portfolio.

This is why there is a debate about the value of **optimization**.

In a now-famous study, Gary Brinson, a fund manager and chairman of UBS Brinson (www.ubswarburg.com), and his associates discovered that 93.6 percent of the return on a diversified portfolio arises from diversification alone. This outcome suggests that investors could pick *any* (random) batch of securities, from any list, and would get the highest return from that set of securities if they are properly diversified within the portfolio. But the reality is that a portfolio of ten losers will still be a losing portfolio, no matter how correctly it is diversified. In addition, if 93.6 percent of the portfolio outcome is due to diversification, there's no point in trying to pick winners or to time purchases and sales. This is counterintuitive, too.

Other studies show that diversification contributes only 15 percent or so (Morningstar gets 16.5 percent), or maybe 40 percent as others have suggested. Confusion regarding the contribution of optimization to total return has resulted in two camps: those who swear by it and those who find that its limitations make it impractical as a management tool. Gradually, improvements are being made on the theoretical level to fix these limitations. One financial professional was actually able to patent his version of a fix (www.rmichaud.com). Whatever the extent of its contribution, diversification reduces risk. The lower the correlation among the securities in a portfolio, the less the risk.

CASE STUDY: OPTIMIZING YOUR PORTFOLIO FOR MAXIMUM DIVERSIFICATION

When diversification is the goal, foreign stocks are the obvious place to look because they may be less correlated with U.S. stocks or not correlated at all. There is a large body of important work on the subject. Most of it appears in issues of *The Journal of Portfolio Management, American Economic Review,* and *The Journal of Finance,* and in books such as *Global Asset Allocation* (Jess Lederman and Robert Klein, eds.). These studies universally conclude that adding foreign securities to a portfolio reduces its risk for the same return, and, if selected properly, these securities can increase return, too. If, however, you add to a portfolio a *security* with a lower return and a higher risk, you get a *portfolio* that also has a lower return and a higher risk.

Consider an article by Katerina Simons, a Federal Reserve economist, in *The New England Economic Review* (November/December 1999): "Should U.S. Investors Invest Overseas?" Simons succinctly captures the analytical process, asks the right questions, and notes the institutional debate on what proportion (if any) of a portfolio should be diversified into international stocks (www.bos.frb.org). Like most studies of this type, the article uses monthly returns on five index funds for a 19-year period to get the needed inputs to the optimization formulas—average annual real returns, annualized standard deviation, and correlation.

Simons points out an important constraint in portfolio diversification exercises. Academics assume that the investor can sell a security short. In practice, many institutions and most individuals cannot sell short. Richard Michaud, a senior vice president at Arcadian Asset Management and Director of the Institute for Quantitative Research in Finance, points out, in the book *Efficient Asset Management,* "Optimization without short selling is more analytically difficult and often leads to qualitatively different results." The day will come when derivatives will allow individual investors to short indices or individual stocks. Many can be shorted today, but most studies constrain their research to the single option of buying or not buying.

The data for the five mutual funds used in Simons's study are shown in Tables 6.2 and 6.3.

As shown in Table 6.4, Simons derives ten optimum portfolios from these five securities. As an individual investor, you can choose the level of return you want and accept the associated risk, or you can select the risk level first and accept the associated return. The point of optimizing portfolios is that they are all "efficient." You cannot get a higher return without accepting more risk.

Table 6.4, showing the ten optimum portfolios, bears some scrutiny. Notice that portfolio 1, the least risky of the ten efficient portfolios, consists of a 99 percent allocation to the U.S. money market fund and a 1 percent allocation to European equities. In efficiency terms, U.S. equities don't make the cut for this level of risk. Portfolios 9 and 10, which have the highest risk, consist exclusively of U.S. securities. Portfolios 5

TABLE 6.2
AVERAGE ANNUAL RETURNS AND RISKS OF FIVE FUNDS
Monthly Returns, 1980–1998

Fund	Annualized Return (Percent)	Annualized Standard Deviation (Percent)
U.S. stock	15.49	15.31
European stock	13.57	16.32
Pacific stock	9.98	22.45
U.S. bond	10.15	6.91
U.S. money market	7.20	0.98

Source: Katerina Simons, "Should U.S. Investors Invest Overseas?" Federal Reserve Bank of Boston, *The New England Economic Review* (November/December 1999), available at www.bos.frb.org/economic/neer/neer .htm.

TABLE 6.3
CORRELATION AMONG THE FIVE FUNDS' RETURNS
Monthly Returns, 1980 to 1998

Fund	U.S. Stock	European Stock	Pacific Stock	U.S. Bond	U.S. Money Market
U.S. Stock	1.00	0.59	0.33	0.29	−0.5
European stock		1.00	0.53	0.22	−0.13
Pacific stock			1.00	0.14	−0.10
U.S. bond				1.00	0.14
U.S. money market					1.00

Source: Katerina Simons, "Should U.S. Investors Invest Overseas?" Federal Reserve Bank of Boston, *The New England Economic Review* (November/December 1999), available at www.bos.frb.org/economic/neer/neer.htm.

and 6 are most like the conventional portfolios that you read about: a blend of U.S. stocks and bonds, plus a few European stocks.

The 10 portfolios show the virtue of portfolio diversification: you get a well-defined choice between higher risk or higher return. The probability is high that these risk and return characteristics will be close to what actually happens in the near future. Instead of haphazardly assembling a list of securities from around the world "from the bottom up"—with no idea what risk you are taking or what return you can realistically expect—in a portfolio diversification exercise you get solid guidance "from the top down" on both risk and return.

Note that the Pacific fund doesn't make it into any of the optimum portfolios offered as choices in this list of 10. The Pacific fund has a very large risk, 22 percent, accompanied by a low return. Moreover, it has a correlation coefficient with the U.S. stock fund of 0.33 and with the European fund of 0.53. If the correlation had been negative instead of positive, the optimization exercise would have come out differently.

TABLE 6.4
FUND ALLOCATION OF 10 OPTIMAL PORTFOLIOS
(All Portfolio Data Expressed as Percentages)

Portfolio Number	Expected Return	Standard Deviation	U.S. Stock	European Stock	Pacific Stock	U.S. Bond	U.S. Money Market
1	7.27	0.96	0	1	0	0	99
2	9.19	3.25	13	3	0	23	60
3	11.12	6.28	26	5	0	47	21
4	12.45	8.44	39	7	0	54	0
5	13.10	9.69	51	7	0	42	0
6	13.75	11.10	63	7	0	30	0
7	14.40	12.60	75	7	0	18	0
8	15.05	14.17	87	8	0	5	0
9	15.38	15.02	95	5	0	0	0
10	15.49	15.31	100	0	0	0	0

Source: Katerina Simons, "Should U.S. Investors Invest Overseas?" Federal Reserve Bank of Boston, *The New England Economic Review* (November/December 1999), available at www.bos.frb.org./economic/neer/neer .htm.

In practice, completely inversely correlated security classes do not exist. If you still wanted Japan (or some other countries in Asia) represented, you would have to start over again with a different set of funds. Alternatively, you could modify the standard deviation of the Pacific fund by lowering it, on the assumption that the Asia crisis of 1997 was a one-time thing that artificially raised the riskiness of the region.

As the author of this study notes, this case illustrates a limitation of the application of portfolio theory, which is extraordinarily important to know. *You sometimes get strange and unacceptable results*—not because the theory is defective, but because you can't apply simple rules to past data. A very small change in the data can have a magnified effect on the outcome, like that light beam traveling to Mars that was mentioned earlier. This possibility has the odd effect of alerting you to be very careful with the data you use, even as you give yourself permission to modify the data.

Changing the Parameters for Your Portfolio Model

You can recalculate a new set of optimum portfolios, or a series of optimum portfolios, by judgmentally modifying the parameters used in the model (e.g., lowering the Pacific fund standard deviation). While you are at it, you may try a version that also raises the expected return, on the grounds that economic recovery, a few years after a crisis, has been robust and should be manifested in rising earnings and stock prices. If you decide to take this approach, you can't just change what you don't like willy-nilly. You need to change the parameters in a reasonable way and perform the simulated optimizations many, many times. When you use "simulated data" (the polite term for your modifications), you end up with a "fuzzy" set of efficient portfolios—a cone of light in contrast to a laser beam. Simons notes that if your existing portfolio falls within the fuzzy set, it may not be worth incurring transaction costs to rebalance the portfolio.

This is a tremendously important conclusion: Not only *should* you use forecasts, you *must*.

HOW TO FORECAST: IDENTIFYING THE REAL RETURN AND THE RISK PREMIUM

As noted earlier in this chapter, when properly done, asset allocation starts with the optimum balance of two asset classes: the risk-free and the risky. Although risk is a well-defined concept using historical data, it is not well defined at all when viewed in light of personal preferences (called "utility" in economists' jargon). It pays to follow the debate on **equity risk premium.** It gives you a clue as to how to establish your own estimates of expected return and future volatility.

> **equity risk premium**
>
> The amount of extra return investors expect from investments that have risks in excess of the risk-free rate—generally assumed to be the rate of return on three-month or six-month Treasury bills.

This is how the argument starts. If you buy a U.S. government bond on its issue date and hold it to maturity, you will get a return exactly equal to the coupon rate. In other words, a 10-year bond that pays 6 percent will give you a return of 6 percent—to the penny. This is considered, in professional financial circles, a "risk-free" return. A U.S. government bond is deemed to carry no risk, because default by the U.S. government is highly unlikely.

Along this same line, the Bank for International Settlements, in Basle, Switzerland, considers the bonds of all the original OECD countries to be risk-free. The OECD—the Organization for Economic Co-operation and Development (www.oecd.org)—is located in Paris. Seven original members represent the world's most developed countries. Membership has been expanded over the years. Today, the OECD has 29 members.

By the time the ten years are up and you get your principal back, inflation may have eaten away the real purchasing power of your capital (which is why the government has now issued inflation-adjusted Series I bonds). Therefore, the "real" risk-less rate of return is as follows: the **bond yield** minus the expected rate of inflation over the life of the bond. Most analysts subtract actual or expected inflation (although some analysts simply use the published bond yield without that refinement). The assumption is that, to compensate them for uncertainty, equity investors

> **bond yield**
>
> The rate of return of a bond, comprised of the notional yield at issuance plus or minus any change in the bond's price arising from a change in interest rates of the same maturity as the bond, converted from price to yield terms. A bond that is held to maturity has the same bond yield as the **nominal return** or yield.

require a rate of return that is higher than the riskless rate. In all financial analyses, we assume that the riskier the stock, the higher the "equity risk premium" has to be. If equity investors thought that the rate of return on a stock would be the same as the rate of return on a bond for the same holding period, they wouldn't bother to take the extra risk.

Academics assume that the average investor is risk-averse. The risk premium encompasses both the dividend return (which is largely known in advance), and the capital gain (which is not). But some investors—such as those who invest in private ventures and IPOs—are risk seekers. Some investors may be irrational; they do not have an informed idea of what extra risk they are taking, or should take, when they invest in equities. Keep in mind that we are always comparing the certain outcome (bonds) with an uncertain outcome (stocks).

What should the risk premium be? Nobody knows. The Fed has an interest in the subject and publishes academic papers on various ways to calculate it as equity market conditions change. One reason for the Fed's interest is the so-called "wealth effect" of individuals' gains in the stock market. The presumption is that people will spend more if they feel rich, even if their gains are only on paper. Efforts to quantify the wealth effect have not conclusively proven this thesis, but it is intuitively plausible and has some bearing (how much, we don't know) on the Fed's interest rate policy.

Another reason why nobody knows what the risk premium should be is that "savings" are officially defined to include bonds and bond funds (on the assumption of a long holding period), and equity holdings are not included. This comes as a surprise to most people; they intend their IRA, 401(k), and Keogh equity accounts to be "savings." Here, the Fed's idea is that there is some break-even point at which the return on bonds becomes high enough—or the risk premium on stocks becomes too low to compensate for the volatility of the stock market—to lure individuals away from stocks and into bonds.

If you try to discover what the Fed is thinking (www.ny.frb.org), you will run into a wall of mathematical formulas and highly technical language. Instead, why not just look at what the risk premium has been in the past, and go on from there? Various studies have concluded that, over a long period of time, the real return on equities in the United States is 6 to 8 percent. In his book, *Stocks for the Long Run,* Jeremy Siegel comes up with 6.8 percent for the period from 1871 to 1996. *The Millennium Book,* by Elroy Dimson, Paul Marsh, and Mike Staunton (London Business School and ABN AMRO, 2000), concurs with that number, having arrived at 6.9 percent for equities and 1.5 percent for bonds over the past 100 years.

Even though the historical record is relatively clear, the implications are not, because the past may not be a good guide to the future. For example, in macroeconomic terms, the information technology revolution is deflationary. If we believe today that this structural change is permanent and ongoing, and if we believe that the Federal Reserve has the ability to prevent high inflation, the past real return on equities is not relevant to what people expect from and demand for the immediate future.

The perception, right or wrong, that inflation has been conquered implies that equity investors require less of a **nominal return** to get the same **real return**. And yet, in 1999, the Nasdaq gained over 80 percent in real (after-inflation) terms. So, which is the correct "expected return" of the average investor: the historical 6.9 percent or the 80 percent? Average investors change their expectations and requirements over time. There is a direct relationship between the equity risk premium—which we must impute to average investors because we have no way of calculating it from scratch—and the volatility that will occur as average investors' requirements are met or not met. In this feedback loop, the expected return is continuously adjusted by real results.

> **nominal return**
>
> The stated, contractual yield a security returns.

> **real return**
>
> The yield a security returns after deducting the current rate of inflation. If a bond has a nominal yield of 6 percent and the current rate of inflation is 4 percent, the real rate of return is 2 percent.

CAKE TODAY OR CAKE TOMORROW?

The democratization of the stock market means that participants put their own interpretation on "value." The traditional measure of value is earnings in relation to price. This can be done in two ways.

The first way is to consider the price/earnings (P/E) ratio, quoted everywhere. The higher the P/E, the more expensive the stock in terms of the firm's past or expected earnings. On this basis, U.S. stocks are relatively expensive today. The P/E ratio of the S&P 500 averaged 27.3 (as of June 7, 2000), compared to a 20-year norm of 16 to 17 percent. Some stocks, especially on the Nasdaq, have P/Es in the hundreds.

The other way of looking at value is to turn the ratio upside down and divide 12-month past earnings by current price. The result, called the earnings yield, shows current profit as a rate of return because, in this form, it *is* a rate of return. It is comparable to the rate of return on a risk-free bond, whereas P/E is not. Current profit is either used to pay dividends, or retained to make investments that will enhance future earnings. Investors today seem to prefer retained earnings (cake tomorrow) over dividends (cake today). The dividend rate in the United States has gradually fallen from 7.35 percent during 1871–1945 to 3.75 percent in 1945–1996, and under 2 percent in 2000.

Growth fueled by retained earnings is assumed to signal stock price rises in the future. This is actually a vote of confidence in corporate management, which is being entrusted by the investing public to keep on producing capital gains—and has to pay a lower cost (the dividend) to get the capital to do it.

According to Standard & Poor's, the average corporate earnings of the S&P 500 in 1999 were $51.58, and the S&P 500 closed the year at 1469.25. That puts the earnings yield of the S&P 500 at 3.52 percent, or a little lower than the real return on the U.S. Government's inflation-adjusted savings bond. If we calculate the earnings yield on a future-earnings basis for the year 2000, we get 3.99 percent as of June 7. For the period from 1946 to 1996, Jeremy Siegel (in *Stocks for the Long Run*) puts the earnings yield at an average of 6.96

percent, considerably higher than the level today. The S&P 500 would have to be at 741 (about half the year-end-1999 level) to match the earnings yield during those 50 years.

This is an anomaly. If we believe in reversion to the mean in financial ratios, either earnings have to rise or the S&P 500 has to fall below 1000. This is the bear case. Another way of looking at it is to say that the new-age investors have so much faith in the stock market as the only place to invest that they don't compare the yield in bonds and stocks. They assume that stocks yield a risk premium, and they don't bother to calculate it. Whatever it is, it's fine. In fact, it could be nonexistent or even negative. They would still want to invest in the stock market. Such an interpretation implies a shift in investors' preferences, matching the shift in attitude toward dividends. Critics who say that, as of 2000, we are in the grip of a stock market mania favor this view—the investors are historically ignorant and economically irrational. A third interpretation would be that the earnings yield is just an academic exercise. Professional stock analysts don't look at it. The average investor doesn't look at it. The fall in the earnings yield is true, but not useful.

THE BEAR CASE

The conventional wisdom claims that equities have been the best-performing asset class during the past 100 years and will continue to outperform other assets. The expected real return will be higher than the historic norm—maybe substantially so—because of the democratization of the stock market, the permanent deflationary effect of technology, and world peace (if not smarter government, too).

But an important school of thought doesn't see it that way. Information technology does not create permanently deflationary conditions, any more than did the spread of electrical power or the invention of the radio, the railroad, or indoor plumbing. We shouldn't overvalue the productivity enhancement arising from technology, given that inflation is "always and everywhere a monetary phenomenon" (in the words of Milton Friedman, the 1976 Nobel Laureate in Economics), and external inflationary shocks, such as oil price rises, natural disasters, and war, are always possible.

Moreover, the **earnings yield** doesn't tell the whole story. The argument is that the U.S. stock market is overvalued on a more sophisticated statistical basis, too. For example, when you calculate the bond yield/earnings yield as a ratio and compare it with the S&P 500 price/book ratio, things are off the chart in the year 2000.

One argument that uses **price-to-book value**, or Q, is put forth in a book by Andrew Smithers and Stephen Wright, *Valuing Wall Street* (McGraw-Hill Professional Publishing, 2000). The authors debunk many components of "stockbroker economics" and make an academically convincing case for a coming crash. Now, to confuse the issue, a growing body of literature suggests that book values are grossly miscalculated in a knowledge-based economy, where assets such as research and development (R&D) and "human capital" are hard to measure and often undervalued. Another book, Gary Shilling's *Deflation* (McGraw-Hill, 1999), addresses the issue of stock market overvaluation from a global macroeconomic point of view.

> **earnings yield**
>
> The inverse of a price/earnings ratio. It converts the value of a stock to a bond equivalency.

> **price-to-book value**
>
> The price of a stock divided by the book value of the company.

Not every value investor wants to be described as a bear, but many don't mind and even choose the appellation. (Further information on the bear view is available at www.prudentbear.com and www.bearmarketcentral.com.) Bear work is worth more than a passing glance because bears say, "It's not different this time" and point out that risk is far higher than is commonly assumed. At issue is preservation of capital. The capital lost in the 1929 crash took 24 years to recover. The capital lost in 1966 took 27 years to recover.

Pondering those statistics might give you cause to adjust your expected return.

IRRATIONAL CAPITAL FLOWS AND IRRECONCILABLE DIFFERENCES

In theory, the risk premium that investors demand over the rate of return on a risk-free asset, has to be higher when the security in question is foreign. If the risk-free asset in the United States has a return of 4 percent and the U.S. risk premium is (say) 4 percent, investors require an 8 percent return to induce them to buy equities. If the risk-free return in the foreign country (its government bond) is 2 percent and its domestic equity investors demand only a 2 percent risk premium, the total return on equities in that country is 4 percent. American investors will never buy equities in that country because its combined total return is less than the total return that can be had by staying at home and not taking any foreign risk. Yet, people invest in Japan, which has such a risk premium profile. In fact, non-Japanese institutional investors poured billions of dollars, euros, and pounds sterling into Japanese equities in 1999 and the first quarter of 2000.

Why has this seemingly irrational capital flow occurred? Because portfolio theory does not use the risk premium concept or statistics in its formulation. It does start with an analysis of risk premiums, but only to arrive at the concept of expected return. It thereafter proceeds on a different path. For example, to those investing in Japan, the diversification benefit far outweighs any theoretical musings on what the local equity risk premium is or should be.

SUMMING UP

In short, there is a giant irreconcilable gap between the "foreign equity premium" construct and modern portfolio theory. What closes the gap somewhat is aggregate security selection, whether based on diversification as a goal in its own right, without regard for the foreign equity risk premium, or based on forecasts of expected return instead of historical returns.

Now that you have some insight into the challenges of portfolio theory, Chapter 7 introduces another level of risk that you need to keep in mind when investing in foreign stocks: country risk.

CHAPTER 7

ASSESSING COUNTRY RISK IN THE 24/7 WORLD

CNBC

Once you've made the decision to "Go 24/7" and invest in foreign securities, you need to keep in mind another risk. When you invest in a foreign stock, you are assuming not only the risk of the enterprise, but the larger risk of the country itself. As Walter Wriston, the head of Citibank in the 1970s and 1980s, famously said: "Countries don't go broke." And although technically this is true (because sovereign countries have the power of taxation), it is not particularly helpful when a country defaults on its loans and its stock market takes a dive. When countries mismanage their public finances, foreign investors in private-sector equities suffer along with multinational bank lenders and government bond buyers. So, in the long run, you might get your money back, but you probably won't like being forced to maintain a position where the expected return has changed dramatically and the exit doors have suddenly slammed shut. Understanding country risk can help you get a grip on some of the additional issues you face in this respect.

The checklist of everything that can go wrong in a country—everything that can damage or even completely destroy the value of your investment—is enough to put off the most intrepid investors. In some cases, therefore, the return on a foreign investment needs to be astronomical to offset these risks. In other cases, the risks can be systematically identified if not exactly quantified, and investors can develop a certain comfort level through research. This chapter demystifies and decodes "country risk" by describing what the real operating risks are and by defining the difference between the risk you assume with the foreign country in general and the risks associated with that country's government. The chapter also offers guidance on how to identify the risks you're taking on when you invest in a particular foreign security, and some cautionary tales from India, Malaysia, and other countries around the world.

UNDERSTANDING THE OPERATING RISKS WHEN YOU ARE INVESTING IN FOREIGN STOCKS

To illustrate some of the challenges of investing in foreign securities, let's consider a case study. Suppose you're thinking of investing in a company that is headquartered in India. India may intrigue you because it is a dynamic country with a fast-growing class of brainy and well-educated entrepreneurs and professionals. Moreover, the Bombay Stock Exchange offers several indices, including a dollarized index, and its well-organized Web site (www.bseindia.com) gives you both the data and the charts of their performance over the past ten years. This looks promising.

Then you read a front-page story in the business section of *The New York Times* (June 1, 2000) titled "In India, The Wheels of Justice Hardly Move." The story presents an astonishing tale of incompetence, corruption, and injustice, not to mention bureaucracy run amuck. It says that some criminals go on trial *after* serving the maximum sentence for the alleged crime. It describes how a civil case is unlikely to be tried in fewer than 10 years, and cases can drag on for 30 or 40 years. The citizens, however, trust that justice will be done and file ever more cases, ignoring the principle that justice delayed is justice denied. Good grief, you think, what if you have a dispute with your Indian broker or with the company in which you have invested (which publishes dividend payments but has not sent them to you).

Global equity firm intltrader.com takes the situation seriously. In *Bloomberg Personal* (July/August 2000), intltrader.com COO Brent Bressire explains that the site is staying out of India even though there appears to be a lot of opportunity there. He thinks it is too difficult a place to do business.

Sometimes you can get insights about the foreign investment environment from human interest stories like the one on India's court system, and sometimes you need to look farther afield. So, if you're interested in investing in foreign stocks, the first type of risk you need to understand and consider (after liquidity risk) is operating risk. In the broadest sense, operating risk is the risk that the broker or the exchange will fail to record your investment transactions correctly and in a timely manner, and will deal with your cash the same way.

Operating failures occur because of fraud or incompetence as well as unintended error. Fraud is universal, but not universally tolerated. Every country has at least a token law against fraud, but enforcement of the law may be a different matter—and you should realize that "different" can mean difficult or impossible—or, at least, not feasible. Fraud comes in countless forms, including stock manipulation and insider trading. Among the causes of incompetence are:

- Corruption (subsets of which are nepotism and crony capitalism).
- Shortages of skilled workers.
- Lack of sufficient investment in infrastructure (from computers at the exchange to the national electric power grid and telephone system).
- An overall lack of discipline because of weak leadership.

Your first line of defense against fraud and incompetence is the foreign stock exchange itself. When you visit the Web sites of foreign exchanges, read carefully the sections on market surveillance, investor protections, and grievance resolution. For example, in India, the Bombay Stock Exchange is one of the foreign exchanges that makes available statistics on investor grievances. These are categorized as to type of grievance and the names of companies against which complaints are lodged. In Bombay, there are five types of grievances:

1. Nonreceipt of the sales proceeds.
2. Nonreceipt of dividends or interest.
3. Nonreceipt of share certificates.

4. Nonreceipt of annual reports and other forms.

5. Nonreceipt of credit at the depository.

In May 2000, the exchange received 4,192 complaints against 432 companies, and resolved 2,912 of them (about 70 percent), although some of the resolved cases are carryovers from complaints made in previous months. The average amount of time to resolve a complaint is not disclosed.

The Bombay Stock Exchange's Web site also lists the top 10 and top 20 companies against which the highest number of complaints are lodged. Something named the Vatsa Company, with 634 grievances pending as of May 31, 2000, has almost twice as many cumulative complaints as the next in line. This information would make you think twice about investing in the Vatsa Company if your other research had identified it as a possible investment candidate.

Although it is comforting to know that there is a grievance resolution process independent of the Indian civil courts, what can you conclude from this information? The only way to put it in perspective is to know the extent of investor grievances as a ratio of volumes traded, and the pace of resolution at all the other exchanges in the world. Note that the New York Stock Exchange Web site has a short blurb on arbitration but offers no statistics, in contrast to the Bombay Stock Exchange. This fosters a presumption that in New York it's not a problem worthy of mention, while in India, it's such a big problem that it must be disclosed in detail.

Yet, that inference is not necessarily warranted. In January 2000, investors in the United States won the right to arbitration by the American Arbitration Association or the Judicial Arbitration and Mediation Service (instead of having recourse to only the National Association of Securities Dealers or the New York Stock Exchange). Disgruntled investors even have their own group of specialist lawyers: the Public Investors Arbitration Bar Association. This is the litigious United States, after all. Type in any combination of those words in an Internet search and you will get thousands of Web sites, some with really catchy names like www.investorfraud.com and others describing the laws and regulations, with extensive case studies. The point is: The securities industry in the United States and worldwide is generally self-regulating, and a fair number of foxes are guarding the henhouse.

It is difficult to assess the operating risk of another country because there is no single source for comparative information on operating risk issues. The International Federation of Stock Exchanges (the FIBV, discussed in detail in Chapter 3) has published a paper on "Investor Protection," but it is dated 1990. In short, at this level of country risk, you would have to make specific inquiries by writing letters to brokers, the exchanges, and the companies in which you are interested in investing.

The Bombay Stock Exchange is visibly striving to project an image of a mature and honest place of business where fiduciary responsibility is taken very seriously indeed. Like most so-called "emerging" markets, India's stock exchanges implicitly acknowledge the benefit of foreign capital inflow. It is in their best interests to be both efficient and transparent. Putting *The New York Times* story in this perspective, what stands out is that the Indians themselves continue to file cases because they believe justice will be done (however slowly). The British colonial legacy, despite class elitism and bad boundaries, is also one of fair play. The implication is that there is an authentic commitment to fairness as a social goal and a social norm in the country (in contrast to other societies where history has led the people cynically to view justice as an impossibly naïve and unattainable ideal).

Protecting Your Foreign Investments from Operating Risks

Investor protection is where the rubber meets the road for an investor in foreign securities. There's no point in investing in a company and making a spectacular return if you never receive proof of purchase and sale, and your cash disappears. In practice, though, you will most likely be using an international broker behind whose skirts you can safely hide. It is the broker's responsibility to disclose operating risks like this to you, in detail. Operating risks include not only the efficacy of market surveillance and regulation, settlement times, document delivery and custodial arrangements, and the like, but also taxation.

In some countries, domestic taxes on dividends are levied at the source (the company). Foreigners may be exempt from the dividend tax, but the procedure for getting a refund is usually horrendously complicated and time-consuming. The paperwork sometimes looks like the paperwork given to tourists for getting a refund on sales tax or VAT (value-added tax)—fraught with semantic difficulties (if they are even written in English in the first place) and stuffed with hopelessly strict validation requirements.

In a foreign country and in your home country, taxes on current and capital gains are another topic on which your broker *should* offer guidance. Often, however, the broker *won't* offer guidance—except in situations where there is a specific securities tax (such as a stamp tax). To be fair to the brokerage houses, if they gave explicit tax advice, they might incur legal liability, not to mention the wrath of the legal profession. After all, a broker's job is to broker trades, not to dispense tax opinions. This is an area of hot debate and some incremental (though glacially slow) change is taking place. Today, the best advice you will get on the subject of foreign taxation is to tackle it on a case-by-case basis and never deliberately seek to evade taxes in any jurisdiction.

SOVEREIGN RISK IS ANOTHER ASPECT OF COUNTRY RISK

Operating risk is the most immediate and specific of country risks. Many of the other country risks are broader and, seemingly, more vague. The vagueness is more apparent than real. You can quickly acquire the analytical tools and the mindset to evaluate events and developments in a foreign country in a simple framework.

The first distinction to draw is between *country* risk and *sovereign* risk. Country risk pertains to everything about a country—its geography, demographics, natural resources, rate of economic development and growth, cultural heritage, political system, and even its food. The reference to food is only partly a joke. For example, consider the fact that the start of the Japanese stock market recovery in 1998–1999 coincided with Starbucks' opening shops on every street corner in Tokyo. Many global equity commentators have noted this strange correlation of good stock market performance with different food.

In contrast, sovereign risk is risk associated with the sovereign or the government. To a banker, sovereign risk is the risk that a government will default on its loan. To an international bondholder, it is the risk that the sovereign will repudiate the bond and refuse to pay either principal or the coupon. (By the way, antique defaulted securities are among the most collectible of antiques. The field is called "scipophily." Type that into a search engine and you can look at some beautiful illustrations engraved on old securities certificates—and on some that are not so old.)

Today, as in the past, there is no recourse to sovereign default except in cases where a supranational organization, or another state, has provided a guarantee. Every time a government defaults on international private bank loans or government paper, the banks scramble to devise repayment schemes that minimize the losses. But losses there are. In the 1980s, we had a slew of Latin American sovereign defaults, starting with Mexico; in the 1990s, it was South East Asia, starting with Thailand spreading to Russia and then Latin America. It seems as though some government, somewhere, is always on the verge of default or just coming out of it.

For private equity investors, the highest sovereign risk is expropriation. The foreign government seizes their property, whether it is real estate, factories, financial instruments, or bank accounts. Since the Russian, Chinese, and Cuban communist revolutions, this happens rarely but it does happen. Consider these examples:

- Nazi Germany expropriated companies left and right.
- The United States expropriated German companies during World War II.
- Mexico expropriated the oil companies operating there in the 1930s.
- Venezuela expropriated the oil companies in the 1980s and nationalized the banks in the 1990s.

Wartime is not the only time expropriation takes place. Consider these examples:

- The United States seized assets belonging to Iran and Iranian companies in 1978.
- France expropriated banks in the 1970s, in the guise of socialist nationalization of what had been private-sector enterprises. Banque Rothschild was only one of 39 banks nationalized by the Mitterand government.

Keep in mind that expropriation is usually without compensation to the private owners, whereas nationalization is usually accompanied by some form of restitution, but at prices set by government fiat, not the market.

Indirectly, despite near-universal claims to American-style capitalism, which puts a high value on private property rights, expropriation is still alive and kicking. It has just evolved. Nowadays, it is manifested through piracy of products, especially software and music, but also clothing design (e.g., knock-offs of Chanel handbags), jewelry (e.g., *faux* Rolex watches), perfume and cosmetics, spare parts for airplanes and other vehicles, and many other goods that are copyrighted or trademarked. Billions of dollars in product value are stolen yearly. Intellectual property piracy requires governmental collusion. Ex-communist countries, in particular, have a long history of expropriation and have merely shifted the focus from bricks and mortar to a less blatant form of expropriation. China is singled out as the chief offender, but, to be fair, countries that were never communist (such as Taiwan, Thailand, and the Dominican Republic) also participate.

The victims of this form of expropriation are mostly U.S., Japanese, and European companies. If you are interested in investing in domestic securities in these countries, you have to ask yourself whether the disregard for property rights might spill over to the company you have invested in, should it fall out of favor with the government. Governments have the ability to bestow tax exemptions and other financially valuable benefits on new competitors, especially if the new competitor is started up by a relative or crony of the present government leaders. This is not discrimination against foreigners *per se,* but it can have the same effect.

If you are investing in a company that has a local market monopoly, it will pay to read the newspaper about a possible change in regime.

Case Study: The Malaysian Stock Market Crisis—An Example of Sovereign Risk

A form of sovereign risk is the imposition of capital controls, and we have a modern instance of it: the Malaysian stock market crisis of 1998. The whole saga of the East Asian crisis can be found at www.stern .nyu.edu/~nroubini/asia/AsiaHomepage, and it makes entertaining and educational reading. Here's a brief summary. The crisis started in 1997 with a private South Korean company's bankruptcy, which was followed by others in Thailand. Very quickly, the inability and unwillingness of governments to bail out overextended private companies (including banks) led to outflows of foreign capital from every emerging market security, including government bonds and local stocks. Deprived of tax revenue and with falling local currencies but debt denominated in dollars, Deutschemarks, and yen, governments (e.g., Malaysia, Indonesia, South Korea, Thailand, the Philippines, and others) defaulted on sovereign debt. The crisis spread to Latin America, Russia, former Russian states such as the Ukraine, and even Japan and Hong Kong. Currencies fell as much as 80 percent, stock markets crashed, civil strife ensued, and governments (most notably, Indonesia's) were toppled.

In Malaysia, Prime Minister Mahathir railed against foreign speculators as the cause of the loss of confidence, and although he still subsidized grandiose public projects, he blocked the remittance of foreign exchange proceeds from the sale of Malaysian equities. (Mahathir also made a series of shocking remarks grounded in a conspiracy theory he said was hatched in the West, particularly in the United States, and implemented by hedge fund managers to bring down Asian economies so that they could impose Western values.)

The ban on foreign remittances was imposed in October 1998 and lasted one year. What effect did the Malaysian sovereign's actions have on foreign investors? During the time it was in effect, they could buy and sell Malaysian stocks, but they could not remit their funds in dollars or other foreign currencies. Approximately $10 billion—which was 10 percent of the total stock market—was blocked. Before the ban, there was a bigger pile of the local currency (the ringgit) on deposit in Singapore (R 32 billion) than there was in Malaysia itself (R 20 billion). These sums were being lent to currency speculators who were shorting the ringgit, which had already fallen from 2.50 to the dollar to 3.80 to the dollar, a devaluation of 52 percent. The government gave depositors one month to repatriate the money, after which it became "external ringgit" and could not be used within Malaysia, the only place where it is legal tender. The government had shut down Singaporean trading in Malaysian stocks the year before, in an overall ban on short-selling.

Technically, nothing was taken from individual investors; they were simply forced to continue to hold Malaysian stocks or Malaysian ringgit for another year. Investors could still sell the Malaysian stocks they had bought, but they couldn't use the ringgit proceeds to buy dollars to remit to the United States. By the time investors' funds were unblocked, the ringgit had fallen considerably, which meant they got a lot fewer dollars for the ringgit than they had paid for them. So although investors lose money in any financial crisis (domestic as well as foreign), in the United States at least you always have access to your actual cash.

If you visit Asian financial Web sites today, you will find little reference to this remarkable story. The Kuala Lumpur Stock Exchange makes no mention of it at all. In fact, you can get news, analysis, and live quotes from the largest Malaysian investment Web site, www.stockk.com, but no mention of capital controls. (For a window on Asian markets, go to www.asiaco.com.) Is this just an unfortunate chapter in world financial history that is now behind us?

It would seem not. Malaysia's Prime Minister Mahathir wrote a book entitled *A New Deal for Asia,* in which he defends the idea that emerging market countries have not only a right but also a *duty* to the electorate to choose their own medicine and not to accept the prescription of the International Monetary Fund. The IMF's demands on the countries that take its emergency loans hew to a particular collection of economic ideas that, to some economists and other critics, lack theoretical coherence and practical effectiveness. They also have unintended consequences that less ivory-tower market observers can easily predict.

Many academic and applied economists in the United States and elsewhere have come to the reluctant conclusion that capital controls may not be such a bad thing, after all. MIT professor and columnist Paul Krugman is among them. He points out that a currency crisis is the market's way of informing a government that it is pursuing unsustainable policies. Capital controls are handy for fending off a destructive crisis, but only for a short time, which the government should use to clean up its act. Prolonged use of capital controls ends up distorting the efficient allocation of resources and results in ever wider discrepancies between price and value, causing a worse shock when controls are eventually lifted.

How do these economic views of capital controls pertain to the country risk you should be aware of when investing in foreign markets? The answer is that because the IMF so far remains opposed to capital controls, you are probably safe from that quarter when you invest in a country where the IMF has mounted an emergency rescue (such as those countries named). Nevertheless, investing in such countries is considered to be "bottom-fishing." In fact, some investors believe that the best time to invest in a country is immediately after it has just had such a crisis, because stock prices are low, the currency is cheap, and the faint-of-heart have not yet returned. And when they do, you are already there on the ground floor.

Elsewhere in the emerging market universe, you are on your own in evaluating the prospect of capital controls. This means you have to read news and analysis of your country. For non-Japan Asia, the *Far Eastern Economic Review* (www.feer.com) is helpful, although Asia also boasts a high number of competently designed financial Web sites. And, of course, there are other specialized publications and Web sites for other emerging markets.

Finally, keep in mind that, in international finance, the hipbone is connected to the thighbone is connected to the legbone is connected to the anklebone. In other words, in Asia, the currency crisis led to the equity market crisis, and they both led to the banking crisis and the sovereign defaults. There is pretty good evidence that the East Asian financial crisis was not the fault of hedge funds at all, but rather the fault of international banks. *Foreign Affairs* magazine (March/April 2000) cites how, in 1996, $47.8 billion in bank loans came into the five Asian crisis countries (Thailand, Malaysia, South Korea, Indonesia, and the Philippines). They then had a $29.9 billion outflow the next year—a turnaround of $80 billion. Consider this excerpt from that article:

> The pattern is not limited to recent crises. Across the world, foreign bank lending is generally more volatile than portfolio investments. During the 1990s, quarterly swings in the total amount of foreign bank lending were far larger than the ebbs and flows of either portfolio bonds or equities. The volatility of bank-loan flows over this period—the standard deviation of flows divided by the average size of capital flows for the entire world—was 82 percent, as against 50 percent for portfolio flows. The same pattern holds for many individual countries. Between 1992 and 1997, for example, the average volatility in annual foreign bank lending to an individual country was 239 percent. During the same period, average annual volatility in bond flows was only 176 percent and in equity flows 150 percent—still turbulent, but much less so than foreign bank loans.

How can you protect yourself against sovereign risk? In general, avoid countries that are run by despots and those where the rule of law is not respected. How you define "despot" is subjective.

EVALUATING COUNTRY RISK: SEEK GUIDANCE FROM PROFESSIONALS

As a practical matter, it will be difficult for you to try to evaluate country risk yourself; instead, you might want to seek guidance from professionals. You can sometimes find online research reports that analyze a country's prospects. Another source of information on country risk is the bond ratings published by Moody's, Standard & Poor's, Fitch/IBCA, and other ratings agencies. If you scour the financial press, you can get these ratings for specific sovereign and corporate issues. The actual country reports are by subscription to institutions only, and they are prohibitively expensive for individuals. Be aware that some critics say the ratings agencies are a day late and a dollar short in downgrading countries in financial trouble.

Another good source is the semiannual "Country Credit" rankings conducted by *Institutional Investor* magazine, available at big bookstores or by subscription. As noted in the *Foreign Affairs* article, the countries to which the big international banks are lending money are probably good equity investment candidates, too. Conversely, where banks are pulling out, you need to take a second look.

In the March 2000 issue, *Institutional Investor* listed "who's up the most?" and "who's down the most?" as well as the ratings—country-by-country, and by continent—for 145 countries. Table 7.1 is an excerpt from this rating. The magazine also asked participants in the survey to rate the countries for likely rises and falls in the upcoming six months. The credit ratings were compiled from information provided by banks, money management firms, and economists. Each country was graded on a scale of zero to 100, with 100 representing the countries least likely to default/most likely to have favorable equity returns. Participants were not allowed to rank their home countries, and in *Institutional Investor's* judgment, more weight was given to the rankings of institutions with the widest international exposure and most sophisticated country analysis. In a way, this publication's rankings are the distillation of the conventional wisdom on country risk—every six months.

If you read newspapers and news magazines, you will not be surprised by these ratings:

- The top 20 countries are the usual developed countries— Switzerland, the United States, the countries of Euroland, the United Kingdom, and Japan.
- The least creditworthy countries are Yugoslavia, the Congo Republic, Sierra Leone, North Korea, and Afghanistan.
- The Czech Republic ranks 34th among the 145 countries. Its former partner in Czechoslovakia, Slovakia, ranks only 61st. Both have issued ADRs.
- China ranks higher than Malaysia, an interesting outcome for a communist country.

TABLE 7.1
INSTITUTIONAL INVESTOR COUNTRY CREDIT RATINGS
As of March 2000

Region/Country	Regional Rank	Global Rank	Rating
Latin America			
Argentina	6	60	43.0
Brazil	11	71	38.5
Chile	1	26	62.6
Mexico	—	47	49.8
Asia-Pacific			**45.1**
Australia	3	21	78.3
Hong Kong	6	30	60.8
Japan	1	10	86.9
Singapore	2	18	80.4
Malaysia	9	42	65.9
China	8	40	56.6
Africa/Middle East			
Israel	3	37	57.6
South Africa	5	58	45.2
Ghana	9	82	31.0
Western Europe			
Ireland	12	15	84.8
Spain	15	19	80.4
Portugal	16	20	79.7
Greece	18	27	62.5
Turkey	20	68	39.0
Eastern Europe			
Czech Republic	3	34	59.1
Hungary	2	33	59.2
Slovakia	7	61	42.9
Russia	13	103	19.6

Source: *Institutional Investor* magazine, March 2000.

- Russia, so interesting to many, is 103rd of 145. Its rating is only 19.6 out of a possible 100.

You could probably have guessed this from the news. An article on the front page of *The New York Times* on April 18, 2000, for example, described how thieves are stripping Russia of its power lines to get the copper. The *Times* reported that hundreds of people were dying of electrocution and electric shock, and more than 15,000 miles of power lines had been pulled down in Russia nationwide. In a single year, 2,000 tons of high-voltage aluminum cable had been literally ripped off power pylons, at a cost of $40 million. A nuclear power plant was shut down when aluminum sensors were stolen. The Russian Navy, in one port, lost all communications for over a week. An article like this one should make you consider whether this is a country in which you really want to make an investment.

An interesting feature of the twice-yearly country ratings by *Institutional Investor* is the list of countries that are likely to rise and fall during the coming six months. A sample is shown in Table 7.2.

EVALUATING COUNTRY RISK BY CONSIDERING LITERACY RATES AND GDP PER CAPITA

The idea of a "stock market" is central to a particular form of economic organization described as "capitalism." Whether capitalism *requires* a particular social and political system is open to debate, but it is clear that some societies and some political systems do not cohabit well with some aspects of capitalism and, thus, with stock markets.

The "crony capitalism" of East Asia is a prime example. The endemic corruption in Russia and West Africa, among other places, is another. Why do the Chinese in the communist People's Republic of China embrace the concept of stock markets so wholeheartedly, while the nominally capitalistic people of East Africa do not? (Such puzzles of history are fully explored in *Guns, Germs and Steel,* by Jared Diamond, W.W. Norton, 1999.)

TABLE 7.2
THE WORLDVIEW FOR POTENTIAL FOREIGN
INVESTORS: LOOKING AHEAD

Countries Most Likely to Rise	Countries Most Likely to Fall
Brazil	Argentina
Greece	China
Hungary	Colombia
Indonesia	Croatia
Malaysia	Ecuador
Mexico	Pakistan
Poland	Romania
South Korea	Russia
Thailand	Ukraine
Turkey	Venezuela

Source: Institutional Investor magazine, March 2000.

To some extent, capitalism requires a meritocracy that exists only at the margin of societies in which family, caste, rank, and other such constructs are paramount. Above all else, a meritocracy requires *education*. Premodern agrarian societies achieve economic development through industrialization, which requires literacy and numeracy. In short, you can't buy and sell stocks if you can't count.

You also can't buy and sell stocks if you are at a subsistence level and cannot save. Thus, the two vital characteristics you might look for in any country in which you might want to invest are *literacy* and *gross domestic product (GDP) per capita.* UNESCO (United Nations Educational, Scientific and Cultural Organization, www.unesco.org)

has been working on literacy for decades. Literacy may seem obvious—people either can read or they can't—but the *degree* of literacy is actually quite hard to quantify, and you will not find statistics that are reliable and accurate. For example, India has 850 languages. Literacy rates range from less than 20 percent to more than 80 percent, depending on the state.

GDP per capita is also an elusive number, chiefly because census taking is not very well organized in many places (and countries that receive international aid have an incentive to fudge numbers). The International Monetary Fund (IMF) and World Bank publish statistics, as do the individual countries. Unfortunately, you will not find the numbers easily by visiting their Web sites, but you can keep an eye out for mention of literacy and education in the press. As you contemplate investing in foreign stocks in emerging markets, you need to be concerned with literacy and GDP per capita because, without widespread stock ownership in a particular country, you are at the mercy of other foreign investors and the country's elite. The elite are often a shockingly small group of people who are usually well connected politically. They can and do send their money out of the country long before the rest of the world knows that there is a problem. This is why the currency often reveals the first signs of strain in an economy.

Two Good Reasons for Investing in Foreign Markets Despite the Country Risk

So why not just focus on the more developed countries of the world and forget about emerging markets? There are two answers. The first is summed up in the word "opportunity." Unless you are exclusively a day-trader, you want to find first-rate, world-class companies that are as yet relatively unknown. When they become well-known, they will become fully priced. For the individual investor, emerging markets are becoming the best hunting ground for such opportunities.

The other answer is that the developed world is so wired together these days that a drop in the Dow or the Nasdaq is often followed by an equivalent drop in the Nikkei 225 (Japan), DAX (Germany), CAC (France), FTSE 100 (UK), and other major indices. A new university study shows that the benefits of international diversification may be exaggerated because a bear market in the United States contaminates other markets, at least in developed countries, and particularly in Japan and Germany. When markets are flat or rising, the correlation is low and you get diversification that reduces risk. When markets are falling, however, the correlation rises and reduces your protection just when you need it most. (If you have a head for mathematics, the study is "Are

TABLE 7.3
EMERGING MARKETS I

Country	Three-Year Average GDP per Capita
Israel	$16,078
Taiwan	12,066
Republic of Korea	10,172
Slovenia	9,332
Argentina	8,519
Chile	4,887
Czech Republic	5,149
Brazil	4,772
Hungary	4,392
Mexico	3,653
South Africa	3,402
Poland	3,357
Turkey	2,900
Thailand	2,837

Source: United Nations Yearbook, 1998.

the Gains from International Portfolio Diversification Exaggerated? The Influence of Downside Risk in Bear Markets," by Kirt Butler and Domingo Castelo Joaquin at Michigan State University, and can be found at courses.bus.msu.edu/fi/fu860.)

This information should help you consider whether you want to invest in emerging markets. If so, you at least need a cutoff point for excluding the least likely prospects for stock market profits. One rule of thumb is GDP per capita of no less than $10,000 per annum, but this excludes some interesting countries, such as Brazil and Poland. Based on the three-year average of GDP per capita (and using United Nations data as of 1998), Tables 7.3 and 7.4 show a selection of some countries you might consider. Keep in mind that these lists may differ from yours. Countries undergoing political problems at the time of writing (e.g., Malaysia, Indonesia, Russia, Sri Lanka, Zambia) as well as those where the situation is extremely complex and rapidly changing (e.g., Pakistan)

TABLE 7.4
EMERGING MARKETS II: SPECIAL SITUATIONS

Country	Three-Year Average GDP per Capita
Lebanon	$4,116
Estonia	2,867
Lithuania	2,106
Egypt	1,067
Ukraine	854
China	668
India	384
Vietnam	305

Source: United Nations Yearbook, 1998.

and those where the environment seems to limit opportunities (e.g., Colombia, Venezuela, Bulgaria, Kenya, Bangladesh) are excluded.

SUMMING UP

Now that you know a bit more about what country risk is and what it encompasses, you can begin to make more informed decisions regarding the countries you want to research further. As with the stock selection process, you can do this top down or bottom up.

"Top down" consists of selecting a region or country and then finding the available news and analysis Web sites, including the country's stock exchange site. For the general "feel" of a place, as well as specific news and analysis, always check the "special surveys" in the *Financial Times* and *The Economist* magazine. On July 4, 2000, the *Financial Times* issued a special report on information technology in India. As of August 1, it began carrying a special survey of Turkey. Surveys like this one are usually available for quite a long time after publication, in the archive section.

"Bottom up" consists of reading about a specific foreign stock and then learning more about the country of issue to be sure that you are not also taking more country risk than you would like. Web sites that feature international stock stories include www.worldlyinvestor.com, www.adr.com, www.ftmarketwatch.com, www.globalnetfinancial.com, and www.global-investor.com. At this writing, the international investment world is fascinated by China, the most populous country in the world. It is at an early stage in the development of its stock markets and could offer fertile ground for opportunity.

You may decide that foreign investing carries more risk than you are comfortable with. Opportunity, yes—but "Why should I leave home at all?" Why not simply invest in foreign stocks that are cross-listed in the United States—usually in the form of American Depositary Receipts (ADRs) or exchange-traded funds, ishares, or international mutual funds. The next chapter explores those questions, and offers some recommendations for 24/7 traders.

CHAPTER 8

24/7 AT HOME

Any investor who wants to know more about 24/7 trading is interested not only because of profit opportunities, but also because diversification into foreign equities reduces the risk of a portfolio of U.S. stocks. In fact, according to proponents of diversification, *not* diversifying means taking a bigger risk. However, as we have seen, when you buy a foreign stock, you are likely to get only minimal news coverage of the country or the company in the United States. (Consider how shockingly little news the U.S. media report on Canada, for example.)

Furthermore, when you trade foreign stocks, you are also taking on country risk (discussed in Chapter 7), currency risk (covered in detail in Appendix B), liquidity risk (see Chapter 3), and operational risk (see Chapter 7). Some—but not all—of these risks are vanquished by investing in:

1. Foreign stocks cross-listed in the United States—directly or in the form of American Depositary Receipts (ADRs).
2. iShares (international shares), the exchange-traded funds that trade like stocks on the American Stock Exchange but are comprised of a basket of foreign stocks in a particular country.
3. Closed-end mutual funds, including "country funds."
4. Open-ended mutual funds.

We noted at the beginning of this book that many investors think that extraordinary returns can be realized from investing in and trading individual stocks rather than investing in mutual funds. Most people would consider mutual funds as belonging in the "long-term holding period" basket rather than in the "actively traded basket." However, trading foreign stocks can be a difficult, expensive, and time-consuming task, despite the speed and efficiency of executing the trade *per se* via an electronic communications network (ECN) once you have figured out what trade to do. Consider these obstacles. You must:

- Evaluate country risk.
- Monitor currency risk.
- Scan the country's universe of stocks for good prospects.
- Estimate the stock's riskiness in the context of your total portfolio.
- Obtain and update fundamental and price data on the chosen stock.

To these tasks we might add "Keep abreast of industry conditions" and other factors, although those chores apply to domestic stocks as well. The point is, we are including some information on international mutual funds because the firms offering these funds are doing the extra homework on your behalf that international investing requires. They visit the countries; sometimes their firms have offices there. They read the local newspapers and keep informed on the local political and economic conditions. They follow the ups and downs of their currency against the dollar, and they determine whether to hedge currency risk. They find and evaluate the risk of specific companies in the context of the fund, which, from their point of view, is a "portfolio."

Before getting to funds, however, there are other choices: individual foreign stocks that are listed in the United States, and funds consisting of foreign stocks that trade like domestic U.S. stocks. We will cover those first.

FOREIGN STOCKS LISTED IN THE UNITED STATES

Many foreign stocks are cross-listed in the United States. These stocks are generally in the form of American Depositary Receipts (ADRs), although a large number of foreign stocks are listed directly. The Nasdaq (www.nasdaq.com) has more international listings than the New York Stock Exchange (NYSE) and the American Stock Exchange (ASE) together.

The American Depositary Receipt (ADR) is a negotiable U.S. certificate representing ownership of shares in a non-U.S.-based corporation. ADRs are quoted and traded in U.S. dollars in the United States, including via ECNs. Dividends are paid to investors in U.S. dollars. ADRs were specifically designed to facilitate the purchase, holding, and sale of non-U.S. securities by U.S. investors, and to provide a means for non-U.S. companies to broaden their shareholder base and raise capital in the United States. You can search for stock symbols and fundamental or technical research information just as you would for any U.S. stock. In fact, many ADRs are more closely followed by the investment community than some small U.S. firms because, in most cases, the foreign companies are important in their home countries. Some firms, such as Sony, are known worldwide.

ADRs offer a means to invest in foreign markets without actually working through foreign brokers or foreign exchanges. The benefit for 24/7 traders who want to invest in foreign securities is, again, diversification. When foreign markets outperform the U.S. market, diversification into foreign stocks pays off (Table 8.1). For example, in 1999, the Bank of New York ADR Index rose 46.07 percent—*more than double* the 20.15 percent achieved by the S&P 500.

As shown in Figure 8.1, the ADR Index published by Reuters DataLink (IXA) gives a somewhat different reading but still shows that the ADR Index, while following the S&P 500, can vary significantly from it and outperformed the S&P 500 in 1999.

One of the chief advantages that ADRs have over direct foreign investment is that, in order to list in the United States and to be traded on an exchange (NYSE or Nasdaq), the foreign company has to conform to U.S. accounting standards. As noted below, ADRs that are not exchange-traded may choose not to conform to U.S. accounting principles. For exchange-traded ADRs, the requirement that they conform to U.S. accounting standards yields some interesting restatement effects when companies have to reveal previously concealed cash reserves or show financial assets at current market value instead of at historical

	TABLE 8.1	
	COMPARATIVE PERFORMANCE, ADR INDEX AND S&P 500	
	Percentage Change Per Annum	
Period	ADR Index	S&P 500
5/12/89–Year-end 1989	26.49%	12.61%
1990	−21.11	−6.56
1991	12.03	26.31
1992	11.92	4.46
1993	36.71	7.06
1994	8.68	−1.54
1995	22.00	34.11
1996	19.23	20.26
1997	1.26	31.01
1998	3.16	26.67
1999	168.36	19.53
2000 to 8/18/00	−0.72	1.53

Source: bofny.com.

cost. Japanese companies' reluctance to restate their balance sheets and income statements according to U.S. accounting standards is one of the reasons that Japan has a disproportionately small list of ADRs, even though it is the world's second largest economy. Japan's market share in the ADR universe is only 11 percent compared to Australia, a much smaller country, with a 9 percent market share. Table 8.2 breaks down the number of ADRs sponsored by the Bank of New York by region and country.

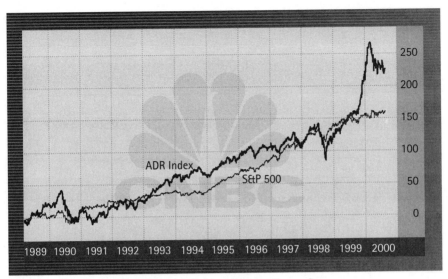

Figure 8.1   ADR Index vs. S&P 500 (Percentage Change)

Data: Reuters DataLink; chart: Metastock.

An ADR is a certificate; an ADS, or American Depositary Share, is the actual share. An ADR can represent any number of ADSs. The term *ADR* is often used to mean both the certificates and the securities themselves. Also, in contrast to the ADR (which is issued in the United States), a Depositary Receipt (DR) is issued in markets outside the United States. For example, Global Depositary Receipts (GDRs) are offered to investors in two or more markets outside the issuer's home country. Sony, for example, is listed in Tokyo, New York, and London. The listing is, technically, a Global Depositary Receipt, although we may call it an American Depositary Receipt because a GDR sometimes subsumes an ADR. As a practical matter, you will probably not be interested in GDRs that are not also ADRs. You would be trading in a foreign stock listed as a GDR in a second foreign country—for example, a British stock listed as a GDR in Germany but not also listed in the United States. This puts you back in the position of needing a foreign broker or trying to convince your U.S. broker that you really do want to execute what is, for him or her, a complex transaction. GDRs are available on the two global ECNs described in Chapter 2. Remember,

TABLE 8.2
ADRs BY COUNTRY

Country	Number of Issues	Market Share
Latin America	227	15.300
Argentina	16	1.085
Bolivia	5	0.339
Brazil	72	4.885
Chile	27	1.832
Colombia	6	0.407
Dominican Republic	1	0.068
Ecuador	2	0.136
Mexico	71	4.817
Panama	2	0.136
Peru	8	0.543
Venezuela	17	1.153
Caribbean and Bermuda	13	0.882
Bermuda	8	0.543
Cayman	1	0.068
Jamaica	4	0.271
Trinidad	1	0.068
Asia	533	35.550
Australia	145	9.837
China	20	1.357
Hong Kong	107	7.259
India	7	0.475
Indonesia	5	0.339
Japan	159	10.787
Korea	7	0.475

Source: Bank of New York.

TABLE 8.2 (Continued)

Country	Number of Issues	Market Share
Malaysia	19	1.289
New Zealand	9	0.611
Papua New Guinea	2	0.136
Philippines	9	0.611
Singapore	27	1.832
Taiwan	2	0.136
Thailand	15	1.018
Africa and Middle East	94	6.378
Egypt	1	0.068
Ghana	1	0.068
Israel	15	1.018
Jordan	1	0.068
South Africa	68	4.613
Turkey	5	0.339
Zambia	2	0.136
Zimbabwe	1	0.068
Europe	550	38.802
Austria	15	1.019
Belgium	4	0.271
Czech Republic	1	0.068
Denmark	5	3.39
Finland	6	0.407
France	46	1.556
Germany	46	3.121
Greece	9	0.611
Hungary	4	0.271

| | TABLE 8.2 (Continued) | |
Country	Number of Issues	Market Share
Ireland	28	1.900
Italy	27	1.832
Luxembourg	7	0.475
Norway	17	1.153
Poland	3	0.204
Portugal	6	0.407
Slovakia	1	0.068
Spain	15	1.018
Sweden	25	1.696
Switzerland	16	1.085
The Netherlands	45	3.053
United Kingdom	224	15.197
Russia and Former Soviet Republics	74	3.189
Kazakhstan	1	0.068
Russia	40	2.714
Ukraine	6	0.407

however, that if you were to buy a UK stock as a GDR in Germany, you would have two foreign exchange rate risks to think about: the euro/dollar and the euro/pound. The discussion of depositary receipts that follows will be limited to ADRs.

Unlike standard shares, each ADR can represent one share, more than one share, or a fraction of the underlying shares. The relationship between the ADR and the home-country share is referred to as *the*

ratio. Many ADRs have a 1:1 ratio (one underlying share equals one depositary share), but ratios can also range from 100,000:1 to 1:100. Keep this in mind if you try to arbitrage ADRs with the home-country security.

How ADRs Are Issued, Managed, Traded, and Cleared

ADR issuers are usually big multinational corporations; many have familiar names. For example, the Citibank Web site (www.citicorp.com/adr) features the list in Table 8.3.

TABLE 8.3 TOP ADR ISSUERS As of June 14, 2000
Nokia Corporation (Finland)
Royal Dutch Petroleum Company (UK/Netherlands)
BP Amoco (UK)
Vodafone Airtouch (UK)
Telefonos de Mexico
L.M. Ericsson Telephone Company (Sweden)
Royal Philips Electronics (Netherlands)
TotalFina SA (France)
Sony Corporation (Japan)
SmithKlineBeecham (UK)

Source: Citibank.

If you're looking for more information on ADRs, the Bank of New York, which is the largest depository of ADRs, has a free 14-page booklet: *The Global Equity Investment Guide—The Case for Investing in Depositary Receipts.* You can order it at www.bankofny.com/adr. As this booklet states, ADRs are familiar to most market participants by now, and they are traded by brokers and on ECNs like any other stock.

ADRs are managed by banks. J.P. Morgan (www.adr.com) created the first ADR in 1927 on behalf of the British department store Self-ridge's, but trading growth in ADRs really took off only in the 1990s. These days, the leader in new depositary receipt programs is The Bank of New York (71 percent), followed by Citibank (15 percent), and J.P. Morgan (11 percent). Banks are the issuers of the ADR certificates, and they manage all the back-office functions—registration of owners, payment of dividends, and so on.

Each major bank that is active in the ADR business has detailed information on the ADRs in its programs. You have to visit each Web site to get the full picture. For example, at www.adr.com, you can easily see a chart of each ADR in the J.P. Morgan program. You will notice that the trading volume of the top ADRs is the equivalent of the volume in any other security in the market, but the trading volume of some other ADRs is quite low, except when special circumstances cause it to spike. Low-but-"spiky" volume is a persistent problem with some ADRs. "Spiky" volume is characterized by long periods of time during which trading volume is below (say) 5,000 or 10,000 shares but suddenly surges to 50,000 or 100,000 shares for a day or two, creating the appearance of a spike on the chart of volume that accompanies most price charts. Low volume is of concern; it implies that the stock lacks liquidity. If you have to exit to get the cash for something else in your life, you may have to offer your shares at a lower price than you had expected.

Offsetting that issue involving specific ADRs is the comforting thought that institutions are major players in the ADR market. For example, J.P. Morgan's site lists the top 10 holders of ADRs (see Table 8.4). Together, these holders have 37.48 percent of the total value of their funds invested in ADRs. They are all "investment advisors," which means they are associated with issuers of mutual funds. Turnover is generally "moderate," which is not quantified.

TABLE 8.4
TOP 10 HOLDERS OF ADRs

1. Janus Capital Corporation

2. Fidelity Management & Research

3. Alliance Capital Management

4. Capital Research and Management

5. Brandes Investment Partners

6. Templeton Investment Counsel, Inc.

7. Putnam Investment Management

8. Smith Barney Asset Management

9. Lazard Asset Management

10. Capital Guardian Trust Company

Source: www.jpmorgan.com.

Mutual funds that follow a policy of international diversification are the natural investor base for ADRs. You, the individual investor, are not alone. You can see the percentage of institutional holders of each ADR, which is, in a general way, a clue to the professionals' judgment on the intrinsic value of the company. For example, top-performing Driehaus International is the largest institutional holder of China Dotcom Corporation, an Internet IPO ADR in 1999. In addition, the Web sites of each of these investment advisors have useful information on their international diversification philosophy.

ADRs trade, clear, and settle in accordance with U.S. market regulations. Investors receive annual reports and proxy materials in English. They also get prompt dividend payments and corporate action notifications (annual meetings, mergers and acquisitions, and so on).

It's easy to get price information on exchange-traded ADRs (NYSE and Nasdaq), but Over-the-Counter (OTC) and "pink sheet" ADRs can take a little searching. Exchange-traded ADRs publish their financial statements according to the U.S. Generally Accepted Accounting Principles (GAAP). Information on OTC ADRs is more limited. Company financials do not have to conform to U.S. standards (although they might), and the SEC does not require companies to communicate with shareholders on a regular basis.

Foreign Investing via ADRs Is Increasing

ADRs and GDRs comprise a huge and fast-growing market. Global investing through the use of depositary receipts is rising dramatically. For example, consider these statistics:

- At the Bank of New York, the number of sponsored depositary receipt programs grew from 352 (representing 24 countries) in 1990 to more than 1,800 programs from 78 countries by year-end 1999. Most of this rise is in the form of ADRs, although some can be attributed to GDRs—companies offering depositary receipts in countries other than the United States. Table 8.5 offers a selected country-by-country summary of depositary receipt dollar-trading volume. Again, not all transactions conducted in dollars occur in the United States or in the American form of depositary receipts per se. The Bank of New York Web site does not break it out between the American version and the global version.

- The market capitalization of companies that have ADR programs exceeded $6 trillion at the close of 1999.

- In 1999, foreign companies (some owned by foreign governments) from 33 countries raised a record $22 billion through 113 depositary receipt offerings in the U.S. and European markets. This was twice the amount raised in 1998. (Again, we do not have a breakout between the two markets, American and "global.") Asia dominated the GDR landscape by raising $11 billion (half of the new capital). Privatization of state enterprises in 15 countries accounted for $6.7 billion.

- Worldwide, trading volume in 1999 exceeded 22.8 billion shares, an increase of 20 percent. (See Table 8.5 for a percentage breakdown by country.) The value of the shares was $758 billion, an increase of 21 percent over 1998.

The technology and telecommunications industry sectors raised the most capital in 1999—more than $11 billion. India, Poland, Qatar, and

TABLE 8.5
DEPOSITARY RECEIPT DOLLAR TRADING VOLUME BY COUNTRY, 1999

Country	Percent of Total
United Kingdom	23%
Netherlands	15
Finland	11
Brazil	8
Mexico	6
Sweden	6
France	4
Ireland	4
Argentina	3
Japan	3
Italy	2
Germany	2
Korea	2
Other	11

Source: www.bankofny.com.

others were pioneers, issuing ADRs for the first time. ADR programs with the highest volume in trading activity were Nokia (Finland), Vodafone Airtouch (UK), and BP Amoco (UK). Table 8.6 shows some of the telecom companies that were privatized in 1999. Telecommunications companies continue to be at the forefront of public attention, as they have for the past several years.

Could You Be an Arbitrageur?

Arbitrage is the art and science of exploiting tiny discrepancies in price that emerge from time to time in different markets. If a stock is listed on several exchanges and its price is even "just a hair" higher on one exchange than on the others, professionals rush in to buy it where it's cheap and sell it where it's expensive. This can be extremely profitable. For example, a mere 1/32 price difference brings a $15,625 gain if you

TABLE 8.6 SAMPLE 1999 TELECOM PRIVATIZATIONS
Korea Telecom
Nippon Telephone and Telegraph (Japan)
PT Telkom (Indonesia)
China Telecom (Hong Kong)
Telstra (Australia)
Estonian Telecom
Telefonica del Peru
Telecom Eireann (Ireland)

Source: Bank of New York, J.P. Morgan.

are trading 500,000 shares. This assumes, of course, that you can switch back and forth between price quote screens in an eye blink, and you can ignore currency risk. Most foreign securities are priced in decimal form but many U.S. securities are still priced in 32nds and 64ths (this will be completely rectified by April 2001). Some ECNs, including Island and Archipelago, beat the deadline and started showing prices in decimals on July 3, 2000. The NYSE and Nasdaq are switching to decimals ahead of the April deadline as well (and CNBC shows stock quotes in decimals).

In practice, acquiring the information tools to conduct international arbitrage is prohibitively expensive for the average investor. Professionals routinely arbitrage tiny price differences between different geographic markets for the same stock, but it is not realistic for the average individual investor to try to conduct the same kinds of arbitrage. The first big obstacle is simply getting the foreign price data. At this writing, live real-time foreign quotes are not available in the United States except through expensive subscription services (such as Bloomberg). When they do become more widely available and affordable, you will need either a second screen or some other way to "window" both the U.S. and foreign stock quote screens in order to monitor both markets simultaneously. You will need a live foreign business news feed. You will also need a third online service to provide real-time foreign exchange quotes, and then a program or utility to keep the foreign stock price continuously translated into U.S. dollars. Many professionals can do currency translations in their heads, especially if they are specializing in a single country (such as Canada). It is not unusual to see four or more screens on the desks of professional arbitrageurs, each for its own special purpose, at a combined cost of $10,000 per month or more. Still, you may want to start looking for ideas and opportunities today, ahead of the day when information becomes affordable.

There are many types of international arbitrage, but the two most common are exploiting price differences across geographic locations at a single point in time, and exploiting price differences across time zones at different times, anticipating that what has happened in one market will logically be followed in the other market when it opens for business again in its own time zone.

ARBITRAGE ACROSS TIME ZONES

If a stock closes in its home country at the dollar equivalent of $25, but fresh news or perspective emerges overnight that will raise its price to $30, you can buy it in ADR form during New York hours or after-hours trading on an ECN in anticipation that it will also rise in the home country when that market opens, whereupon you will sell it. This is one of the benefits of 24/7 trading.

As another example, consider that in the United States we get news of Fed rate changes after the Federal Open Market Committee meetings. This news usually comes on a Tuesday and usually around 2:15 P.M. Eastern time. At this hour, Far East exchanges are closed. Let's say the Fed lowers rates. This benefits a country like Australia, which competes with the United States for long-term bond investors and often matches U.S. rate changes. The implication of lower rates in the United States is that Australia will benefit from capital inflows, and its stock market may rise in tandem. The general Australian stock index may go up when the market opens there. It is roughly tracked by the Australia iShare, available on the Amex during U.S. hours (and extended-hours trading) today.

Time zone arbitrage has been around a long time. The Rothschilds, who specialized in getting the news first and complained when the telegraph destroyed their monopoly, took great advantage of time zone arbitrage, especially when they had news through their special contacts with sovereigns that wars were starting or ending. One of the more interesting accounts of time zone arbitrage involves Bernard Baruch, the speculator who rose to political prominence during World War I. On July 3, 1898, Baruch (who was 28 at the time) heard that the Spanish fleet had been defeated at Santiago Bay. The battle would mark the end of the Spanish-American War. The next day was the Fourth of July. The New York Stock Exchange would be closed, but the London Stock Exchange would be open. Baruch reasoned that by buying American stocks that traded on the LSE, he could profit in the coming market rally. Train service was shut down for the weekend, and Baruch had to hire a locomotive and carriage from New Jersey. When Baruch got to his Wall Street office, he had forgotten the key and Baruch's brother was hoisted through the transom to open the office so Baruch could cable London with his orders. Sure enough, when the New York markets reopened after the holiday, prices soared.

Time zone arbitrage is conducted routinely by professionals who have accounts in foreign countries (and foreign currencies). As a practical matter, the individual investor is limited largely to using foreign stock ADRs as a substitute for the home country stock. For example, at the end of September and the beginning of October 2000, revenue and earnings warnings were issued by Apple (APPL) and Dell (DELL), following an earlier warning by Intel (INTC). The individual investor wishing to take advantage of this news could sell Japanese companies in the same sector in ADR form, in anticipation that the next day they would fall in Tokyo. In fact, Hitachi (HIT) and NEC (NIPNY) ADRs started to fall in after-hours trading in the United States and vindicated the speculation by falling in Tokyo in the ensuing days. Going the other way, when Nokia announced on July 26, 2000 (in Helsinki), that revenues would not be as high as previously expected, Motorola stock fell the next day in New York, as well. These examples illustrate that to do time zone arbitrage, it pays to know in advance not only which stocks are sensitive to industry and sector announcements, and correlated with one another as a result, but also the schedule of earnings and other important releases.

ARBITRAGE ACROSS MARKETS

The arbitrage process becomes even more complex when the opportunity involves simultaneous trading across markets in the same time zone or when both markets are open. For example, the Brazilian government-owned oil company, Petroleo Brasiliero ("Petrobras"), launched a new ADR in New York in August 2000 (in addition to two other ADRs it had in the United States, one listed in the "pink sheets" and one traded only privately). It was the biggest issue out of Latin America so far in the year, $4.5 billion, and thus attracted a lot of attention. The day before the launch, the existing listed ADR traded at three times the usual volume. This was due to arbitrage between the existing ADR and the shares traded in Brazil (denominated in Brazilian reals). Meanwhile, on the Sao Paulo Stock Exchange, Petrobras traded at four times the usual daily volume—and it fell on the day before the launch. This is counterintuitive—you'd think the price would rise in anticipation of buying interest in the "new" shares in the United States. Instead, the professionals were driving the price down in Brazil in the hope of having the launch in the United States priced at a bargain rate. In the end, the launch was delayed by two days for various reasons. Petrobras is one of the most liquid stocks in Brazil, with a 10.2 percent weighting in the Bovespa Index, and expected to attract U.S. investors partly because of its liquidity. The Petrobras ADR was issued (symbol PBR) on August 10 at an opening price of $25.25; like many new ADRs, it rose to $32.25 by the close on August 30, 2000.

The chief lesson of this story is that to participate in this event, you would have needed a quote screen showing the "right" Petrobras price in Brazil (the preferred), another showing the price of the existing ADR in the United States, a screen showing the ever-changing price of the Brazilian real against the U.S. dollar, and a news service that was keeping up with the delay of the launch. Otherwise, you might have bid for the new Petrobras ADR on an ECN at an unnecessarily high price. Knowing that new ADRs often rise immediately was not enough information in this case, a neat application of the rule that a little knowledge can be a dangerous thing.

Keep in Mind the Currencies You're Dealing With

If you're interested in conducting arbitrage, remember that the stock will always be traded in its home currency in its home country, so you must be sensitive to any change in the exchange rate that would offset your expected return on the stock. Argentina is the only major country today that has "dollarized" its currency, the peso (although Ecuador has plans to dollarize, too). Every peso is backed by dollars held in the government's reserves. Thus, the peso moves one-to-one with the U.S. dollar against other currencies. If you reside in the United States, you take no currency risk when you buy and sell Argentine securities, unless the government, at some point, devalues the peso. Hong Kong's currency, the HK dollar, is also linked to the U.S. dollar, albeit in a narrow band rather than a fixed price. In every other country, you face exchange-rate risk when you arbitrage between the U.S. ADR market and the market in the home country. (See Appendix B for more information on exchange-rate risk.)

If you have a long holding period, the risk is inherent in the position, and you have to decide whether to hedge it away. If you are conducting arbitrage, the currency risk really arises from the exchange rate that your broker chooses to give you. For example, let's say you are selling short a Japanese company in ADR form (in U.S. hours) because the company has just lost a lawsuit in the United States. You plan to buy it back at a lower price on the Tokyo exchange, denominated in yen, when the stock opens during Japanese trading hours. If the exchange rate stays the same, you anticipate a gain of $5 per share on 100 shares costing $100 each. But let's say the yen rises by 5 percent between your short sale and covering the trade in Tokyo. The loss on the exchange rate exactly offsets the gain on the stock. If the broker executing your Japanese trade marks up the exchange rate by 1 percent, you would lose 1 percent, even though your arbitrage idea was correct.

Foreign Stocks Follow Their Home Indices

Most ADRs trade in parallel with their home country market index. Nokia is a great example of this, as Figure 8.2 indicates. When you own Nokia, it's as if you own the Helsinki Exchange Index (HEX) and its currency, the euro. ADRs are denominated in U.S. dollars, but the company is headquartered in Finland and issues its financial statements in euros. It is conceivable that the stock, as traded in Helsinki, could rise 5 percent while the euro is falling 8 percent. In this case, you are down a net 3 percent in your ADR through no fault of Nokia.

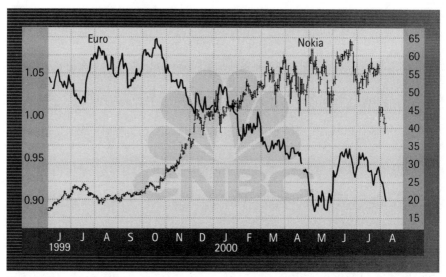

Figure 8.2   Nokia (light line, right-hand scale) and Euro (heavy line, left-hand scale)

Data: Reuters DataLink; chart: Metastock.

The currency effect can also be seen in the chart of Rio Tinto (RTP), an Anglo-Australian natural resource company that trades in Sydney, London, and New York. It is quite highly correlated with the Australian dollar, which is in turn quite highly correlated with the country index, as shown in Figure 8.3.

In addition, ADRs may have a correlation with other stocks in their sector. For example, Biacore (BCOR), a Swedish biotech company, appears correlated (as shown in Figure 8.4) with the Merrill Lynch Biotech HLDR (BBH), a sector "basket" security that tracks the top names in the sector.

Similarly, Telmex, the Mexican telephone company, is correlated with the Mexican index (MXY), as shown in Figure 8.5. It could also be evaluated in terms of the ADR Latin Telecom Index, published by the Bank of New York.

To date, there doesn't seem to be a Web site devoted to correlations. Such a site would allow you to quickly find out which ADR is correlated with what index. You can compare performance on a chart at

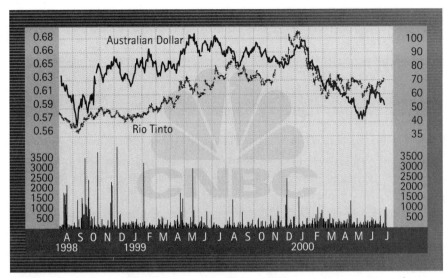

Figure 8.3   Rio Tinto (light line, right-hand scale) and Australian Dollar (heavy line, left-hand scale)

Data: Reuters DataLink; chart: Metastock.

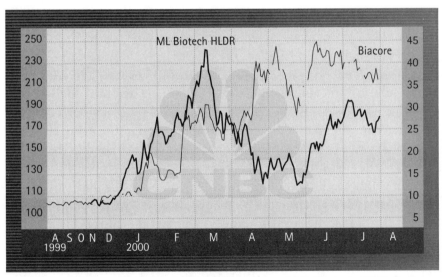

Figure 8.4   Biacore (light line, right-hand scale) and ML Biotech HLDR (heavy line, left-hand scale)

Data: Reuters DataLink; chart: Metastock.

Figure 8.5   Telmex (light line, right-hand scale) and the Mexican Peso (heavy line, left-hand scale)

Data: Reuters DataLink; chart: Metastock.

www.bigcharts.com, although it is not generally safe to trust eyeball comparisons or to make assumptions about how an ADR "should" trade. For example, if oil and gas prices are rising, it's possible—but not certain—that oil and gas ADRs will benefit. Oil and gas are priced worldwide in U.S. dollars. If the dollar is rising against other currencies—including, for instance, the British pound—a British oil company could have most expenses and costs denominated in the rising currency (the dollar price of crude) but most revenues denominated in the falling currency (the pound).

You would want to know whether the company has the flexibility to change prices in its main market. You would also have to look at the geographic distribution of sales, to guess whether the currency effect will outweigh the commodity price effect. Also, did the company hedge forward its oil purchases, as well as its currency risk, when prices were lower? Sometimes you can find this information in the annual report or 10-K footnotes, and sometimes you can't.

In short, you get diversification when you buy ADRs, but you also get additional risk exposures and additional analytical complexities.

ADRs Can Behave Like IPOs

Even though a company may have been in existence for many years as a publicly traded company in its home country, when it lists in the United States for the first time, it may behave somewhat like an initial public offering (IPO). This is logical because, for most U.S. investors, it is a "new" stock. A research paper published by the NYSE in 1996 (and available free at its Web site, www.nyse.com) reports that non-U.S. companies listing in the United States get an average annualized 12 percent return in the first week after their listing. Better yet, there is a nice liquidity effect: total world trading volume of the stock rises, and there is a significant decrease in the **bid–offer spread** in the home country. The paper also notes that the home market beta and the U.S. market beta change after listing, as does the cost of capital for the companies conducting the cross-listing. They become cheaper, which is the intent. As Table 8.7 shows, buying ADRs may reduce the volatility of your return when you invest in a foreign country.

In some cases, the new issue may actually be an IPO, as were China Dotcom Corporation (CHINA) in 1999, and the spin-off of Terra Networks (TRRA) from Telefonica de España in the spring of 2000. Figure 8.6 shows that, like many IPOs in the Internet and telecommunications sectors of late, a true IPO that is also an ADR can take off like a rocket.

As with domestic IPOs, the average investor is unlikely to be able to secure an

> **bid–offer or bid–offer spread**
>
> The price quote at which another market participant bids to buy a specific quantity of a security from you and offers to sell a specific quantity to you. When you are a seller of a security, you are always responding to the other party's bid and when you are a buyer, you are responding to his offer. A narrow bid–offer spread implies an active market with frequent trades, while a wide bid–offer spread implies an illiquid market with few trades.

TABLE 8.7
SELECTED STATISTICS FOR NEW ADR LISTINGS

	Australia	Canada	Europe	Asia	United Kingdom
Home Market Betas					
Before listing	1.414	1.110	0.646	1.185	0.992
After listing	0.991	0.997	0.627	0.991	0.853
U.S. Market Betas					
Before listing	−0.081	0.036	0.006	0.072	0.082
After listing	0.248	−0.053	0.104	−0.002	−0.199

Source: www.nyse.com.

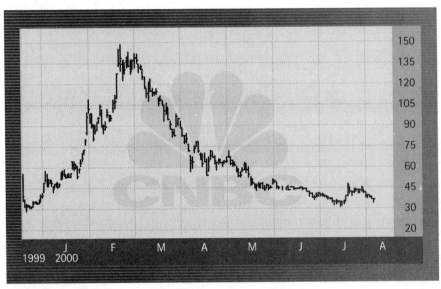

Figure 8.6　Terra Networks
Data: Reuters DataLink; chart: Metastock.

allocation at the very beginning of the new issuance. You can find ADRs on lists for upcoming issuance, however. Here are some Web sites where you can find lists of upcoming IPO issues:

- www.freeedgar.com—lists SEC filings that you can scan.
- www.ostman.com—lists filings by country, and links to dozens of free international newsletters, such as "German High-Tech Watch." Ostman ranks IPOs according to bullish or bearish technical indicators as well as specific information on the expiration dates of the "quiet period" and the "lockup period."
- www.bloomberg.com—Bloomberg makes a point of being on top of new ADR issuance.
- www.ipocentral.com—a Hoover offshoot Web site where its analysts give a "chili rating" to how "hot" the upcoming IPOs are likely to be.
- www.redherring.com—also has a rating system.
- www.ipohome.com—offers in-depth evaluations of IPOs and has a unique IPO mutual fund, but is a subscription service.

These and other Web sites are reviewed by the founders of www.ipoguys.com in their book, *Trade IPOs Online*. More information on some of the hair-raising characteristics of the IPO market can be found at www.iporesources.com.

ADRs of companies that are already established in their home countries may or may not behave like IPOs when they first appear on the scene in the United States. Early price experience seems to depend on the sector and the reputation of the company; for example, Nokia and Telmex were popular from the very beginning. ADRs that are authentic IPOs seem to behave like other IPOs, at least initially. Not every ADR IPO rockets to the moon in its first trading period, but many do. Many also have the unfortunate habit of doubling or tripling, only to fall back after a few months as the institutional investors clear out and individual investors come to own the majority of shares. Figure 8.7, a chart of China Dotcom, makes the point.

Investing in IPOs as a class, for the longer term, is a risky proposition whether the stock is an ADR or not. It's important to know your

Figure 8.7   China Dotcom
Data: Reuters DataLink; chart: Metastock.

holding period. If you are a long-term investor, ADR IPOs may not be for you. *Trade IPOs Online,* quoting data from a University of Florida study (bear.cba.ufl.edu/ritter/ipoall), shows that the average first-day return of IPOs was 17.4 percent during the period from 1977 to 1999, and ranged from 9.5 percent (1988) to 68.7 percent (1999). This is delightful for the stouthearted, but they also need to recognize that, on average, 16.9 percent of IPOs were dropped from the exchange or liquidated within five years, during the period from 1980 to 1993. Only 31 percent of IPOs outperformed the market over five years, during the period from 1980 to 1997.

Therefore, it's important to know when to take your profit. A good rule from the professional trading world is to have a stop order that trails the price and serves to lock in profit if and when the stock starts to fall. The stop order can be a function of how much money you have at stake—say, 5 percent—in the early days of holding it. Later, the stop order can be a function of securing *x* percent of your gain. Stop orders are a problem in global and foreign ECN trading—again, most do not offer the capability—so you need to have a mental stop and then be disciplined in checking prices regularly.

INVESTING IN EXCHANGE-TRADED FUNDS

Exchange-traded funds (ETFs) were invented at the American Stock Exchange in 1993 to serve as an alternative to passive index-tracking mutual funds. All ETFs trade at the Amex. The first one was the S&P 500 Index Depositary Receipt, with the ticker symbol SPY and thus nicknamed "spider." As of late summer 2000, there were 15 ETFs that track major indices. The one tracking the Dow is named "diamonds" after its ticker DIA, and the one tracking the Nasdaq 100 has the ticker QQQ. You can also get ETFs that track the Russell 1000 (IWB), 2000 (IWM), and 3000 (IWV), and other indices. Most are issued by Barclay's Global Investors. The most comprehensive description of ETFs is at the American Stock Exchange Web site, www.amex.com.

Then along came ETFs that track sectors (also usually called "spiders"). They cover energy, financials, transportation, technology, utilities, health care, and so on. As of July 2000, there were 22 sector spiders, issued by Barclay's Global Investors and by State Street Global Advisors.

"World Equity Benchmarks," a form of exchange-traded fund, first appeared in 1996. It raised $79 million in that year and was valued at $2 billion as of April 2000, according to a research paper by PaineWebber, "The Future of Indexing and More," at www .cefa.com/ETFunds.pdf). This six-page paper is highly informative. It accurately outlines what ETFs are, how they compare to closed-end funds (which we'll cover later in this chapter), and who the managers are (Barclays; Nuveen and State Street have announced plans to enter the market). In July 2000, World Equity Benchmarks (WEBs) were renamed "iShares" by the issuer, Barclays.

ETFs are, generally, passively managed portfolios modeled after an index. Passive management causes ETFs to have a low fee structure. They track their respective indices fairly closely, although not perfectly, and give rise to some arbitrage opportunities.

Like a closed-end fund, and unlike many mutual funds, ETFs can be traded intraday and are traded like shares on markets. Standard commissions are the norm for ETFs, unlike the hidden expenses that are sometimes attached to the buying, holding, and selling of some open-ended funds.

ETFs have some advantages over closed-end funds. For example, ETF units can be redeemed, which prevents big disparities between discounts and premiums to NAVs. ("NAV" refers to "net asset value," the combined closing prices of all the component stocks in a mutual fund.) Because NAVs are calculated only once a day, after the close, most mutual funds are rendered unsuitable for active trading, and trading intraday is virtually impossible. Closed-end funds generally trade at a discount or a premium to the true net asset value of the component parts. These funds are, literally, "closed"; they do not add more of the underlying shares in proportion to new money flowing in. A popular fund will therefore become priced at a premium to the basket of underlying shares and, thus, the NAV. A less popular fund will trade at a discount. These discounts and premiums are complicated, and we won't go into them any further here, except to say that closed-end funds report their holdings only twice a year. This makes it impossible to know what the underlying holdings are at any moment, whereas you always know the component parts of an EFT, including the country iShares. ETFs' liquidity and transparency make them more attractive to institutions than closed-end funds, and, as we noted in Chapter 3, institutions are valuable allies in the quest for sufficient liquidity.

INVESTING IN FOREIGN INDEX SHARES (iSHARES)

Foreign index shares were originally named WEBS (for World Equity Benchmark Shares) and were renamed iShares by their issuer, Barclay's Global Investors, in June 2000. Each iShare tracks the Morgan Stanley Capital International (MSCI) index in the country. The MSCI index sometimes differs from the established country index; for example, the iShares Germany index is not perfectly parallel to the German DAX, but the correlation is extremely high in all cases. Nineteen country indices are available. Table 8.8 gives the complete list. For more information, go to www.ishares.com and also check out www.bglobal.com.

iShares trade exactly like common stocks, even though technically they are a "fund" comprised of the basket of underlying foreign stocks. The issuers charge expenses, as do mutual funds, but the charge tends to be considerably lower than for mutual funds. Foreign iShares are charged 0.84 percent of the face amount at the moment, although Vanguard (almost universally considered the lowest-cost mutual fund provider) has announced it will be going into the business, and competition may drive down the fee. In contrast, the average foreign stock fund has an expense charge of 1.71 percent, according to Morningstar.

The ability to trade iShares all day, instead of being an end-of-day price taker, as with mutual funds, is a key benefit. Institutional investors use iShares to arbitrage or to hedge positions in the underlying securities. Because of institutional arbitrage, the iShare price tends to diverge from the fund's underlying portfolio value by very little.

TABLE 8.8 iSHARE INDICES BY COUNTRY		
Australia	Japan	Spain
Austria	Hong Kong	Sweden
Belgium	Malaysia	Switzerland
Canada	Mexico	Taiwan
France	Netherlands	United Kingdom
Germany	Singapore	
Italy	South Korea	

Source: iShares.com.

Recently, the Consumer Federation of America complained that, with some exchange-traded funds, traders could be buying the shares at a premium and selling them at a discount—in other words, the arbitrage is not perfect. The discrepancy between share price and portfolio value is highest in the international iShares—presumably because the foreign market is closed while global iShares are being traded on the Amex.

Another issue is that trading in iShares depends on Morgan Stanley Capital International, which devises the baskets of underlying stocks in the international iShares. MSCI seeks to cover 60 percent of each market—a lower proportion than Standard & Poor's 70 percent target. MSCI includes the full market capitalization of each stock when calculating its proportion in the country basket, even though many foreign stocks are closely held and these shares are not really available to the investing public—or the arbitrageurs.

MSCI rebalances its country benchmarks periodically. This provides both opportunities and pitfalls. Global fund managers took losses when specific Hong Kong stocks they were holding were deleted from the MSCI index for Hong Kong, in favor of other stocks. They had been holding the stocks in order to mimic the MSCI index for Hong Kong, which differs somewhat from the Hang Seng, the main Hong Kong index. The deleted stocks fell in popularity and price, and the replacement stocks rose, simply because index-tracking fund managers are required by their own internal rules to follow suit, whatever the merits of the individual stocks. Because the Hong Kong iShares track the MSCI index for Hong Kong, you can get volatility in the iShares that has nothing to do with the index *per se,* the country risk of Hong Kong, or any other macro variable.

As with some ADRs, another challenge with iShares is liquidity. In some cases, despite institutional interest, daily trading volume is less than 5,000 shares. Some of the same spikiness in volume is present, too. Often, this is inexplicable, and combing the news for the reason behind sudden interest in a country index yields no clues. iShares are therefore less than ideal for hedging a position in specific country stocks. For example, let's say you own Ericsson (ERICY), the Swedish telecommunications company. You figure that a short sale of the Sweden iShare constitutes a hedge of your position, or a hedge against a drop in the Swedish krona in dollar terms. Technically, iShares can be shorted like any other stock—but your broker may have a hard time finding them to borrow on your behalf.

If you believe you have a good head for country analysis—or you have good currency forecasting skills—iShares are an excellent vehicle. Unfortunately, the correlation of currencies with their country's iShares is not consistent across countries or across time. Sometimes they are highly correlated and sometimes they are not. And sometimes a currency that is correlated with its stock index will suddenly stop being correlated. iShares may not be the best way to make a strategic trading move in currencies because the currency is only one factor in determining the iShare price in dollars. It is possible to have the iShare go up because the underlying stocks in the index it tracks are going up, while the currency is falling. This means that the index on which the iShare is based is rising when denominated in its home currency, but rising by less when converted to dollars, because of the currency's decline. For example, the index may rise by 10 percent when denominated in its home currency (euros, Australian dollars, Japanese yen, and so on). But your iShares may rise by only 6 percent if the currency fell 4 percent that day. You may not want to consider iShares a way to play in the currency market, but you should be aware of currency effects. If a currency is on a long-term downtrend, you may want to defer your purchase of iShares until it hits bottom and has started to turn back up. Then you have the opportunity of getting a "double-dip" gain—a gain on the underlying stocks and the index, and a gain on the currency. Together, these are reflected in the price of the iShare.

THINKING THROUGH THE CURRENCY EFFECT

If you had invested in the FTSE-100, the main stock index in the United Kingdom, on January 2, 1986, by August 23, 2000 your gain would have been 362 percent, or almost 26 percent per annum (acknowledging that 2000 isn't over yet as of this writing). Since the FTSE-100 is denominated in pounds sterling, let's look at what it did over the same period—it rose from $1.4461 on January 2, 1986, to $1.4776, or 2.18 percent. Assuming that your home currency is the U.S. dollar (i.e., you sold dollars to buy pounds to buy the FTSE-100 and 14 years later reversed the process to get dollars again), we should add the 2.18 percent to the FTSE gain for a total gain of 364 percent. In the context of a 362 percent gain, an incremental 2 percent is almost insignificant.

Figure 8.8 shows the FTSE-100 and the UK pound for a shorter time period, starting in 1990. The FTSE-100 rose 170 percent from 1990 to mid-2000 (including the October 1998 hiccough all world markets experienced).

However, look also at the movement in the pound. It did not meander neatly near the starting point around $1.4461 in 1986. By 1990, it started the year 1990 at $1.6852, and over the course of 1991 and again in 1992 it reached highs around $2.00. If you had bought the pound and the FTSE-100 at those levels, your gain in the FTSE-100 would have been substantially reduced. Calculating from January 2, 1990, to August 2000, the loss on the pound would have been 12.3 percent. Again, in the

Figure 8.8   UK Pound (heavy line, right–hand scale) and FTSE 100 (light line, left–hand scale)

Data: Reuters DataLink; chart: Metastock.

context of a 170 percent gain, perhaps a 12 percent loss is trivial—but consider that, over shorter periods, it is not trivial. For example, if you had chosen September 8, 1992, to buy pounds, you would have paid $2.0042. If you had then sold them the following June 24, 1993, they were worth only $1.4664, or a loss of 27 percent. Over those dates, the FTSE gained 24 percent. Net, you would have lost 3 percent by venturing into a foreign stock market.

Of course, the converse is true, too. You may be able to discern that a currency is undervalued and choose to buy stocks in that country expecting to get a gain on the currency without a lot of concern for the stocks themselves. During 1985, for example, the pound reached an all-time low of $1.0350. If you had bought and held securities denominated in pounds until it reached $2.00, you would have practically doubled your money—and then it would be the stock return that was trivial.

One of the virtues of iShares is that you don't have to conduct any foreign exchange transactions or even think about the pound if you don't want to. iShares are U.S. dollar-denominated and trade in the United States. In the case of the iShare U.K., it doesn't track the FTSE-100 perfectly, because (as explained above), the MSCI index on which the iShare is based is not identical to the main stock index in any of the countries, including the U.K. Figure 8.9 shows that there is little difference between the FTSE-100 and iShare U.K.

Just because you can't see the pound in the iShare doesn't mean it isn't there. Notice how in 2000 the FTSE-100 is higher than the iShare. This is due to a combination of things: first, the difference in the composition of the two indices; and second, the fall in the pound since the beginning of the year, which is visible in the previous chart.

How does the pound relate to the British stock market as exemplified by the FTSE-100? As things stand today, there is little correlation between currencies and their home stock markets—and in some cases, the correlation is negative. The pound and FTSE-100 is one such case. Over the 1986–August 2000 timeframe, the correlation coefficient is −0.181. This means that if the stock index rises, the pound is likely to *fall*, but only a little (remember, perfect positive correlation means that a 10 percent rise in one is accompanied by a 10 percent rise in the

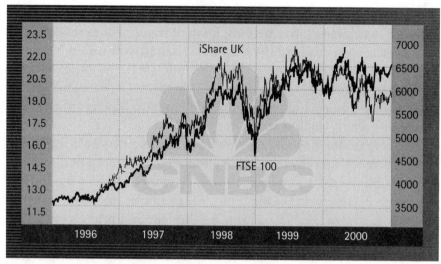

Figure 8.9   iShare UK (light line, left-hand scale) and FTSE-100 (heavy line, right-hand scale)

Data: Reuters DataLink; chart: Metastock.

other, and perfect negative correlation means a 10 percent rise in one is accompanied by a 10 percent fall in the other).

Looking a little more closely and running the correlations for each calendar year, we find that the correlation is negative in 13 of 15 periods, and ranges from −0.038 to −0.761. It was positive only in 1986 and over the first eight months of 2000. In fact, the wide range of outcomes alerts us to a problem with conducting the correlation exercise. Two series can be correlated by coincidence. Correlation does not necessarily imply causation. If we want to estimate expected return from a foreign stock investment and factor in the currency effect—or figure out whether to hedge the currency effect—we should understand why the currency and stock index are correlated (or not).

Professional international analysts who work for the big financial institutions have spent a great deal of time and effort trying to understand this issue, and the relationships among markets in general. Intermarket analysis can be very tricky, not least because things change. How do grain and metal prices (commodities) relate to interest rates (short- and long-term) and how do they both relate to currencies and stock markets? How do currencies and stock markets relate to one another? Until recently, this was not a particularly important question to anyone but specialists. Cross-border portfolio investment was limited to a few large institutions with relatively long-term investment horizons measured in years. Some percentage of a global portfolio was going to be allocated to British stocks and kept in British pounds, even if the stock selection within that allocation changed over time. Now, transactions are a lot easier to execute and managers are more responsive to developments across a broad spectrum of economic and financial events. Money has become "hotter"—i.e., more willing to flee unfavorable events. In practice, this is likely to make currencies more highly correlated with their stock markets than they have been in the past, although many factors affect currencies, including the unmeasurable factor of "confidence" in government.

One country in which the link between the currency and the stock market is sometimes clear is Japan. To a large extent, the Japanese economy is driven by exports. When the yen is relatively weak, Japanese companies find it easier to sell cars, electronics, and machinery abroad. Corporate investment and corporate earnings rise, helping the stock market to rise, too. When the yen is strong, Japanese exports are not competitive with domestic products in Europe and the United States, and in other markets where the buyer can choose between Japanese or other suppliers. Therefore a strong yen causes the stock market to fall in anticipation of lower corporate earnings and the capital investment that produces the productivity gains that contribute to the bottom line. Note that the effect is not consistent, however. A falling yen does not necessarily result in a higher stock index, or vice versa.

Figure 8.10 shows the Japanese yen and the Nikkei 225 stock index. The yen is inverted so that when the line on the chart is rising, it means the yen is rising against the dollar.

As you can see, the Nikkei 225 crashed in 1990 from over 38,000 to lows in 1992, 1995, and 1998 below 15,000. This is a unique case of a prolonged recession in a major world economy, and it is reflected in the Nikkei—but not the yen. In the middle of this, the yen rose to

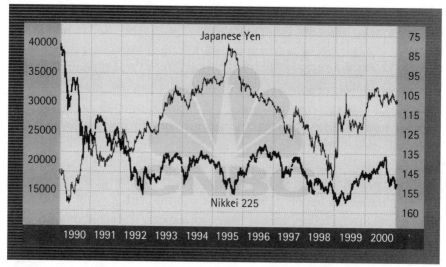

Figure 8.10   Japanese Yen (light line, right-hand scale inverted) and Nikkei 225 (heavy line, left-hand scale)

Data: Reuters DataLink; chart: Metastock.

80 yen to the dollar, an extraordinary movement that was partly the market punishment for very high trade surpluses with the rest of the world. The yen was so overvalued that it was said that the land under the Imperial Palace in Tokyo was worth more than the entire state of California. At the same time, the Nikkei was returning to lows under 15,000.

The correlation coefficient for the entire 1990–August 2000 period is 0.488, but this masks significant variation in the year-to-year relationship. This ranges from a relatively high negative correlation of 0.651 in 1990 to an equally high positive correlation of 0.765 in 1997. In the eleven periods, five show a positive correlation and six show a negative correlation. This confirms that we cannot draw a hard and fast rule about the relationship between stock markets and currencies that is valid over all time periods—you have to follow each situation closely to see whether there is an effect during any single period.

You will not be investing in the yen-denominated Nikkei directly, though, if you invest in iShares Japan. In that situation, as shown in Figure 8.11, the correlation coefficient of the iShare price series and the yen is more consistent—0.868 over the life of the iShare (starting March 18, 1996 to August 23, 2000). The correlation obtains for all years and ranges from 0.442 to 0.890 although it doesn't look like a strong correlation on the chart. This observation only serves to highlight the obvious fact that if you buy a security whose underlying currency is falling, the country iShares will fall, too, unless there is an offsetting rise in the underlying equities.

iShares have benefits and drawbacks. Having been introduced only in 1996, they are still relatively new, partly accounting for low volume. One the benefit side we can include "playing a country." If economic conditions suddenly take a turn for the better or some other "event" occurs that favors a country, its stock market and currency are likely to rise, giving the investor a double dip. If conditions suddenly worsen,

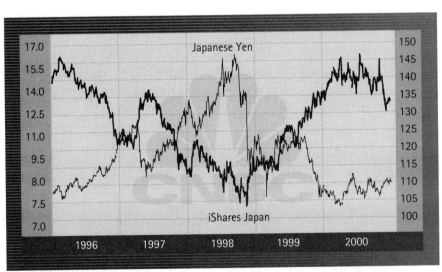

Figure 8.11   Japanese Yen (light line, right-hand scale) and iShares Japan (heavy line, left-hand scale)

Data: Reuters DataLink; chart: Metastock.

the U.S. investor can exit (during regular or extended hours) without the hassle of dealing with a foreign broker or with foreign exchange issues. Another benefit is that iShares fully reflect the true value of the underlying shares, most of the time, and do not display the wide discounts/premiums of closed-end funds, discussed below. This is partly because iShares give institutional investors the option of creating new shares by actual delivery of stock. This is termed "PIK" for "payment in kind," and is restricted to 50,000-share blocks and thus professionals, who use the feature to arbitrage away any price differences between the iShare and the underlying securities in the index.

Keep in mind that iShares are like mutual funds in that return is reduced by the amount of the management fee, while the risk stays the same. More importantly, it is possible that one company or one sector (or the currency) can affect the entire index on which the iShare is based disproportionately, as in the case of Nokia and the Helsinki Exchange Index. The iShare Japan, as noted above, is highly correlated with the yen. Because iShares have been around only a few years, we don't yet know whether the currency effect will continue to be high and positive, or will change (as it does with the domestic stock index denominated in the same currency). Finally, a drawback of any index-tracking vehicle is that total return is dragged down by whatever poor stocks, commonly called dogs, are in the index. When the sole criterion for index membership is market capitalization, you are sure to get some bad performers that you would not select individually.

FUNDS

This is not the case with funds. The chief advantage of funds generally is that the professionals managing them are doing the homework. Their goal is to select the best performing and most promising stocks, and to winnow out the dogs. In addition, they have market clout (to greater or lesser degree) in local markets, and know local economic conditions, local accounting standards, and local customs. Mark Mobius, in *Passport to Profits,* says that fund managers can more effectively exert pressure when companies try to play "fleece the foreigner," whereas the individual investor would have virtually no chance at all.

CLOSED-END INTERNATIONAL FUNDS

Today, 517 closed-end funds trade in the United States. Their combined NAV is $123 billion. The Closed-End Fund Association (www.cefa .com) labels 129 funds as not fully domestic (U.S.-oriented) in the following categories:

Categories	Number of Funds
1. Emerging Market Equity	6
2. Emerging Market Income	7
3. Global Equity	6
4. Global Income	30
5. Non-U.S. Equity	80
Total	129

You would have to dig into the composition of each fund to discover the exact difference between "Global Equity" and "Non-U.S. Equity." "Global Equity" implies the inclusion of some U.S. companies and is not entirely "foreign" from a U.S. perspective. The word "international" usually means non-U.S. investments only. These international funds hold roughly $20 billion in total NAV.

A closed-end fund has a fixed number of shares, and the issuance and redemption of those shares are limited. As a general rule, the fund changes the composition of the shares infrequently and aims for long-term capital appreciation (i.e., a long holding period). Closed-end funds may sell at a premium or discount to NAV. Country funds can be illiquid (hard to sell), especially when the country is suddenly experiencing political or economic turmoil. Country funds (e.g., the Korea Fund) specialize in the stocks of the country named. Some are also industry-specific. ASA Ltd., for example, specializes in South African gold mining stocks. One benefit of closed-end funds is that they may choose securities that are unavailable to the average investor, such as venture capital investments, real estate, and private placements. There are over 80 single-country funds. Recently even more specialized closed-end funds are appearing—Emerging Markets Infrastructure (EMG) and Emerging Markets Telecoms (ETF), for example.

Price information on closed-end funds is made available by the National Association of Securities Dealers (NASD) through most electronic quotation services. Additional sources for statistical data include Lipper, Morningstar, and Wiesenberger, a Thomson Financial Company. There are also brokerage and advisory firms that specialize in closed-end funds. The Closed-End Fund Association's Web site (www .cefa.com) is free and provides daily NAVs and performance histories for all reporting closed-end funds.

Trading Strategies for Closed-End Funds

As noted, closed-end funds are designed to be buy-and-hold securities, and the annual returns that you may see advertised for particular funds disguise sharp variations in price during the course of the year. Combining trading strategies with a macro, top-down picture of a particular country's stock market direction would increase the effectiveness of these trading strategies. Donald Cassidy, a Lipper manager and author of *It's When You Sell That Counts* (McGraw-Hill, Rev. Ed., 1998) and *30 Strategies for High-Profit Investment Success* (Dearborn, 1997), says that to trade closed-end funds successfully, you have to remember that the world changes, and as the world changes, the discount/premium on closed-end funds changes disproportionately. He recommends a contrarian approach whereby you seek extremes in fund valuation. Counterintuitively, when the NAV of a fund collapses because of unfavorable developments in the underlying country or region, the premium for that fund may rise or it may switch from a discount to a premium. This arises from individuals' reluctance to sell into falling NAV, and fund holders are overwhelmingly individuals, not institutions. Institutions would be more likely to abandon ship, while there is a distinct lack of individual sellers when there is "blood on the street."

Cassidy says there is often a year-end tax effect, though. Depending on whether the fund did extremely well or extremely poorly, selling may occur in December or January, and it has nothing to do with the fund itself, but instead with whether the taxpayer wants to book a profit or loss for his own tax reasons. Further, the discount/premium band of each fund has a distinct personality. Some traders become expert in trading a fund's price range.

Cassidy warns against raising your hopes when a vote is about to be taken on opening or liquidating a fund. If a fund has been consistently priced at a discount and investors have been disappointed that it never rises to the NAV, they may be hopeful that opening the fund or liquidating it will finally give them full value. The problem is that most funds are structured in such a way that it takes two-thirds or even an 80 percent vote of all investors to override a decision by the board of directors of a fund. If the board votes against opening or liquidating, there is no hope of an override because the fund investors are fragmented among many individuals and there are hardly any institutions to mount a campaign for opening or liquidation. "It has never happened," says Cassidy.

For more active traders, then, here are some ideas.

- *Bottom-fishers/contrarians* would want to pay special note to funds in the worst 10 categories, and keep an eye open for a change in conditions.

- *Momentum players* can take the opposite tack, looking for improvements in discounts/premiums, NAV, or market price moves. Buyers of closed-end funds are thought to be of the buy-and-hold school, so it is generally assumed that news is factored in more slowly than in more actively followed and traded securities. Hence, a closed-end fund may take a few days, or longer, to have positive or negative news factored in. For instance, favorable news out of India may not be reflected in an Indian-focused closed-end fund for a month or more.

- *Arbitrageurs* could compare the one-week change in market return (i.e., the stock market price of a unit of a closed-end fund) with a one-week change in NAV (i.e., the underlying value of the holdings per unit) to find market inefficiencies. For instance, the sample Wiesenberger Weekly Review (June 25, 1999) revealed a stark difference between the China Fund's one-week NAV change (5.96 percent) and one-week market price change (0.55 percent). This suggests a 5 percent gap in valuation, which the market may or may not factor in at some later point.

The Discount/Premium Debate in Closed-End Funds

The "Internet Closed-End Fund Investor" published, in late 1994, a discussion of why closed-end funds develop short- and long-term discounts and premiums (more often, discounts). This is a comprehensive review and while the examples given are not updated, it explains how to think about and trade discounts and premiums. For example, in the 1993–1994 spurt in emerging markets, three closed-end funds overshot their significant rises in NAV, yielding triple-digit returns. India Growth Fund had a 120 percent rise in market price—but only a 56 percent rise in NAV. To see a graph, go to www.icefi.com/icefi/tutorial/igf_1.htm.

According to this Web site:

> Sometimes, the market price lags the NAV. This is especially true when the NAV drops suddenly and sharply. In such cases, the closed-end fund tends to trade at a premium for some time, possibly because investors expect a market rebound and are reluctant to sell. Examples include the Turkish Investment Fund (early 1994) when the Turkish market crumbled under currency turmoil. The NAV slumped from a little over $14 to a little under $4 in a period of a few weeks. The market price however held its ground better, but at premiums of as high as 100 percent. Similarly, the sudden devaluation of the Mexican peso in December 1994, led to drops of 40 percent in the NAVs of the Mexico-related funds (e.g., the Mexico Equity & Income Fund). However, the market price held up better, but again, the funds traded at sharp premiums to the NAV (30%+) when they traditionally trade at moderate discounts.

The key attractions and risks of closed-end funds are their low trading volume and, often, their large discount/premiums to NAV.

Arbitrage opportunities, or simply trading windows, arise because of the often sluggish market reactions to relevant news. When news does get factored in—such as Indonesia's transition from Suharto's rule during the Asia crisis in 1997—more people become interested, moves often become exaggerated, and quite different longer-term market inefficiencies are created.

The Internet Closed-End Fund Investor (ICEFI) provides a long discussion of the factors that create inefficiencies in how closed-end funds trade. "Inefficiency" is defined as the degree of discount or premium to NAV. Long-term factors include lack of widespread knowledge about the funds, because they do not advertise as much as mutual funds. Further, a closed-end fund that consistently underperforms the relevant benchmark index will trade at a discount as investors leave. In like manner, those that consistently outperform the benchmark will trade at a premium. Examples of funds that have traded consistently at a premium are the Asia Pacific Fund and the Templeton Emerging Markets Fund, according to the ICEFI Web site.

The ICEFI also discusses the tax liability and gives the following example:

> New investors who buy such funds may find themselves with a large capital gains tax liability if the funds unwind some of their older profitable positions. For example, if an investor buys shares worth $100, and the next day the fund returns $20 as a capital gains distribution, the investor essentially puts in only $80. Worse still, on the $20 returned to him, he pays taxes (assuming it is a taxable investment), even though he did not own the fund during the time it racked up the substantial gains. So the investor shows a loss immediately. Such funds tend to trade at a discount.

Moreover, there is often a distinct year-end tax effect, especially in the prices of funds that have shown a big loss. Investors sell the fund to realize the loss and offset gains earned elsewhere.

Among other factors contributing to discounts are risky or hard-to-evaluate investment components, such as real estate, venture capital, "distressed securities," and other special situations.

Trading at a premium may be possible because the fund is offering a unique opportunity. It has traditionally been difficult for individual investors to participate in the market in some countries, and funds targeting those countries have historically traded at a premium. The site names the Korea Fund and the Indonesia Fund.

In practice, the discount or premium will fluctuate around a mean level and will vary according to the news, especially in emerging markets. The site mentions that the First Israel Fund moved dramatically from a deep discount to a sharp premium when peace seemed to be developing between Israel and its Arab neighbors.

There is what we might call an "overflow effect," too. When investors generally feel bullish or bearish, sentiment spills over into closed-end funds as much as into any other security. The phenomenon is reminiscent of "A rising tide raises all boats." Another surefire trigger for discounts or premiums to converge on NAV is a takeover or an announcement that a closed-end fund will go to an open-end structure. On the other side, discounts can widen when new funds are introduced, because the new funds divert money from existing funds. Funds also, upon occasion, execute new offerings, secondary offerings, or distributions. These are usually aimed at reducing premiums.

Closed-end funds are controversial and the premium/discount debate can become quite heated. Each side has equally passionate proponents and critics. For ongoing analysis and discussion, the most thorough coverage can be found at www.worldlyinvestor.com. Worldly Investor provides the only internationally focused commentary on mutual funds. Paul Merriman's column discusses key themes of diversification by using international funds. James Welsh's mutual fund articles are not limited to international funds, but when they are the feature, he also provides macro commentary on international fund groups. For instance, he recently took on why Asian funds are slumping despite the improvement in fundamentals.

Other worldlyinvestor.com writers (many of whom are also money managers) address closed-end funds, too. For example, Peter Marber, author of *From Third World to First Class: The Future of Emerging Markets in the Global Economy* (Perseus, 1998), likes the semiconductor chip sector and Taiwan. While he recommends specific Taiwanese stocks which trade as ADRs in the United States, he also likes a closed-end fund named ROC Fund (ROC), which has over 50 percent of its holdings in

Taiwan's high-tech sector. As of mid-August 2000, Marber writes that the fund tracked the local market all year and is down some 10 percent since January, trading at a 20 percent-plus discount. Another fund is the Taiwan Fund (TWN), whose price is down 13 percent and trades at a 21 percent discount to the NAV of the underlying shares. These funds are of interest because uncertainty is high in Taiwan about China's unification intentions, a new government, changes in the tax regime, and other issues—but the high-tech sector itself is booming.

As both Mobius and Cassidy say, the best time to enter a closed-end fund is when conditions seem terrible and everyone else is exiting. This is also a situation where you could buy the fund and short the iShare as a hedge. Note that the New Taiwan dollar is essentially unhedgeable except for large amounts in the professional foreign exchange market.

Where to Go for Information on Closed-End Funds

The first place to go is the Closed-End Fund Association's Web site, www.cefa.com. It provides a great deal of educational material, case studies, and research studies. It also compares closed-end funds to open-end funds.

A full list of closed-end funds by name, and useful information, such as NAV, 12-month change in NAV (which, barring dividends, constitutes NAV), and the top 10 holdings and top 10 sectors are available at www.site-by-site.com/usa/cef/cef.htm.

A graph of the growth of closed-end funds from 1990 to 1999 can be viewed at www.ici.org/facts_figures/closed-end_statistics.

Two newsletters on closed-end funds are available at www.site-by-site.com and www.wiesenberger.com. Site-by-site publishes a weekly Closed-End Fund newsletter at a cost of $8.95 a month or $83.40 a year. It compares the current week's data to historical averages, and it highlights potential buy-and-sell opportunities through twelve top-10 tables, as well as occasional in-depth country/region reports. A sample 19-page report is available at www.site-by-site.com/usa/cef/weekrev .pdf. International closed-end funds are noted as "FOR" (for "foreign") in the tables, so readers can easily pick out international funds from U.S.-focused ETFs. ETFs such as iShares, while technically not closed-end funds, are included for comparison. The sample weekly review, from June 1999, scanned 527 closed-end funds, of which 95 were International Equity closed-end funds, including all WEBS (now iShares).

The Weisenberger site is designed for mutual fund and other financial professionals, and is part of the Thomson Financial network. It follows 500 closed-end funds and publishes newsletters on in-depth research. Some data are available at the site, as well as a glossary and other educational materials.

For newsletters on closed-end funds and mutual funds in general, financialweb.com (www.financialweb.com/fdsIndex.asp) provides daily commentary on open- and closed-end funds. The commentary is not limited to international funds but usually recommends some. For instance, the August 2, 2000, column highlighted changes to the structure of the Mexico Fund (MXN), a closed-end fund. Mutual fund data can be sorted by ranking and performance within a fund category. The fund screener is easy to navigate.

The Internet Closed-End Fund Investor (www.icefi.com), in addition to providing good education on closed-end funds, posts a discussion forum where some enlightened discussion occurs. Roughly 10 messages get posted a month—not a lot, but some provide clues on trading strategies, including shorting of iShares and closed-end funds. Yahoo! (quote.yahoo.com) posts messages about closed-end funds, too.

Open-Ended Mutual Funds

"Open-end fund" is simply another term for mutual fund, which was invented in the 1800s. Mutual funds offer shares to investors continuously, and they stand ready to redeem shares at all times. The price is based directly on the NAV, determined at the close of each business day. Sometimes the transaction price includes an adjustment for a sales, redemption, or other charge. Mutual funds are generally very liquid—often, more liquid than closed-end funds. According to Morningstar (see below), international funds compose roughly 14 percent of the mutual fund universe available to U.S. investors.

If your purpose is to invest in a highly specialized industry or region, a mutual fund may offer greater diversification and therefore less risk than a closed-end fund, but there are no guarantees. The mutual fund has to sell shares in a falling market to meet redemption demand. The closed-end fund manager may stick with the amount of shares, in the same proportion, using the long-term buy-and-hold strategy.

A discussion of open versus closed-end funds can be found at www.site-by-site.com/usa/cef/cef.htm as well as www.cefa.com. Both sites favor closed-end funds, so "consider the source." One distinction to keep in mind is that closed-end funds are specialized and focused, while most open-ended funds are regional or global in scope and thus fully diversified. Open-ended funds will therefore often have a high proportion of multinationals and blue chips. This makes for a fair amount of confusion if you are engaging in one of the optimum portfolio diversification exercises described in Chapter 6. In other words, you are trying to get international diversification by buying an international fund, but by buying some "global" mutual funds, you are in fact getting a high proportion of U.S. names. You may inadvertently be getting less diversification, not more, if you already own those U.S. companies individually.

Where to Get Information on Open-Ended Mutual Funds

Industry Statistics   The Investment Company Institute, www.ici.org, based in Washington, DC, provides basic figures on mutual fund ownership in the United States:

> Today, more than 83 million individual shareholders own mutual funds, or nearly one in two American households. The typical mutual fund shareholder is 44 years old, married, middle income, and employed. Mutual fund assets total more than $7 trillion in the United States.

ICI's Web site is fairly dry and industry-insider-focused, but does provide a useful and long alphabetical listing of fund managers' Web sites, for both open-ended (www.ici.org/aboutfunds/members

_websites.html#Open-End Funds) and closed-ended funds (www.ici .org/aboutfunds/members_web sites.html#Closed-end Funds). Roughly half of the managers are listed, along with their Web sites. These sites provide more detail on individual funds, although many of the links appear to be dead.

Education on OEFs   Mutual Fund Education Alliance, www.mfea .com, provides fund basics, but little coverage specifically on international fund investing.

International Mutual Fund Screening Tools   MAXFunds.com, Morningstar, Lipper, and Standard & Poor's provide standard and highly similar scanning tools. MAXFunds.com (www.MAXFunds .com), has a user-friendly drill-down feature, and screening that is slightly more specific than Morningstar's. MAXFunds.com's data come from Lipper. MAXFund improves, or at least processes Lipper's data uniquely by ranking according to MAXFund's proprietary green, yellow, and red classification, which uses an unconventional evaluation technique, taking into account not only a fund's peformance but also its asset size, expenses, momentum, and vulnerability to disruptive short-term movements. High expenses and turnover hurt a fund's rankings; over- or underdiversification also demotes a fund. The site also provides intelligent, high-level but clearly written education on mutual fund investing. Closed-end funds are not included, but iShares are included for comparison to mutual funds.

Lipper Inc. provides mutual fund data to many other financial sites, but does not provide data or screening tools directly to the surfing public. Forbes, Kiplinger's, Go.com, and roughly 15 other sites use Lipper data. Each user slices it in slightly different ways. Typically, these sites focus on screening for low expenses and low taxes, or on investment categories.

Morningstar (www.morningstar.com) offers a screening tool for all funds, including international mutual funds. Morningstar categorizes 1,582 funds as international, and tracks 11,006 funds—presumably, roughly the number of listed, publicly traded mutual funds.

Morningstar also offers the returns (organized by time frames of one week, year-to-date, and one, three, and five years ago) of various categories of international funds. The international fund world is categorized as:

Europe

International Hybrid

World

Latin America

Pacific/Asia ex-Japan

Emerging Markets

Precious Metals

Pacific/Asia

Japan

Morningstar's "Fund Tool Box" provides various screening devices. Its "Fund QuickRank" (www.screen.morningstar.com/fundsearch /fundrank.html) provides best and worst rankings of international funds based on short- and long-term returns, Morningstar's proprietary ranking system, and volatility (standard deviation).

The proprietary star-ranking system is based on risk/return ratios. According to the site:

> The Morningstar Risk-Adjusted Rating, commonly called the star rating, brings both performance and risk together into one evaluation. To determine a fund's star rating for a given period (three, five, or 10 years), the fund's Morningstar Risk score is subtracted from its Morningstar Return score. The resulting number is plotted along a bell curve to determine the fund's rating for each time period. [T]he Morningstar Risk statistic evaluates the fund's downside volatility relative to that of other funds in its broad investment class (domestic stock, international stock, taxable bond, or municipal bond).

The proprietary risk measure attributes returns that differ from the expected amount to a change in volatility, as we describe in Chapter 4. The basis of Morningstar's comparison, however, is the risk-free rate of return an investor can earn on the 90-day U.S. Treasury bill. Preservation of capital is highlighted as the chief objective.

From the list of top-performing funds, one can click through to quite rich data on individual funds: total returns; a graph mapping "Growth of $10,000" against the S&P 500 and other funds in its category; and rankings of a fund's risk, including modern portfolio theory statistics (such as beta), against the S&P 500 and Wilshire 5000. This is a useful measure for whether a fund historically has provided diversification away from U.S. blue-chip and broader benchmarks. Under "Portfolio," Morningstar lists a fund's asset class and regional and country allocations. Very useful, also, is a list of the top 10 holdings. For a premium fee of $9.95/month, one gains access to a fund's top 25 holdings, as well as a tax analysis of the fund.

This screening tool is useful not only for ferreting out attractive mutual funds, but also for identifying the underlying holdings—another version of "bottom-up" research. Searching the top holdings category of high-performing funds may lead to useful companies to research individually, especially in undiversified, small-cap funds. A single holding may represent a large portion of a fund's value and may be largely unknown to Wall Street—and thus undervalued or inefficiently priced (assuming it is not efficiently priced on its local exchange).

WorldlyInvestor (www.worldlyinvestor.com) lets users search U.S.-traded mutual funds by return, category (i.e., Asia ex-Japan), and load/no-load. Value Line provides the data. Drill-down information on funds appears neatly in four categories: (1) profile, (2) chart, (3) top holdings, and (4) fees and expenses. Unfortunately, the top holdings data come from annual reports and, being rather outdated, are perhaps not a useful source of foreign stock ideas. Worldly Investor excludes data on U.S.-only funds, making searches much easier, and provides internationally focused fund analysis and commentary.

Value Line (www.valueline.com) sells what it calls a sophisticated mutual fund screening service. It is updated weekly, sold for $345 a year, and offered for $50 as a two-month trial. It claims to have "Advanced portfolio analytics, including Stress-Tester" and "asset allocation capabilities, which may include the ability to test for proper interfund, portfolio-wide diversification."

Folio (www.foliofn.com), a subscription service geared toward individual investors, lets the average person create his or her own 50-stock (maximum) portfolio. It is meant to be like a mutual fund without the fees. The service supplies off-the-shelf portfolios, including a global folio (which includes the United States) and an international folio (which doesn't). Holdings in the global folio are selected not because they are likely to perform better than other stocks, but because they are the largest-cap stocks from five major geographic regions: (1) North America, (2) Latin America, (3) Asia, (4) Europe, and (5) Africa. The folio is reviewed every month. The company also proposes geographic portfolios, weighted by market cap and limited to ADRs.

You can create or buy up to three FOLIOs for a flat fee of $29.95 a month or $295 a year. Free trading during two daily "windows" is included. Each additional folio is $9.95 a month or $95 a year.

SUMMING UP

As mentioned at the beginning of this book, the president of the Nasdaq, Frank Zarb, says with enthusiasm that within a few years we will be able to trade 500 international stocks 24/7.

The theory of portfolio diversification is intuitively sound, even if we don't grasp the complex mathematics. All we really need to know is that diversification reduces risk, and optimal diversification reduces risk while enhancing returns. Because foreign stocks may be uncorrelated with U.S. stocks, they are a natural place to search. And, the ability to track (and buy or sell) U.S. (and foreign) stocks after regular trading hours is valuable in that it gives us more control over our portfolios. However, as a practical matter, getting from the theory to a list of actual tradable stocks and profitable opportunities is challenging. As of mid-2000, the major scanning and screening Web sites do not include foreign stocks, and after-hours liquidity is often lower than ideal. A few foreign Web sites exist, but when you have selected a few foreign stocks, you still need to integrate them into your portfolio—and the portfolio optimization Web sites do not yet include foreign stocks! To do the job really well and as close as possible to the way the professionals do it, you would need their databases and their software, and both are very expensive. You can approximate the professionals' level with software like Decisioneering's CrystalBall, but you must be statistics-literate and you must input price data yourself on a daily basis.

This could easily turn into a full-time job—and you may like your daytime job. The alternative would seem to be ADRs, for which you can get the scanning and price information and which you can include in diversification exercises. You can also include some closed-end and some mutual funds in some diversification exercises. However, the optimization Web site managed by the Nobel prize winner for portfolio theory, www.sharpe.com, will not integrate individual stocks, let alone foreign stocks, with funds. In short, we are probably going to get the execution capability for those 500 stocks Frank Zarb mentions before we get the analytical capability, because the analysis is computationally so complex.

Nevertheless, to "trade like a professional," we need to grasp the concepts and processes introduced in this book, and be ready for the 24/7 trading and investing world.

APPENDIX A

BASIC CHARTING
FOR BEGINNERS

Throughout this book, one of the recurring themes has been that 24/7 investors who are interested in foreign securities should find out as much as possible about the security that has piqued their interest. And logically, this research often involves checking out Web sites of foreign stock exchanges and the foreign companies themselves; reading financial news publications specific to the region of interest, annual reports, and other materials from the companies being considered for investments; and, at times, talking directly to international brokers or others who are located in the home market of the country of interest.

But unless you plan to learn Turkish or Japanese, for example, the language barrier is obviously a very high obstacle to international investing. You are in the dark about whether a security is fundamentally a good investment when you can't read the business news in the local newspaper, the annual report, or a professional analyst's research report. This situation is rapidly being rectified, and a lot of information is available in English. But in addition to these research methods, and until everything is available in your native language, you should know that you also have technical analysis to put in your toolkit.

Technical analysts seek value in the form of rising prices, and then quantify how strong—and therefore how long-lasting—the rise might be.

Technical analysis has long been a controversial subject because many analysts have believed it to be inherently antithetical to "fundamental investing." This is less the case today. Even the Federal Reserve has studied the efficacy of certain technical indicators and found them to be helpful predictors (see www.ny.frb.org/rmaghome/staff_rp/sr4 .html—12-Nov-1999 for the full report).

Essentially, good market timing means you buy stocks that have identifiably hit a bottom and you sell stocks that have identifiably hit a top. If you get a lead on a stock, the first thing you should do is check the chart. If the price is in a downtrend, you have to question whether the stock is a worthwhile investment. Maybe it's a great stock, but most technicians would think that it makes more sense to wait for the bottom to be reached before buying.

It would be accurate to say that technical analysis simply *ignores* fundamental analysis—but that doesn't mean you have to. It just means that when you are wearing your technical analysis hat, you are temporarily suspending any and all reference to fundamental factors. This appendix offers a primer in technical analysis for readers who want to brush up on this approach to investing. It then applies the lessons of technical analysis to the specific subject of investing in foreign securities.

THE DIFFERENCE BETWEEN FUNDAMENTAL ANALYSIS AND TECHNICAL ANALYSIS: VALUE VERSUS PRICE

> **net present value**
>
> The current dollar value of the future revenue stream known or expected to be generated by a security which is discounted using the current rate of interest.

Fundamental analysis is the study of the likely intrinsic value of a security. Modern financial analysis views a security today in terms of the **net present value** of future cash flows that will accrue to the owner of the security, although other ways of valuing securities are also used. For example, the rock-bottom value of a company is correctly measured by its

> **book value**
>
> The value of a company's tangible assets carried on its balance sheet.

book value—what all the bits and pieces can be sold for at market prices today. A metal fabricating company may lose all its sales to foreign competition and thus no longer qualify as a "going concern," but it may still have money value in its inventory of the metal, real estate, machinery, office supplies, and so on.

In contrast to fundamental analysis, *technical analysis* draws a distinction between the *value* of a security and its *price*. Oscar Wilde said a cynic is someone who knows the price of everything and the value of nothing. That definition can apply equally to technical analysts, who believe that all the relevant information about supply and demand for a security resides in its price. It would also be fair to say that a technical analyst would trade a security that has *no* intrinsic value, as long as a liquid market exists to trade it. The point is proven when you consider that currencies possess no inherent intrinsic value except their purchasing power (as Ben Franklin said, "The use of money is all the advantage of having money"). Yet traders speculate in the foreign exchange market, often using technical analysis, with great gusto.

BENEFITS OF USING TECHNICAL ANALYSIS TO EVALUATE SECURITIES

To consider a security only in terms of price rids you of the normative impulse to attach assumptions to your thinking about price—that is, that a stock *should* be at such-and-such a price level. It teaches you one of the most valuable lessons of investing: You cannot control the outcome of trading and investing. You cannot influence the market, let alone control it. You can control only the *risk* you take and the *outcome* of your own actions.

In a sense, technical analysts believe part of the efficient market theory—the part that says prices correctly and almost immediately reflect all information about a security. They do *not* believe the part that says past price activity does not influence current activity. Technical analysts study past price activity; nontechnicians also study past price activity, in building their expectations of what a given security is likely to return. Any single move in a price series may be random, but all moves in a price series are not random.

"DON'T BOTHER ME WITH THE FACTS"; INSTEAD, LET'S FOCUS ON PRICE TRENDS

Technical analysts focus on trends in price movement. Trends tend to remain in place until something significant comes along to change them. Then prices move into a sideways or consolidating phase until the old trend resumes or a new trend begins. The "something significant" can be a new fact or a new interpretation about something that may or may not be happening with a company. The technician doesn't care what it is and often will not bother to find out. The technician is liberated from facts, opinions, and hypotheses.

Charles Dow, who founded the Dow Jones News Service and is credited with the idea of stock indices (later named after him), essentially started what we know today as technical analysis. The first major book on the subject, Edwards and Magee's *Technical Analysis of Chart Trends* (first published in 1948 and still in print today) says that, in Dow's editorials in *The Wall Street Journal,* there is evidence that Dow himself did not view the "Dow Theory" as a device for forecasting the market, or even as a guide for investors.

Technical indicators *indicate,* they do *not* dictate. All technical indicators are based on the observation that markets repeat their behavior, and their behavior can be measured. In applying the measurement to current conditions, there is only a *probability,* not a certainty, that the behavior will be repeated. Thus, when we say that a technical indicator forecasts a particular outcome, the forecast is valid only in the sense that it is probable and only until the technical exercise is conducted again after fresh data have been added.

This brings up two further issues. First, some technicians start with an assumption of cyclicality. Most of today's cycle theorists are students of the **Elliott Wave theory** and of the obscure work of W.D. Gann. Elliott was a financial writer and investor in the 1930s and 1940s. He produced a booklet entitled "The Wave Principle." Later, it was incorporated in a book entitled *Nature's Law*. Many other analysts and writers have been attracted to Elliott's theories. The most prominent is Robert Prechter, coauthor, with A.J. Frost, of the book, *The Elliott Wave Principle*, and founder of the Web site www .elliottwave.com. William Gann was an investor and writer who also used "natural law" to forecast the market and specific stocks, although, some say he died broke. He was profiled in the December 1909 issue of *Ticker Magazine* by its editor, Richard Wyckoff, a technical analyst who is still quoted today. Gann published many books but never revealed his entire theory in a single place in a unified way. Students of Gann have been trying to reconstruct it ever since.

> **Elliott Wave theory**
>
> A securities price prediction method described by Ralph Nelson Elliott in the mid-1930s. It holds that a complete price movement has five waves, three aligned with the current trend, and two that are countertrend. Long-term waves that last for decades are composed of smaller waves with lengths of years. They, in turn, are made up of progressively smaller waves. The final waves last a minute or less. Regardless of scale, all Elliott Waves have the same characteristics, and the rules for their behavior apply at all levels.

The prerequisite of any cycle theory is a view of history that imputes a certain order to the course of human events. This order is mathematically ordained or is in some other way inevitable and predestined. The events arise outside the boundaries of markets themselves but are so powerful that they cause certain market behaviors. Edwards and Magee wrote (again, in 1948) that the cyclical approach, "although still beset by a 'lunatic fringe,'" promises to contribute to our understanding (as a third element alongside the fundamental and technical approaches). Many people, including Prechter, have had outstanding investment success using these ideas. Most individuals, however, find it difficult to apply these ideas profitably, at least in their initial efforts.

The second issue is the observation that any moderately experienced market technician can look at an unlabeled chart and come up with a forecast for the next price action, and can do so correctly far more often than mere chance would allow. A stock market technician can predict the next period's price in, say, soybeans or Swiss francs with uncanny accuracy. The use of the phrase "next period" is significant. A chart can be of any periodicity for this to be true. It may be a chart of prices taken at ten-minute intervals, one-hour intervals, one-day intervals, or weekly, monthly, or yearly. It is not a parlor trick, but a reflection that markets are "fractal," the word used to describe this effect. "Fractal" is oddly difficult to define; the founder of fractal geometry, Benoit Mandelbrot, does not offer a definition, according to Edgar Peters, author of *Fractal Market Analysis: Applying Chaos Theory to Investment and Economics* (Wiley, 1994). Fractal analysis is a third way of analyzing events, including price series; it sees them as neither completely random nor linear. Readers may be daunted by the mathematics, but the fractal market hypothesis emphasizes that liquidity and investment time horizon have an important impact on investor behavior—precisely the point we have been making in this book.

If you stop and think about it, the ability of technical analysts to predict upcoming price behavior based on recent past price behavior is not as remarkable as it appears at first blush. Market prices are a function of human behavior, and human behavior tends to be repeated, whatever the time frame. For example, a trader whose holding period averages ten minutes will exhibit the same behavior as a trader whose holding period is three weeks, or one whose holding period is three years. If each is using a stop-loss limit that is a function of variability away from a mean, the exit point will be equally obvious on a 60-second chart, a monthly chart, or a three year-chart. Like a set of nesting Russian dolls, each time frame is susceptible to the same rules of technical analysis. This is yet another reason for you to determine your own best time frame for trading and investing. A technical system built on an hourly time frame will lead to catastrophic loss if it is applied in a daily trading regime.

MARKET TIMING

Technical analysis is often associated with "timing the market"— a controversial subject, to say the least. Some people believe passionately that they can time the market (buy low and sell high); others believe, equally passionately, that timing cannot be done successfully. The statistical record shows that some practitioners achieve above-benchmark returns with market timing techniques; others do not. *The Hulbert Financial Digest* evaluates market timing advisors—both fundamental and technical—on a risk-adjusted basis. Of the top five performers during the past 15 years on a risk-adjusted basis, two are technically based (*The Hulbert Financial Digest*, April 26, 2000).

Whichever way you choose to go in this debate, you do not have to become a full-time market timer in order to apply technical analysis to your benefit. For example, let's say you hear a wonderful story about some security. As discussed in detail in Chapter 5, the first thing you should do to check out the story is *not* to comb the Web for industry and company information. Instead, look at the security's *price chart*. If this is a stock that has been falling for weeks or months, you may still have an interest—but no urgency to buy. In falling price conditions, you will want to buy after a bottom has been reached. This is simply common sense and requires no technical knowledge or ability. Similarly, if you get a lead on a stock that has been on a rising trend, you will want to know where current prices stand relative to historical prices. Is it the beginning of the trend or is the trend peaking? In this case, some technical study is desirable.

You can use technical analysis in any amount you wish—a little or a lot. To use it a little and with only a little knowledge of the discipline,

> **double top**
>
> A charting term describing two highs with almost equal prices connected in a V-shaped pattern of lower prices that technical analysts believe signals a reversal of an upward trend to a downward trend.

however, is to risk getting it wrong. You may see a **double top** (an approaching price decline). A more practiced technician may see a bottoming in some other indicator and, thus, a coming price rise. Often, there is no single correct answer (until the next price is recorded; then you know). Indicators only indicate.

It often happens that two or more patterns are present on the same chart at once, each pointing in a different direction. One chartist may read into a chart what he wants to see, such as his wish for the security ("talking his position") or one of the limited number of patterns he is capable of seeing. As Thomas Bulkowski writes in *The Encyclopedia of Chart Patterns* (Wiley, 2000), people are forever seeing a head-and-shoulders pattern where none exists—but where some other pattern does exist that could give them guidance if they only knew about it. As with fundamental security analysis or any other field, the more you know, the more likely you are to excel or at least to avoid errors.

TECHNICAL ANALYSIS MEASURES MARKET SENTIMENT

To embrace technical analysis is not to exclude all other research. One of the chief criticisms of the dot-com phenomenon is that so-called momentum investors bought these issues simply because they were rising, without regard for their fundamental value. They were grumpily lumped together as young whippersnappers who had never seen a bear market. To some extent, technical analysis as a discipline became tarred with the brush of irresponsibility and irrationality, although every momentum investor is not a technical analyst. Momentum investors are said to be in the grip of a mania, which is an emotional state, yet technical analysis is supposed to be deliberately rational and emotionally neutral.

It is true that technicians will not let a huge price rise change their decision to buy, unless they see indications that a run is near its end. Because it is based on price alone, technical analysis is the measurement of *market sentiment*. If market sentiment is wildly bullish, as shown by various indicators, the technicians accept the evidence of their eyes. They are pragmatic. They look to empirical work rather than anything judgmental.

For example, to say a P/E ratio of 150 means you shouldn't buy a security *when it is still rising* is to impose a *value* judgment. This value judgment is irrelevant to many technical analysts. It is, of course, of interest to fundamental analysts and to some technical analysts, too, who may override their technical opinion on a security for this or other fundamental reasons. To override a technical judgment for fundamental reasons does not alter the technical judgment.

When the majority of participants come to believe the judgment and buying power is exhausted, those developments will be seen on the chart and that is the time for the technical analysts to plan their exit. The technical analysts may exploit the mania; they do not start trends, they take advantage of them. It's the nature of the discipline that technical analysts wait until a move has been formed before acting.

TECHNICAL ANALYSIS RESULTS IN SMARTER TRADING BECAUSE IT IS DISPASSIONATE

Technical analysis doesn't have a motto, but if it had one, it would come from the Edwards and Magee book:

> The secret of success lies not in buying at the very lowest possible price and selling at the absolute top. It is in the avoidance of large losses.

Technical analysis can inject your investing with rules that keep you on target. For example, stop losses are important tools to help you avoid large losses. A stop loss order is an order given to a broker to sell a security at a specific price that is lower than the current price (if you own the security). The order can be placed as a function of the maximum amount of cash money you are willing to lose—the percentage of your stake or equity—or as a function of the maximum move a security is likely to make in a certain time period, or both.

For example, let's say you own only one stock. It has risen 30 percent and you believe that it has sufficient momentum to rise some more, or at least not to fall more than 15 percent. You place a stop loss order with your broker to sell the stock at the current price minus 15 percent, securing half your gain if the worst-case scenario materializes. How do you derive the 15 percent potential-decline number? By looking at the historical **maximum adverse move** over the time frame in question. If this particular security has a habit of moving 15 percent every day and you cannot tolerate a 15 percent loss, you will be a nervous wreck. You have picked the wrong security for you.

> **maximum adverse move**
>
> The maximum price move away from an average, even when occurring rarely.

Many day-traders fail because they neglect to observe the maximum daily range of their chosen securities in the context of their *total equity at risk* and the maximum loss they can tolerate in any single trade. It stands to reason that if a stock trades in a daily average range of 15 percent and they have just bought at the top of the daily range with a 15 percent stop loss, the trade is doomed.

The practice of setting stop losses arises from two factors: (1) the technical analyst's acknowledgment that any particular trading decision may be wrong—because, as noted, indicators only indicate; and (2) a cold-hearted refusal to fall in love with a position. Many investors ignore this valuable lesson because it comes from technical analysis and they suspect the legitimacy of technical analysis without understanding its basic premise: The purpose of trading and investing is to make money and to preserve capital, not to be right.

TWO TYPES OF TECHNICAL ANALYSIS: PATTERN-BASED AND STATISTICS-BASED

Aside from analysis based on cycle theories (discussed earlier in this Appendix), two types of technical analysis are popular today. The first is based on recognition of patterns—triangles, double tops, head-and-shoulders, and the like—and the second is based on statistical models.

Using Chart Patterns

Chart patterns, first described in the Edwards and Magee book, were thoroughly updated and catalogued in *The Encyclopedia of Chart Patterns* by Thomas Bulkowski. It takes experience and skill to recognize chart patterns, and Bulkowski warns against common misconceptions and facile and hasty identifications. He has refined the definition of each pattern and has backtested the patterns to discover the range of returns, average return, rate of failure, and so on—all amply illustrated.

Figure A.1 shows a good example of a chart pattern.

You do not need to learn the 25 or so standard patterns if you decide that pattern technical analysis is not your cup of tea. You should, however, understand the one pattern that is inescapable in all discussions of stock prices today: "support and resistance." The core concept is that followers of a specific stock have an idea of what the price should be, based on fundamental knowledge, fresh news, and wishful thinking. When the price falls well below that value, they perceive the stock to be a bargain, and they buy. When the price rises to what they consider to be an overvalued level, they sell to take profit—with the expectation of buying the same security back when it is cheaper.

Technical analysts exploit this behavior, and they are able to exploit it because the process is generally quite orderly. To identify the lower level where followers of the stock are likely to appear as buyers, we draw a support line connecting a minimum of two recent lows. When that line is extended out into the future, we have an estimate of the level

Figure A.1   Example of a Chart Pattern: DJIA and Triangle Breakout

Data: Reuters DataLink; chart: Metastock.

at which supporters of the security will emerge and provide support. A support line is not a hard-and-fast rule. Buyers will often show up before the price hits the line—if the security has been in an overall uptrend. This is the fear part of "fear and greed." These investors fear missing the opportunity. It also happens that the support line will be broken on the downside, sometimes a little and sometimes a lot. Traders never know whether buying will resume below the line and restore its legitimacy, or whether the breakout below the line means the line is no longer valid and should be discarded.

Resistance, a line connecting two or more recent highs, works in a similar fashion. Holders of a stock think they know where it is overvalued to such an extent that further price gains are unlikely (i.e., where only a fool would keep buying). This is the level at which they themselves buy no more or sell to take profit. In a bull market, resistance lines are routinely broken.

Most technical analysts are persnickety about support and resistance lines, and they insist that the lines be drawn to connect at least two high or two low points without crossing any price bars in between. Victor Sperandeo, author of *Methods of a Wall Street Master,* advises this approach because it prevents drawing lines to suit personal wishes. Sometimes, however, "sloppy" lines that do cross some price bars are warranted if that's the only way to get a grip on what's happening. In a very real way, allowing support and resistance lines to cross price bars is to generate a more robust support-and-resistance channel. Here, "robust" refers to excluding extraordinary events and focusing on the "normal" price action.

Support and resistance lines are often not parallel. Because the stock market reflects the ebb and flow of knowledge and emotion, we can hardly expect such tidiness. When a support line connects ever-higher lows, and the resistance line connects ever-lower highs, you get what looks like part of a triangle (you have to imagine the third side). A triangle can also occur with ever-higher highs and ever-higher lows. The lines still represent support and resistance, but, in this case, the implication is that the price is "consolidating" (making up its mind) about whether to break to the upside or the downside. As Bulkowski warns, it's easy to make mistakes with triangles (which can also be wedges, or pennants, or nothing at all).

Basic support and resistance lines define the current likely maximum price range. A breakout from the range is significant because it means some piece of information that is new on the scene has changed the market's attitude toward the security. The overbought and oversold levels are not fixed, though. They are influenced not only by the ever-changing perception of fair value, but also by the trend of the overall market. As a practical matter, you have to draw them afresh with some frequency. This exercise has the added virtue of forcing you to examine whether you are using the right time frame. What appear to be perfectly legitimate support and resistance lines may cover only days that turn out to be worthless, whereas the same lines drawn over a few months give better guidance. Therefore, whenever the market is misbehaving—that is, rising too far or falling too far—look at charts that go further back in time, and start your support and resistance lines there. Something may pop out at you. There is no single "correct" time frame to use. The key point about patterns is that they are subjective. One person's "head and shoulders" is another person's "double top." As stated repeatedly, indicators only indicate, and they are right only some of the time.

Using Statistical Models

The second popular type of technical analysis is the use of statistical models. Don't let the word "statistical" intimidate you. Most of the concepts used in statistical technical analyses are either easy or can be adequately grasped with only an intuitive understanding. Most formulations can be expressed in high-school algebra, if not grade-school arithmetic.

For example, the workhorse of statistical techniques is the moving average, which can be calculated by hand if need be. Let's say you have 10 days of closing prices for a security. To construct a five-day moving average, here's what you would do:

- List the first five days' closing prices.
- Add them up and divide by five.
- Drop the first day, add the sixth day's close to the remaining four days, and then average again.
- Keep doing this until you run out of data.

When you plot the averages on graph paper and connect the dots, you see a line that has smoothed the daily price fluctuations. The smoother moving average line eliminates small daily random movements and allows you to see the price trend.

On many charting Web sites, you will often see a 50-day moving average and a 200-day moving average. When a major index like the Dow or Nasdaq approaches or breaks through the 200-day moving average, people take note. (See Figure A.2.) Just about everybody in the investing universe has heard of the 200-day moving average (the only one shown in *Barron's*, for example). Thus, when a major index has fallen below that level, the spread of pessimism becomes very broad and deep. The spread of pessimism fuels negative commentary, which fuels further sales, and so on. (By the way, there is nothing magic about 200

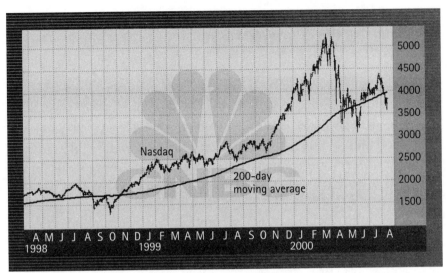

Figure A.2   Nasdaq and a 200–Day Moving Average

Data: Reuters DataLink; chart: Metastock.

days, or 40 workweeks. Years ago, a financial writer named Donchian observed that time span to mark impending market lows, and it became market tradition.)

This brings up the issue of self-fulfilling prophecies. Logically, if a majority of market participants believe a particular price level is a target of some kind, that price will usually trigger whatever action was predicted. The 200-day moving average is one example of that outcome. The all-time high and the all-time low are often mentioned as benchmarks. Others crop up from time to time in various securities.

The self-fulfilling prophecy is not a problem unless a majority of participants believe in and act on a specific indicator. With market participation expanding every day, and with dozens of competing theories (both fundamental and technical), we seldom see a single indicator grab the market's full attention, although now that charts are shown on many Web sites (and on TV) with a few canned indicators, it's conceivable that self-fulfilling prophecies will multiply.

KEEP IN MIND THAT EVERY SECURITY IS UNIQUE

Every security has its own price rhythm because each security has its own set of market participants. The price moves reflect the psychology of that specific group of people. This often extends to an entire sector, such as oil and oil services, chip makers, utilities, and the like. In fact, the bigger the sector (i.e., the more companies in it), the more likely it is to be appropriate for technical analysis. This is not to say that a stand-alone monopoly (such as Microsoft) cannot be analyzed using technical indicators; rather, it's a reminder that when you are analyzing the behavior of a crowd, the bigger the crowd, the better. When you keep in mind the uniqueness of each security, you will be less likely to be flummoxed and misled by a large movement that turns out to be random. An example is a big price drop that actually reflects only selling by the CEO of a company because he or she needs to raise cash for a daughter's wedding. (Sales like these do happen, more frequently when stocks are closely held.)

Linear Regression

> **linear regression**
>
> A statistic that expresses the value of a time series. It draws the most efficient line through the prices in a series, minimizing the distance between itself and a price.

One indicator that is much neglected and doesn't appear on standard canned charts is the **linear regression**. (See Figure A.3.) A linear regression, the purest of trend identifiers, is simply the line that minimizes the distance of every data point from itself. Investors can then draw support and resistance lines parallel to the linear regression line, crossing through outlying price bars or not, as they wish.

Although a linear regression is the purest form of a trend line (i.e., it has no subjective judgment), deciding where to start and end it entails some judgment. As a general rule, start a linear regression at an unmistakable high or low point. The idea is to extend it to the present

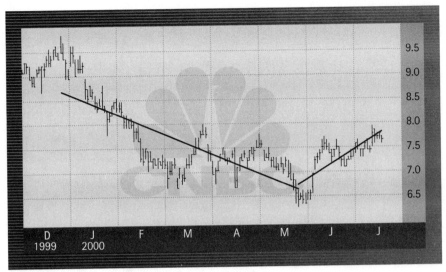

Figure A.3   Linear Regressions, iShare Singapore

Data: Reuters DataLink; chart: Metastock.

and then outward into the unknown future, to get an estimate of where prices should cluster as trading goes forward in time. The purpose is negated if this trend line is drawn through several trends on the same chart.

For example, say you have a 90-day chart where the price action is V-shaped (i.e., you have two trends), one down and one up. It would be silly to draw the linear regression from the first top to the second top. You would get no useful information. As with the support and resistance concept, however, if you go back far enough in time, you can cut through multiple minitrends to get the overall picture. You can't derive immediate trading implications from it, but such an exercise is sometimes useful.

Figure A.4 shows a specific example from the recent past. To address the issue of the U.S. market "bubble" in the fall of 1999 and the winter of 2000, we drew a linear regression from the October 1998 low to the October 1999 low on a long-term chart of the Nasdaq. We chose the lows in order to skew deliberately the linear regression to the downside. We then extended it out into the present. Everything far above

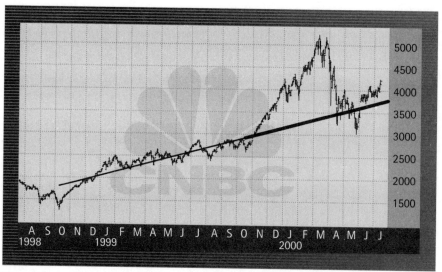

Figure A.4   Linear Regression from 10/8/98 to 10/15/99 Extended into Future
Data: Reuters DataLink; chart: Metastock.

the linear regression line became defined, somewhat arbitrarily, as the "bubble." The Nasdaq *should return* to this longer-term regression line once overvaluations are punished and those who bought under the line are rewarded.

Moving Linear Regression   Another linear regression technique is the moving linear regression. The conventional linear regression line is a straight line that uses all the data within its starting and ending points. For example, if a chart has 500 days, the linear regression is for the entire 500 days.

In contrast, a 60-day moving linear regression takes the linear regression value for the first 60 days and puts that value dot on the chart, as shown in Figure A.5. It adds a day and drops a day, calculates the new 60-day period's linear regression value, and drops down that dot. The result is not a straight line but one that curves like the price series itself. The virtue of this technique is that you don't have to select starting and ending periods. Again, we assume reversion to the linear regression line. If the current price is quite far above the moving linear

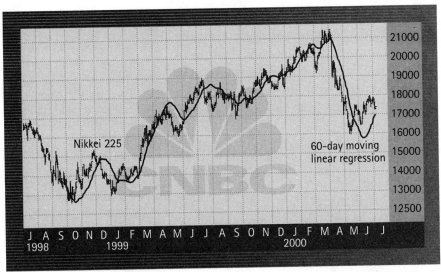

Figure A.5 Example of Moving Linear Regression: Nikkei 225 and 60-Day Moving Linear Regression

Data: Reuters DataLink; chart: Metastock.

regression, you might want to sell. If it is far below, you might have a buying opportunity.

This brings out a key point about technical analysis: Every indicator involves the application of some judgment as to the parameters. Should you use a 30-day or a 60-day moving linear regression? Without back-testing, you won't know how reliably and effectively a technique indicates a change in trend. For some securities, 30 days is right; for others, it is not.

Some numbers and clusters of numbers appear time and again in optimization tests; they are used as the "default" parameters in canned software programs and on chart Web sites on the Internet. One number in particular stands out: 21 days. This is almost the number of trading days in a calendar month (the actual number is 22). A calendar month roughly approximates the lunar month, which affects ocean tides. Therefore, 21 is not a surprising number to see.

The confirmation approach is a useful tool. Because no indicator is right all the time, it's important to get confirmation of a buy or sell signal by applying more than one technique. The confirmation approach will save you from hasty trading decisions. The second technique should not be merely a repetition of the first technique but "in different clothing." For example, the **Williams %R** is a variation of the **stochastic oscillator.** The Williams %R method compares today's close with the highest high over a period of days. The stochastic oscillator includes a parameter that compares the close to the lowest low. Therefore, to use both indicators is to engage in redundancy that adds no value.

Not every technique is effective when applied to a security. For example, the crossover of two moving averages is a common indicator. First, you take a long-term moving average, such as 25 days. This establishes the trend, either up or down. Then you take a shorter moving average—say, 12 days. When the short-term moving average rises above the long-term moving average, market sentiment is becoming more optimistic about the stock. When it falls below the longer-term trend, the mood is becoming more pessimistic (sellers outnumber buyers). We assume the shorter-term trend is likely to prevail.

The problem is that the crossover technique, using two moving averages, may not work to signal good entry and exit points on many stocks and indices.

> **Williams %R**

An indicator that estimates bullish and bearish sentiment, defined by the close in relation to the highest high and lowest low over a recent period. The formula uses the ratio of the close today minus the low over N number of days, divided by the high minus the low over the same N period.

> **stochastic oscillator**

An indicator made up of two stochastic oscillators. It estimates bullish and bearish sentiment, defined by the close in relation to the highest high and lowest low over a recent period. The first oscillator uses a formula that is the ratio of the close today minus the low over N number of days, divided by the high minus the low over the same N number of periods. A second oscillator is the ratio of the high divided by the low. The intersection lines plotted by the two oscillators generate buy or sell signals.

For example, it doesn't work at all on the Nasdaq. The only way to know whether it is likely to work today is to test it on historical data. To chart a standard set of parameters without testing, such as 25/12, is to say "One size fits all." This is hardly ever true in life, and it is almost never true in technical analysis. To say that a particular indicator is signaling a buy, when you don't know how well that indicator performed in the past, is dangerous to your financial well-being.

Figure A.6 shows a standard application of a "canned" set of two moving averages, 25 days and 12 days. Note where the buy and sell signals land. Following this system, you would have made $1.38 per share on an initial cost basis of $67.00 per share over the 150 days shown.

Now look at Figure A.7, which shows the same security back-tested for the two-moving-averages concept. To back-test is to experiment with every combination of numbers of days in the moving average—in other words, to apply perfect hindsight. You are discovering what would have worked best over a given time period, if only you had known it at the beginning. In this instance, using a short-term moving

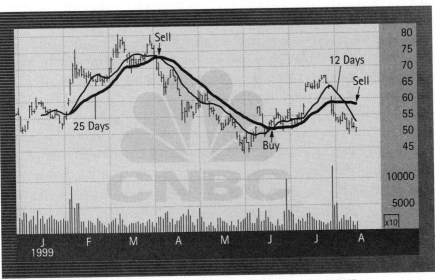

Figure A.6   Telefonos de Mexico: Two Moving Averages "Canned"

Data: Reuters DataLink; chart: Metastock.

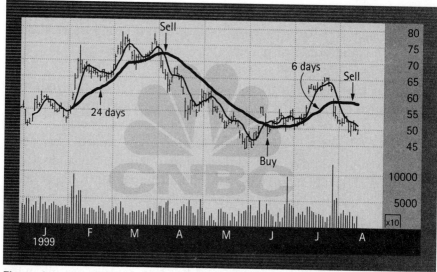

Figure A.7   Telefonos de Mexico: Two Moving Averages Back-Tested for Best Profit

Data: Reuters DataLink; chart: Metastock.

average of six days (instead of 12) and a longer-term moving average of 24 days, improves profitability by 14.8 percent.

Using variables customized to this particular security improves profitability to $9.99 in the same period, or a total return of 16.9 percent on an initial starting investment of $59.13 per share. But you can't count on that profitability going forward. A big drawback of optimizing variables like this is coming up with the most profitable solution and then *assuming* it will also be the most profitable going forward in time. This is a terrible assumption. Conditions change, the overall market changes, the basics of the specific security change, and even the security's band of followers changes. The biggest change is a change in volatility. Think about it: A moving average system that generates six good trade signals per year when volatility is low might generate 50 signals when volatility rises, and 75 percent of them may be wrong. Anyone with a computer can build a system with high profitability on a back-tested basis. But such systems usually fail in real-time trading.

The technical analysis literature is full of caveats about **curve-fitting.** The optimum answer may not work in real time, so what can you do about it? The most sensible solution is to back-test five years' historical data, say, but end the sample data at today's date two years ago. Get the optimum system, and then try it on the out-of-sample data covering the past two years. This is called the **walk-forward technique.** It is laborious, but does result in parameters that are likely to be "robust" (effective) over different volatility conditions.

The confirmation approach (you don't put all your eggs in one basket) is another protection against relying on optimization. If you like the two-moving-averages concept but lament that it lags, you can and should add other indicators that use entirely different concepts and will generate buy–sell signals independent of the two moving averages. One indicator that works well with moving averages is momentum.

> **curve-fitting**
>
> Relying on the assumption that a technique optimized over past data will generate the same gains and losses when applied to future data.

> **walk-forward technique**
>
> To test a trading system on historical data, determine the optimum parameters, and then test the system on out-of-sample data (data not previously used)—historical data that were excluded either from the original study or in real time.

At its most basic, momentum is nothing more than dividing today's price into the price x number of days ago. Therefore, a chart of momentum will show you not only whether the security is rising or falling, but also at what pace. Is it accelerating or decelerating?

For example, let's say that a stock is bottoming. The price is just starting to rise above its short-term moving average, but it hasn't yet built up enough steam to drag the short-term moving average above the long-term moving average. A glance at momentum will tell you whether it is likely to do so. If momentum is rising and the slope of the rising line is zooming upward, buying pressure is building.

Many kinds of momentum indicators have been devised. Some employ the relationship of today's high and/or low to the highs and lows over the recent past. Others combine momentum with a moving average concept *and* a high–low concept. The combinations and permutations are endless. A good reference book is *Market Momentum* (McGraw-Hill, 1993) by Martin Pring.

Another set of indicators that will show market sentiment involves volume. If a price is rising on falling volume, it is not a promising sign. If volume is rising but the price rise is not commensurate, it is another unpromising sign.

In all cases, the purpose of the indicator is to point you toward the most likely direction—is the indicator going up or down?—and to estimate the strength of the move. All the techniques compare current price data to data from the recent past. When a trend is in place, you can look at the current chart and move on to something else. A harder look is required when determining a reversal point—say, from a downtrend to an uptrend. This doesn't usually happen overnight. Some analysts believe that most stocks spend only about 15 to 20 percent of their price lives actually being trended. The rest of the time, they are moving sideways in a patternless and trendless manner. This number seems low to dedicated technicians, but most would agree that, on many occasions, the chart of a particular security simply does not give useful technical information.

In conclusion, bear in mind that not all indicators work all the time, not all indicators work in the canned version but some might work in a customized version, and, at times, no indicator will work at all.

LEARNING MORE ABOUT TECHNICAL ANALYSIS

Technical analysis can be as simple or as complex as you like. Almost any technical indicator, if properly done, is better than none. It's an easy subject to read up on, too, unlike conditions twenty years ago. The literature is quite large and growing all the time. One of the best features of technical analysis is that techniques never go out of date. A moving average is a moving average is a moving average. Once you have mastered a few core concepts, your knowledge base grows by leaps and bounds.

TECHNICAL ANALYSIS OF FOREIGN SECURITIES

The electronic world has yet to catch up with foreign securities. You can't perform technical analysis without historical data, and it can be very difficult to get historical foreign stock data today. You can get daily information from the *Financial Times* or another source, but you must perform the work of typing it into your computer.

You can almost always find foreign stock indices, and that is not a bad place to start. The first thing you want to know is whether the foreign market is booming or swooning. The crowd psychology you will see in the chart of the principal foreign index is, to some extent, the national investor group's psychology—chiefly its institutional investors, but the public at large, too.

You should start with an idea. Of the almost 200 countries in the world, perhaps 100 have stock markets that might be of interest. Let's say you want to get your feet wet in a Western European country, and leave Ghana for later. You know that Greece will join the European Monetary Union in January 2001, and will adopt the euro as its currency. Meanwhile, you read that most European economies are recovering from a semirecessionary condition and may have 3 to 3.5 percent growth over the next few years, with low inflation. Greek companies should benefit. What does the Athens stock exchange look like? Figure A.8 offers some insight.

Right away you can see that a linear regression channel is a simple and effective tool for identifying the current downtrend and determining its range. You now have to ask yourself whether you want to look any further for a specific Greek stock to buy in this environment right now. Obviously, not every Greek stock is falling, but the overall trend of the market is down. At some point, the Athens General Index will hit bottom and reverse to an upward trend. Try to have a good individual

Figure A.8   Athens General Index and Linear Regression Channel
Data: Reuters DataLink; chart: Metastock.

stock candidate ready to be bought, so that you can take advantage of favorable market sentiment spillover.

DO-IT-YOURSELF TECHNICAL SCREENING

More than 40 broadly used technical indicators are popular today. Some sites scan the universe of stocks and funds, and publish the best-performing and worst-performing stocks according to these indicators. Here's a list of just a few sites you may want to look into:

- www.investtech.com—tracks stocks and funds in the Nordic countries, Germany, the Netherlands, and a few other countries
- www.marketradar.com ($150/year)
- www.stkwtch.com (to $49.95/year)
- www.charttrend.com ($15/month)
- www.clearstation.com (free)

- www.prophetfinance.com (some free and some for fees)
- www.barchart.com
- www.tradingcharts.com
- www.tradingmarkets.com
- www.nni.nikkei.co.jp
- www.windowsonwallstreet.com

Most of these sites except investtech and nni.nikkei.co.jp focus on U.S. stocks only, although they include ADRs and iShares, which enable you to invest in foreign stocks (as discussed in detail in Chapter 8).

You can do your own scanning of the universe, too. The least expensive way is to get the TC2000 software and training materials offered by Worden (www.tc2000.com). The software is free and the data updates are $29.75/month. The data are also exportable to other applications—a valuable feature. The site has free training notes and reports on interpretation, and the company offers free two-hour training sessions in cities around the country. For example, with TC2000, you could scan the entire universe of stocks for those that have the highest price momentum coupled with the highest increase in volume. Once you have their names, you can research each stock for value considerations.

Another way to do technical screening is to buy the technical analysis software and database separately. The top two software programs are divided into less expensive and more expensive categories. On the less expensive end of the spectrum is Metastock (www.equis.com), which costs $399 for end-of-day analysis or $1,495 for real-time analysis. Data for end-of-day analysis can be from several vendors, including Equis's Reuters DataLink ($24.95/month). For real-time technical analysis, e-signal is available (www.esignal.com) at prices ranging from $25 to $150/month, depending on how you combine packages. If you want to experiment, you can get a free demo and use the software for a month before paying. Equis includes a huge historical database on a CD to practice on.

Note that if you buy a database such as Reuters DataLink, some 9,000 securities are available. To filter and rank all of them, you need a lot of memory in your PC. The data are organized by type (commodity, index, indicator, stock, or bulletin board) but not by sector or industry.

To scan everything in the biotech industry, for example, you would need to find and enter the symbol for each company to assemble a list. Once you have the list, though, it takes seconds to activate the "Explorer" to filter and rank stocks according to your own criteria.

A more expensive but more feature-intensive program is available from Omega Research (www.omegaresearch.com). It's called Radar Screen 2000i and is available for $2,399.40, which can be paid in monthly installments. You choose from a library of more than 70 built-in indicators that can be applied to your list of securities, and you see them updated in real time. At the moment, the historical and real-time data feed is free. Omega Research also sells TradeStation 2000i and OptionStation 2000i, each at the $2,399.40 price, or you can get all three in ProSuite 2000i for $4,800. TradeStation itself, which is used for the actual back-testing of technical indicators (as opposed to using the canned versions), allows the development of more complex custom indicators than any other program. However, many users do not find its "EasyLanguage" computer language particularly easy.

Other technical analysis software programs are reviewed in *Technical Analysis of Stocks and Commodities* magazine (www.traders.com). The reviews cost $3.95 each. The year-end bonus issue that comes with a subscription contains a summary of the reviews.

There are dozens of useful books on technical analysis. Go to any online bookseller and search on "technical analysis." Your search will result in a list of dozens of books.

BASICS OF FOREIGN EXCHANGE

An investment in a foreign stock is always a dual investment. You are buying the security itself and the currency in which it is denominated. You should consider that you are investing in the currency as an asset class in its own right because it can have as big an effect (or a bigger effect) on your total return as the return on the security.

When you invest in foreign securities, you obviously have to deal with the currency of the country where the security is issued. Foreign exchange is viewed as exotic and difficult, and this description is enough to put off some investors. That's a pity, because there is nothing terribly difficult or complicated about currencies. In fact, you already know most of what you need to know about foreign exchange. You may just need to reorganize the knowledge a little to become comfortable with foreign stock investing.

The information in this appendix is intended to give you a better understanding of all of the issues involved in foreign exchange—beginning with understanding the different quotation conventions and recognizing that the exchange rate you will get is determined by the broker with whom you're working. This appendix also offers several detailed case studies to illustrate some of the challenges of foreign exchange.

THE FOREIGN EXCHANGE RATE IS DETERMINED BY YOUR BROKER

Foreign exchange can give you an unpleasant surprise because when you buy and sell foreign stocks, your broker gets to choose the exchange rate you are charged. For example, suppose you are buying a British stock denominated in pounds. On the very day of your purchase, you may see the British pound quoted with as much as a two-penny variation in U.S. dollar terms—for example, $1.5800–$1.6000. Because currencies are always priced four places past the decimal point, your broker may be buying pounds at $1.5800 and "selling" them to you at $1.6000, or buying them at $1.5880 and selling them to you at $1.5920. It's an extra little profit center for the broker, and you have no way of knowing how much extra you are being charged. Over the course of the day, the price of the British pound can actually vary as much as two cents.

Moreover, the price of the pound quoted in newspapers or on CNBC or other financial news services may be a standard quote for large amounts ($1 million and more), whereas the price of pounds for smaller amounts—like your $10,000 stock purchase—is always higher to accommodate back-office processing costs. Therefore, at each end of a foreign stock transaction, you may be losing a little (or a lot), but be assured, you are almost certainly losing something, and you have no recourse unless you are a really big customer and the loss is a particularly egregious one.

So why put up with such an expense when, elsewhere, everyone is watching transaction cost pennies? The answer is simple: Foreign stocks may offer the opportunity for a higher return or a less volatile return. (Now we are counting in dollars, not pennies and fractions of pennies.) What you consider to be a nuisance expense—e.g., $50 on a block of 100 shares—has to be offset by getting a higher or at least a less volatile return.

UNDERSTANDING DIFFERENT CURRENCY QUOTATION CONVENTIONS

Another big issue in foreign exchange is the "quotation convention." Of all nationalities, Americans have the hardest time with currency quotations, and not because they are provincial or lack the cross-border experience of (say) Europeans. Since World War II, the U.S.

dollar has been the main world reserve and transaction currency. In fact, approximately 65 percent of all foreign trade is U.S. dollar-denominated. For example, oil and most commodities are denominated in U.S. dollars.

Depending on where you are in the world, there are two ways to express the value of a U.S. dollar. For example, sometimes the Canadian dollar is expressed as worth "$1.45" (in U.S. dollars); at other times, you will see it quoted as "0.6897." These two numbers are actually the same price, quoted in different formats. In the interbank "spot" foreign exchange market, where participants are professionals and the amounts traded are large (i.e., a minimum of $1 million), nearly every currency is quoted as a function of the U.S. dollar. This explains the first quotation convention above: 1.00 U.S. dollar will buy 1.45 Canadian dollars.

Alternatively, you could say each Canadian dollar is worth 68.97 U.S. cents, or $0.6897. Arithmetically, you get from one to the other by dividing into the numeral 1.00, which, divided by 1.45, equals 0.6897, and divided by 0.6897 equals 1.45. This is called the reciprocal. Some experienced currency traders can do the division in their head, but you don't have to. You only need to know which quotation convention is being used in any particular situation.

The quotation convention challenge is further complicated by the British pound (and, often, the Australian dollar). The pound is quoted in the "American quotation convention," or dollars per British pound (such as £1 = $1.65). It is very seldom quoted in the "European quotation convention," wherein one dollar equals 60.61 British pence. Then along came the euro, also quoted in the American convention. The euro is the currency that replaced the Deutschemark, French franc, Italian lira, and other currencies of the European-11. These countries formed the European Monetary Union and "issued" the first euro (it was actually just a bookkeeping entry at that time) on the first business day of 1999. In practice, the notes and coins will not be mandatory for a few more years, but all accounting systems have to keep track of both the euro and the national currency until the transition is complete. Meanwhile, the individual currencies still exist for domestic transactions.

Different Quotation Conventions Are Used by Different Markets

Returning to the subject of quotation conventions, the two coexist side-by-side, and usage has not been standardized because the *European* quotation convention is used in the professional foreign exchange market and the *American* quotation convention is used in the Chicago and other futures markets. Although there is active and efficient arbitrage between the two markets (ensuring that prices are almost perfectly equivalent at all times), the participants in each market are very different.

The Professional Market   The professional (or **spot**) **market** is dominated by commercial and investment bank "proprietary traders" who are essentially speculating with the banks' credit lines, as well as corporations conducting transactions overseas, governments, hedge funds, and brokers buying and selling stocks and bonds for customers.

> **spot market**
>
> A market for commodities, including currencies, in which the price is agreed upon today for actual delivery of the goods for cash payment in a short period of time, usually two to five days.

This market is the largest and most liquid market in the world, with about $1.5 trillion in transactions per day, according to the Bank for International Settlements in Switzerland. This makes it bigger than all the world stock markets put together. It is open almost twenty-four hours a day. The only downtime is the few hours between the U.S. close and the Australian open, and even that is mitigated by most big banks' having overnight foreign exchange (FX) desks in every money-center city.

Futures Markets   In contrast, futures markets are patronized by smaller businesses whose transactions are not big enough for the professional market (or they do not qualify for bank credit lines), and by speculators of all levels of expertise, from the amateur day-trader working from a downstairs den to sophisticated proprietary traders at banks and brokerages. In the United States, currency futures are traded at the International Monetary Market (IMM) division of the Chicago Mercantile Exchange, as well as at other exchanges. The cross-rates (e.g., the euro/yen) are traded at the Finex, a division of the New York Cotton Exchange, and contracts that are one-half the usual size are traded at the Mid-Am, a market affiliated with the Board of Trade in Chicago. Electronic trading is offered to the public by many brokers, but only for the so-called day session, which, at the IMM, starts at 7:20 A.M. and ends at 2:00 P.M. Central Time. To trade outside these hours, the customer has to call the broker, who then enters the trade, electronically, in a system named Globex.

To make life more complicated, FX trading outside IMM hours can be conducted in two ways. Globex trading is an auction-style matching system rather than the open-outcry system used on the floor of the exchange; that is, it has less liquidity, although the Exchange hired market-makers to ameliorate this problem. The hours are not continuous, and you cannot place a stop order on Globex, although some brokers will allow a stop order on their EFP desk, if they have one, as a control on a position in the Globex market. To fill in or as a substitute, orders may also be executed in the professional spot market and then converted to futures contracts when the Chicago market opens. This method of executing transactions is called "exchange for physical" (EFP), a name that means a spot contract is created in the cash market (the "physical") and will be exchanged into a futures contract as soon as Chicago opens. The cash market contract is the same size as the futures contract itself, but, technically, it does not enjoy the same customer protections as a real futures contract which is guaranteed by the Exchange.

There's a lot of process in the background that you, as an average investor, do not need to know about, but be aware that if you trade currencies—either as a stand-alone asset class or to hedge foreign equity positions—your brokerage statements will sometimes show price quotes in the spot market quotation convention and other mysterious and indecipherable information. This occurs because a limit order may have been executed in the EFP market—if you did not specify Globex—and the trade was actually done in the cash market and exchanged for a futures contract when the Chicago exchange opened. But don't worry—it's a highly regulated and very efficient process.

American versus European Quotation Conventions

If you look at a CNBC screen and see that the British pound has gone up, you know that your shopping trip to London just became more expensive. In contrast, however, when you see that the Japanese yen just went up, it means exactly the opposite. If yesterday one dollar would buy 110 yen and today it will buy 115, the yen *quotation number* went up, but the yen *value* went down. This occurs because the British pound is quoted in the American convention (i.e., dollars per foreign unit) and the yen is quoted in the European convention (i.e., foreign units per dollar). To make matters even more confusing, if you are looking at a spot market quotation, the price is for a transaction in which money will change hands in two days. If today is Monday, the party selling British pounds will deliver them on Wednesday and will expect to carry away the equivalent dollars.

If the futures screen is displayed, you can breathe a sigh of relief—at least every quotation is denominated in U.S. dollars and cents—but you must also consider that it is for actual payment on some date *in the future*. The standard contract dates are March, June, September, and December. If it is now January, the **front-month** contract is March—i.e., the payment will be made in March. The spot quotation for the British pound (two-day delivery) may be $1.6000, but when you check the futures quote, you see $1.6040. What accounts for the extra 40 points?

> **front month**
>
> A term used in futures markets to describe the most active (and liquid) contract in the market today, usually the one that will mature the soonest. Contracts that mature later in the future are called "back months."

> **basis point**
>
> A basis point is 1/100 of a percentage point. Basis points are frequently used to quantify yields in bonds.

(Note: These points are not the same as **basis points**. That term applies to interest rates, not currencies. In foreign exchange, the term is simply "points" or "pips." This last arises from the British term for the seeds in oranges or lemons—thus, something very small.)

As for the extra 40 points, understanding them is relatively simple and straightforward. The futures contract quote differs from the spot quote because it embodies the interest rate differential between the two countries. In a futures contract, you are agreeing today to a price at which you will exchange dollars for pounds on some date in the future; meanwhile, you get to earn interest on your dollars, and the counterparty gets to earn interest on his or her pounds.

For example, let's say you can earn 1 percent flat on your dollars in two months (6 percent per annum/12 months × 2 = 1 percent). You are a buyer of British pounds today for delivery in two months. The seller of the pounds gets to keep the interest that will accrue over those two months. (The outright two-month interest rate in Britain is 0.75 percent.) At the current spot price of $1.60 per pound, one British pound futures contract of £62,500 is equal to $100,000. Here's the math:

You earn: $100,000 × 0.01 = $1,000; $100,000 + $1,000 = $101,000.

The counterparty earns: £62,500 × 0.075 = £468.75; £62,500 + £468.75 = £62,968.75.

Divide your $101,000 by £62,968.75, and you get $1.6040.

The pounds you will be getting are slightly more expensive, to make up for the fact that you earned a little more interest while you were still holding the counterparty's dollars ahead of delivery to him or her. If the pound were not more expensive for future delivery, everybody and his brother would buy dollars to earn the extra 0.25 percent interest and still be able to sell their dollars without penalty (and the U.S. money supply would balloon).

ALL FUTURES CONTRACTS ARE FORWARD CONTRACTS

All forward or future exchange rates are set this way. A **forward rate** is the exact same thing as a **futures rate,** and they will be identical values for the same delivery date. The only difference is that in the professional foreign exchange market you can name your delivery date, whereas, in the futures market, you are limited to the delivery dates specified by the exchange. In the professional market, the process by which the interest rate differential and the forward rate are continuously kept in this balance is named **covered interest arbitrage.** In other words, a forward or future rate is *not* a forecast of what the price will be in the future, but solely a function of the two interest rates.

> **forward rate**
>
> A contractual price, determined today, at which a security will be bought or sold on a specific date in the future. It includes the cost of financing the holding of the security in the interim or the net interest earned by holding the security in the interim.

To say that a forward rate is an unbiased predictor of the future rate is to miss this critical point. Many Ph.D. dissertations have tortured the arithmetic to make the forward rate a predictor of the future rate, usually without much luck. Something else is happening, though. Often, the forward rate is a predictor of the future rate, because the reason for the high interest rate is high inflation. The country

> **futures rate**
>
> A contractual price, determined today, at which a security will be bought or sold on a specific date in the future. It includes the cost of financing the security in the interim, or the net interest earned on a security in the interim.

with a higher interest rate usually has either higher inflation or an expectation of higher inflation. Higher-inflation countries usually experience a drop in their exchange rates because of the mechanism described below. A country's higher interest rate causes its currency to sell at a forward discount (i.e., less valuable in the future), and

> **covered interest arbitrage**

The simultaneous purchase and sale of goods in two different markets where the cost of financing the securities for the period they are to be held—sometimes called "the cost of carry"—is included in the price at which the *arbitrage* is entered.

its currency falls because its purchasing power is being eroded by inflation.

How Exchange Rates Are Determined

In a world where trade in physical goods dominates the determination of exchange rates, a country with inflation will have goods that are (or will become) more expensive via price inflation than every other country's goods. Therefore, it will not be able to export, and it will have to use foreign currency *reserves* to pay for imports. When its reserves run low, it will be forced to depreciate its currency in order to restore purchasing power parity.

The purchasing power parity/balance of the foreign trade model dominated exchange-rate analysis at a time when exchange rates were fixed, and in the early days of floating rates (which started in 1974). At that time, government-imposed capital controls prevented a free flow of capital into and out of countries. Gradually, starting in the early 1970s and continuing even today, capital controls were relaxed. For example, if you were a Briton who wanted to invest in the U.S. stock market, you had to pay a premium of 15 to 25 percent to buy the dollars to do it. Upon being elected prime minister in 1979, Margaret Thatcher made good her campaign promise of abolishing that capital control.

Nowadays, we have mostly free capital flows among the major countries. A country can run a huge trade surplus and not face a decline in its currency as long as capital is flowing in. This is, of course, the situation in the United States today. Some analysts persist in saying that the dollar must fall because we buy so much more from countries overseas than we sell to them. Others point out that foreigners have an undiminished appetite for American government and corporate bonds, Wall Street stocks, and direct purchases of U.S. companies and real estate. Very little of the capital inflow is "hot money" (able to exit on short notice)—

less than 10 percent of the U.S. stock market is owned by foreigners. In 1999, the inflow was more than double the trade deficit.

FORECASTING EXCHANGE RATES

Combining analyses of trade flows and capital flows, as well as other domestic conditions such as inflation, leads to the forecasting challenge. Forecasting corporate earnings pales in comparison to the complexity of forecasting exchange rates. Every month, we hear that the U.S. trade deficit has risen again to a historic high level, and commentators say the dollar should fall. But, month after month, it fails to fall. Then one month it does fall, but only a little and only for a short time.

The capital flow model of exchange rate determination says that the country with the highest interest rate will get the biggest inflows (all other things being equal), and they will more than offset the trade deficit. This is true, up to the point where foreigners own as many U.S. assets as they want in their portfolios. As Chairman Greenspan and other Federal Reserve Bank officials have reminded us, at some point you have to wonder when they will feel they have as much as they could possibly want.

As noted above, the country with the higher interest rate sells at a **forward discount,** that is, it is cheaper for delivery on a date in the future. The country with the lower interest rate sells at a **forward premium,** that is, it is more expensive for delivery in the future. It's important not to attach value judgments to the words "discount" and "premium." The dollar currently sells for a forward discount because

> **forward discount**
>
> Describes a condition when the price of a security that is to be delivered in the future is lower than the price for current delivery.

> **forward premium**
>
> Describes a condition when the price of a security that is to be delivered in the future is higher than the price for current delivery.

it has a higher interest rate, *not* because it is expected to fall and actually be worth less in the future. If that were true, you'd have a hard time figuring out how much less. This arises from the different quotation conventions described at the beginning of this appendix.

In the professional interbank market, a two-month forward rate for the Canadian dollar may be a 0.46 percent premium to the spot rate. In futures, the same two-month rate may be 0.62 percent different from the **spot price**—solely because when you calculate a percentage difference, it matters arithmetically whether you are using numbers with values less than one or more than one. Academicians consider this a puzzle of finance. It's not. It's simple arithmetic.

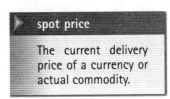

> **spot price**
>
> The current delivery price of a currency or actual commodity.

For this reason, you need to be wary of statements that forecast future exchange rates using the interest rate differential. For example, some might say that the two-month interest rate for Greek drachmas is 10 percent and the two-month rate for euros is 3.75 percent, and therefore the drachma must devalue by the interest rate differential of 6.25 percent. This is not true. The interest rate differential equalizes the principal-plus-interest of money invested in short-term instruments in each country where the interest rate is accessible to all (i.e., there are no capital controls) *and the foreign exchange risk is hedged with a forward or futures contract.* The differential equalizes the cash flows, not the exchange rates.

A SAMPLE HEDGING EXERCISE

In the following example, the Swiss franc is quoted using the European quotation convention. Each dollar is worth 1.6703 francs at the start, or $0.5987. The forward price for delivery in two months is 1.6663, a lower number but a higher value—$0.6001. The dollar has the higher interest rate and sells at a discount, while the franc has a lower interest rate and sells at a premium. Suppose a Swiss millionaire decides he should investigate the U.S. money markets to maximize the return on his investments. He has Swiss francs (SF), and he decides to invest SF 1,000,000 in the domestic Swiss money market for one month at 2.93 percent per annum:

$$SF\ 1,000,000 \times 2.93\% = \frac{SF\ 29,300}{365} \times 30\ (days) = SF\ 2,408.22$$

He could choose, instead, to invest in the U.S. market. He can sell his SF 1,000,000 in the spot market at 1.6703 and invest the principal at 5.88 percent per annum, today's one-month Eurodollar rate. The math would look like this:

$$\frac{SF\ 1,000,000}{1.6703} = \$598,694.85 \times 5.88\% = \frac{\$35,203.26}{365} \times 30 = \$2,893.42$$

Our Swiss millionaire now has a foreign currency exposure. What if the dollar depreciates against the Swiss franc? After all, the only reason to make an investment in a foreign currency is to get a real after-tax return in the *home* currency. The millionaire needs to know the amount that the dollar can depreciate and still allow him to break even with the Swiss franc investment. In simple terms, the answer is:

5.88% U.S. investment rate per annum
2.93   Swiss investment rate per annum
2.95% Break-even U.S. dollar depreciation/12 months = 0.2450%

He will be indifferent toward the two investments if he can be sure the dollar will depreciate exactly 0.2450 percent over the one month of his U.S. investment. Applying this percentage change to the spot price, we get the following:

1.6662 (0.002450 × 1.6703 = .0041; 1.6703 − 0.0041 = 1.6662)

Another way to calculate this is on a cash basis:

Principal + interest in SF = SF 1,002,408.22
Principal + interest in $ = $601,588.27

The break-even exchange rate is therefore:

$$\frac{P + i\,(SF)}{P + i\,(\$)} = 1.6663$$

The one-point difference is due to rounding. Let's say our Swiss millionaire doesn't want to take a chance on the future value of the dollar. To avoid the dollar exposure, he can sell the U.S. dollars one month forward instead of holding the dollar asset unhedged. This would be a **swap**—the simultaneous purchase of dollars for one date (now) and the sale of the same currency for another date (30 days). If he does this, he has engaged in covered interest arbitrage. He has no exchange rate exposure, and he has "covered," or hedged, his investment.

> **swap**
>
> The exchange of one security for another, where no cash is included in the deal and any differences in interest costs or earnings are reflected in the price.

The cost of a one-month forward is quoted by the forward dealer at 44 points. We subtract the points from the spot rate to derive the outright forward rate:

1.6703 − .0044 = 1.6659

The hypothetical break-even rate calculated above is 1.6663, and the actual one-month forward rate available in the market is 1.6659. In other words, the actual rate is *worse* than the indifference point. The Swiss millionaire would get fewer Swiss francs per dollar using the forward market than he needs for a break-even status with the Swiss investment. The fact that the two rates are nearly the same, however, is testimony to the efficiency of the market. Hedging via the swap market is not the only option; he can still do the deal unhedged.

Look at Table B.1, which shows forecasted possible Swiss franc rates. (The formula used is at the top of the relevant columns.) If the dollar were to depreciate to 1.4500 against the Swiss franc, the unhedged position would result in a cash loss of SF 127,698, which can be likened to a negative interest rate of 12.77 percent. On the other

TABLE B.1
POSSIBLE FUTURE SWISS FRANC RATES

P + i Earned ($) ×	Possible SF Rates =	New SF Amount −	SF Principal =	Imputed Interest (SF)	Imputed Interest (%)
$601,588	1.8000	$1,082,850	1 MM	$ 82,850	8.29%
601,588	1.7500	1,052,779	1 MM	52,799	5.28
601,588	1.7000	1,022,699	1 MM	22,699	2.27
601,588	1.6703	1,004,832	1 MM	4,832	.48
601,588	1.6693	1,004,230	1 MM	4,230	.42
601,588	1.6663	1,002,426	1 MM	2,426	.24
601,588	1.6649	1,001,583	1 MM	1,583	.16
601,588	1.6000	962,540	1 MM	(37,460)	(3.75)
601,588	1.5500	932.461	1 MM	(67,539)	(6.75)
601,588	1.5000	902,382	1 MM	(97,618)	(9.76)
601,588	1.4500	872,302	1 MM	(127,698)	(12.77)

hand, if the dollar were to rise to 1.8000, the millionaire would get interest earnings of SF 82,850, which is the equivalent of an effective interest rate of 8.29 percent.

The forward and futures markets are always available. If the underlying exchange rate moves in the Swiss millionaire's favor, he can call his bank or broker, at virtually any time, and order execution of the second leg of the swap. Of equal interest to him is that if the interest rate changes in either country, the cost of the forward-to-close will also change—in his favor if it narrows, and against him if it widens.

For U.S.-based investors in foreign stocks, there are a few lessons in this story. First, the direct case of how professionals equalize cash flows between countries illustrates that the forward rate is not a forecast, a guess, or a hope. It is the result of hardheaded exploitation of small arbitrage opportunities. In other words, there is no point in criticizing the forward rate for being "wrong." It can't be wrong: It is set by the interest rate differentials, and nothing else.

Second, you may buy a stock in a foreign country, and although the stock continues to rise and you are happy with it, the currency starts to fall. Should you hedge your currency exposure? The only way to know whether to hedge is to estimate your break-even point. To what level can the currency fall so that it exactly offsets the investment you have made in the stock? At that break-even point, you are starting to take a net loss if the currency continues to fall.

HOW TO FORECAST EXCHANGE RATES

Unlike gold, currencies do not have intrinsic value. There's no book value in currencies. Logically, each currency has a country (or a group of countries, in the case of the euro), and each country has a government that is more or less solvent. Just as we assume that a company is a "going concern" (i.e., it will stay in business), we assume countries are going concerns, too. The ongoing finances of a country depend on its ability to tax the public. The ability to raise extra money by privatization of government-owned businesses is a one-time thing, but is often useful. (If we were to evaluate countries like companies, the United Kingdom would have to be the best among the major world countries when judged by the going-concern criterion. Not only does it have a budget surplus, it also has a fully funded social security program. It is the only major country of which this can be said.) And yet, fiscal excellence is only one contributing factor among all those by which currencies are judged.

As a rule, the country with the highest interest rate will lure the most money from other countries, but it doesn't do this without regard for other factors. That country also has to have:

- A stable and honest government.
- The confidence of the financial sector that the central bank is proactive against inflation.

- Nonpunitive taxation.
- Other conditions conducive to foreign investment—including such mundane things as a telephone system that always works, and competent bankers—as well as loftier attributes of civilized society, such as the rule of law, and commercial codes of conduct that are actually enforced.

This last point is not trivial. For example, a bank in Nigeria may offer 150 percent for one-month deposits, but can depositors be confident that they will get back their dollars at the end of one month, plus the interest payment? Nigeria has been the source of several international frauds and scams; the Nigerian Consul General often has to run ads in U.S. newspapers (such as *The New York Times*) warning people that promises of extraordinary gains are seldom true, and they should not trust specific offers coming from Nigeria.

Whenever you make an investment in a foreign country, you will want to evaluate beforehand whether the exchange rate is fair, and by how much it is likely to change during your expected holding period. We have already learned that the forward rate is not an unbiased predictor of the future rate. Just because a country has higher interest rates does not ensure that its currency will remain high via capital flows. It may actually develop real inflation, despite the efforts of the central bank (recall the one-time oil shocks of 1973 and 1978), or foreign investors may simply have as much of that currency as they deem appropriate for their portfolios. The Fed now fears this response toward the U.S. dollar.

For example, the Fed raised U.S. rates by 50 basis points on May 17, 2000; two days later, the dollar fell against the Japanese yen from 109.50 to 106.90. At the time, the Japanese short-term interest-rate equivalent of Fed funds was *zero*. This makes no sense at all under the capital flow theory. The reason? A Japanese research institute had just forecast that first-quarter GDP growth would be 13.1 percent—extremely high under any circumstances, and especially high in the context of Japan's 10-year recession. If the forecast is correct, the Bank of Japan will be able to abandon the zero interest rate policy sometime in the next six to nine months. The interest rate differential will still be in favor of the U.S. dollar by a huge amount, but by less than it was before. Ergo, traders rush to "buy on the rumor" well in advance of any actual "fact."

You have to face the unhappy fact that currencies can be undervalued or overvalued for long periods of time, and establishing fair value is an endless and often fruitless quest. For example, the Australian dollar is highly correlated with commodity prices. When commodity prices fell dramatically after the Asian crisis of 1997, the Australian dollar fell and has continued weak into 2000. And yet, Australia's interest rates are almost as high as those in the United States, and Australia qualifies as a foreign investment destination on the criteria named above—phones that work, the rule of law, a stable society, and so on.

Estimating the Value of Foreign Currency: The "Big Mac Price Test"

Let's say you are able to travel internationally and you decide to make your own estimation of the fair value of a currency by traveling to the country and comparing the prices of key items to the prices charged in your home country. For example, you would deem a foreign currency undervalued if a can of Coke that costs $1.00 at home costs 50 cents, and overvalued if the Coke costs $2.00. This is a dangerous approach. There are many factors that render the comparison invalid—transportation expense, import tariffs, lack of local demand for the item, and so on. Cornflakes cost $30 a box in Nairobi. That doesn't mean the Kenyan shilling is overvalued.

The Economist magazine publishes a purchasing power comparison based on the price of a McDonald's Big Mac in 39 countries around the world. This started out 14 years ago as a tongue-in-cheek exercise and has become wildly popular—and often correct. For example, if a Big Mac costs $2.50 in the United States and $5.00 in some other country, that country's currency is up to 100 percent overvalued. As of April 2000, the Big Mac Currency Index shows that the Japanese yen, for example, "should" be at 117 per dollar when it is actually at 106—11 percent overvalued. Table B.2 is an excerpt from the Big Mac Currency Index.

				Undervaluation
		Implied	Actual	(–) or
		Purchasing	Exchange	Overvaluation
	Dollar	Power	Rate	Against the
Country	Price	Parity	(04/25/00)	U.S. Dollar
Australia	$1.54	$ 1.03	$ 1.68	–38%
Britain	3.00	1.32	1.58	+20
Canada	1.94	1.14	1.47	–23
Germany	2.37	1.99	2.11	–6
Japan	2.78	117.00	106.00	+11
Switzerland	3.48	2.35	1.70	+39
Argentina	2.50	1.00	1.00	0
Indonesia	1.83	5,777.00	7,945.00	–27
South Africa	1.34	3.59	6.72	–47

TABLE B.2
BIG MACCURRENCY INDEX

Source: *The Economist,* April 29, 2000, p. 75. The Economist Newspaper Group, Inc. © 2000. Reprinted with permission. Further reproduction prohibited. www.economist.com.

Does this comparison mean that stocks in Switzerland are 39 percent overvalued solely because of the exchange rate, and stocks in Australia are 38 percent undervalued for the same reason? No, not exactly. Currencies can be overvalued and undervalued on a purchasing power basis for long periods of time, even when considering a larger basket of goods than a McDonald's meal. For example, Switzerland has appeal to many foreigners because of its bank secrecy and political neutrality. It is a "safe haven" in times of world troubles, whatever its interest rate. At one time in the 1970s, you had to pay Swiss banks to take your money—a negative interest rate, so to speak. Thus, the Swiss franc is almost always overvalued against the U.S. dollar, year after year.

In contrast to Switzerland, Australia is a different kettle of fish. The Australian dollar (A$) is considered a "commodity currency," like the Canadian dollar. If and when commodity prices start to rise again, the A$ will probably follow, and may overshoot to the upside.

Over the past 15 years, the A$ has been as high as 87.92 cents and as low as 58.10 cents. If you draw a linear regression (the ultimate trend line, as discussed in Appendix A) over those 15 years, the value should be 69 cents as of May 20, 2000. The current spot price is 57.50 cents. Does that mean the A$ should go up by 11.5 cents to meet the long-term trend? That would be a 20 percent rise. The best answer we can give is a resounding "Maybe." It may also gain back the 38 percent it is undervalued on the Mac Currency basis, which would take it to 82.14 cents.

So, we have the A$ at 57.50 cents with a long-term trend value of 69 cents and a purchasing power value of 82.14 cents. To get to the bottom line, Australian stocks are probably undervalued in U.S. dollar terms, and an American investor will probably get, from the currency effect alone, a 20 to 38 percent gain from an investment there, even if the stock does not change in price. If the stock goes up, the investor will get a double benefit. If the stock falls but the A$ rises, the American investor could break even. The question is: How long might it take for the A$ to rise to its trend or purchasing power level? Nobody knows. It might not happen at all—again, currencies can be mispriced for long periods of time.

HOW PROFESSIONAL INVESTORS HANDLE EXCHANGE RATES AND CURRENCY VALUATION

When professional fund managers allocate funds to foreign equities, they agonize over whether to hedge foreign stocks against falling currency values that result in unfavorable translation of returns in dollar terms. A lot depends on whether their firms judge performance in local currency terms, where the managers may have excelled in stock-picking, or in dollar terms, where the same excellent stock picks may show a net loss solely because of translation into dollars. Major newspapers such as the *Wall Street Journal, Barron's, Financial Times,* and *New York Times* show stock market index performance in both local currency and dollar terms. The contrast can be shocking. Nearly all managers are judged according to the MSCI indices, which are quoted in both local currency and dollar terms. There's a further argument, though. Some professionals consider that the exchange rate at any one time is immaterial. If you have a permanent holding period, the currency will always be incorrectly valued—currencies almost never trade at an equilibrium rate. Sometimes it will be undervalued and sometimes it will be overvalued. To keep it hedged when you plan never to remit the funds back into dollars is to waste time and money. In other words, you would want to hedge a foreign investment only if you have a short-term investment horizon.

As with other investment decisions, whether to hedge or not to hedge is a function of the expected holding period. If the expected holding period of the currency is "forever" because asset allocation rules mandate that some portion of the portfolio must always be in that country and currency, there is no pressing need to hedge the currency exposure.

As noted throughout this book, what's appropriate for the professional is not necessarily appropriate for the individual investor. For example, let's say you invest in Stock A in a foreign country in which the currency is, by your estimation, undervalued. Stock A rises 40 percent and the currency rises 40 percent, too. Now you have a windfall gain of 80 percent—an extraordinary return that is far above the "expected return" in any country, over a short time frame. If you do not take profit on this dual investment, and if both the stock and the currency revert to their means, you will be passing up an extraordinary opportunity. (Of course, once you have taken profit, you have to search out another opportunity, but that is a separate issue.)

Suppose you then invest in Stock B in a foreign country—a country that you feel has overvalued its currency. The currency reverts to its long-term mean, falling 20 percent. Your Stock B rises 20 percent. You have therefore made no net gain, and you have incurred the opportunity cost of tying up your money in an investment with a zero net return when it could have been employed elsewhere to better total effect. In this case, if you had hedged the currency (i.e., sold it forward), you would have protected the 20 percent gain on the stock. In terms of asset and liability management, you are "long" the stock (denominated in the foreign currency) and "short" its currency. You have no net foreign exchange position, but, in cash terms, the loss from translating the value of the stock into dollars would be offset by the gain on the currency contract.

To clarify this hypothetical example, let's consider two case studies.

Case Study 1: Investing in SmithKline (SBH)

SmithKline is a British pharmaceutical company. (See Figure B.1.) You bought it as an ADR denominated in U.S. dollars, but it's actually denominated in British pounds in its home country, so you correctly consider that you have a hidden pound exposure. You bought the stock on October 1, 1999, when the stock price was at a low of $56.50 and the pound was

Figure B.1 SmithKline Beecham (bars, right–hand scale) and UK Pound (line, left–hand scale)

Data: Reuters DataLink; chart: Metastock.

at $1.6496. You decide to sell the stock on December 3, when the price reaches a high of $69.88. You have a gain of $13.38. But the pound on December 3 is at $1.5992—a 50-cent ($0.50) drop. If you had sold the pound forward (or in the futures market), you would have made a profit on the short sale (buying it back when it was less expensive), and gained the additional 50 cents. A similar situation developed in early 2000, when you could have bought SmithKline at the low of $53 on February 16 and sold it on April 4 at $70.50. The decline in the pound then was only $0.0035—less than a penny. The gain would have been negligible, or you might have even had a loss, depending on transaction costs.

But wait a minute: The ADR is denominated in dollars. You have no direct foreign exchange risk. To hedge the currency is to add an unnecessary level of complexity to the trading or investing decision. This is perfectly true. The only reason to hedge an ADR is to acknowledge that it is a foreign stock and there is an indirect, underlying exposure to a currency risk. If the British pound were to fall dramatically—say, to $1.35—U.S. professional fund managers might reduce their exposures to all British stocks, or sell the pound forward to hedge their positions, if they need to hold them for strategic reasons. Either way, the dollar price of the British stock is likely to fall. Because you can't hedge a single stock (so far), you hedge the currency.

Case Study 2: Investing in Sony (SON)   This is another ADR; Sony is the famous Japanese electronics firm. (See Figure B.2.) You buy the stock at $63.81 on August 30, 1999. You note that the yen is at 111.01 to the dollar. You sell the stock on February 29, 2000, at $156.80; the yen is at 109.92. In this instance, the change in the yen is trivial—less than one U.S. cent—but the gain in the stock is significant. Hedging the yen would have been a waste of time and money—although it is not always so.

Sometimes, both the stock and the currency are in the same upward trend, and it is definitely not in your best interests to hedge. For example, on January 6, 1986, Sony sold for $9.091 and the yen was at 202.60 to the dollar. By April 4, 1995, the stock had risen to $24.75, a

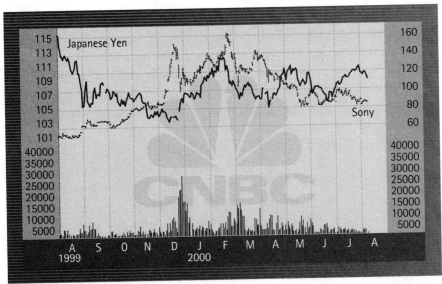

Figure B.2   Sony (light bars, right-hand scale) and Japanese Yen (heavy line, left-hand scale)

Data: Reuters DataLink; chart: Metastock.

gain of 172.2 percent, and the yen had risen to 83.85 to the dollar—a gain of almost 250 percent. This is an instance in which it would have been preferable to have invested directly in Sony in Japan, with the investment denominated in yen. You would have not only made the stock gain, but also directly made the currency gain.

To Hedge or Not to Hedge?
That Is the Question

How do you know in advance whether to hedge or not? You don't—not for sure, anyway. At the launch of the euro at $1.17, just about every professional foreign exchange forecaster predicted the euro would rise to $1.30. People believed the new single European currency would foster a rush of cross-border M&A deals, productivity gains, and other efficiencies that would make Europe a wonderful place to invest, and draw in foreign capital flows. Moreover, foreign countries would want to hold euros in their official reserves.

It didn't happen, partly because the euro came into existence at an inflated price, according to the Big MacCurrencies' reckoning. Other causes contributed to its decline, too, including the problem of a one-speed interest rate being applied to multiple-speed economies that have not yet "harmonized" their growth and inflation rates. As of September 1, 2000, the euro was at $0.8884.

In addition to seeking diversification of your portfolio, you probably want to invest in foreign stocks to obtain a return higher than the one available in the home market, or a return that is less risky because the foreign market is less volatile. Translation of the investment into your home currency should not show inordinate variability of return due to translation alone, or you are violating the purpose of the foreign investment in the first place. You may not know your holding period in advance, but you will know it when you see it. Either you have taken the maximum possible loss you are willing to take with that particular amount of money, or you have made such an extraordinary gain that you feel to hold any longer is only to risk losing the gain.

The only reason to make an investment is to get a cash return—not to get a big-percentage capital gain on paper that vanishes when you have to convert the foreign currency into home currency cash. There's no point in making, say, 50 percent on the stock and losing 75 percent on the currency.

Currency risk can enhance or diminish overall home currency *returns*. You do not have to make a currency-hedging decision at the same time that you make the investment decision, but the hedging decision does have to be a dynamic process of continuous reevaluation of the currency trend. As stated at the very beginning of this Appendix, every foreign stock investment is really a dual investment in the currency as well. By definition, it doubles the work you have to do. If you decide to hedge, your purpose is to protect the expected return on the underlying security. It is not to make money in currencies as a tradable asset class in their own right, although they *are* a tradable asset class. It's important to maintain clarity on this point.

THE MECHANICS OF HEDGING

When you hedge a foreign stock position, you will always be selling the foreign currency against your home currency. When you buy a security denominated or based on a foreign currency, you are long the foreign currency. A hedge of a foreign stock holding is always a forward sale of the foreign currency. Let's say the foreign currency starts to rise. As a dynamic investor, you remove any hedge you may have placed (a forward sale of the foreign currency), because it is not needed at the moment. If you also put on a long position in the currency, you are now a currency speculator, not a hedger. To go long the currency is to increase your exposure to the currency, not to hedge it. If you are an American buying Australian stocks, you will always be a seller of Australian dollars in the forward or futures market, never a buyer, when you are wearing your "stock investor" hat. If you are an Australian buying American stocks, you will always be a seller of U.S. dollars, if you are putting on a true hedge.

It may happen that you have a real talent for spotting currency market trends. You may switch from being a foreign stock market investor to being a currency trader. Actually, you may inadvertently become a currency market speculator when you become a hedger. This may happen because the interbank forward market, in which you could customize the amount and the forward date, is essentially closed to individuals with smaller amounts to hedge. Gradually, brokers and new specialized nonbank foreign exchange trading firms are starting to accommodate such trades, but, in practice, the amounts are usually restricted to the standard contract sizes and the contract dates prevailing in the futures market. Unless you are a very high-net-worth individual, chances are your foreign stock market ventures will be smaller than the standard contract sizes listed in Table B.3.

In some contracts, an "e-mini" contract half these sizes is available. The Chicago Mercantile Exchange (CME) site (www.cme.com) is educational and worth a visit. The CME and other exchanges will also mail you helpful free materials on using currency futures. Note that the list

TABLE B.3
CHICAGO MERCANTILE EXCHANGE IMM
CURRENCY FUTURES CONTRACTS
As of May 19, 2000

Currency	Local Currency Amount	U.S. Dollar Equivalent
Australian dollar	$ 100,000	$ 57,340
UK pound	62,500	92,850
Canadian dollar	100,000	66,900
Euro	125,000	112,587.50
Japanese yen	12,500,000	117,662.50
Swiss franc	125,000	71,675

Source: www.cme.com.

in Table B.3 is not complete—you can also hedge or trade in the South African rand, Russian ruble, French franc, Mexican peso, Brazilian real, and other currencies. You will not, however, find futures contracts in so-called exotic currencies such as the Indonesian rupiah, Czech krone, or Turkish lira. Stock market investments in those currencies are essentially unhedgeable.

This picture is changing. New services are springing up to allow individuals to hedge equity investments (or to speculate) in the spot and forward market in smaller sizes than in the professional market or the futures market. Among the sites worth a visit are matchbook.com, gaincapital.com, and midas.dk.

A word of caution: You may see advertisements that say currency trading is easy, cheap, and low-risk. *It isn't.* You may have to put up only a small amount of capital to be allowed to execute a trade, and trades can be executed electronically for low commissions, but if the position goes against you, you could owe a truly large amount of money. For example, a one-penny change in the euro futures contract is the equivalent of $1,250. The average daily high–low range in the euro over the past 18 months has been 1.03 cents. If you had sold the euro to hedge an equity investment and it moved against you by this amount on each of 10 days, without your paying attention, your loss would be $12,875. If you had ten contracts, the loss would be $128,750. Trade very carefully.

When the European Monetary Union launched the new currency, the euro, on the first day of 1999, the majority of analysts believed that it would bring new efficiencies to Europe, facilitating cross-border trade and investment, and becoming a rival to the U.S. dollar as a currency of denomination for commodities and official government reserves. Instead, the euro fell from an initial valuation of $1.1732 to as low as $0.84 in September 2000. It was not a completely unbroken fall and several times over the course of its first seven quarters the euro seemed to be pulling out of its slide, but each time resumed the decline. On September 22, the European Central Bank intervened in the foreign exchange market in coordination with the central banks of Japan, the United States, Great Britain, and Canada. It was the first coordinated intervention since June 1998, when the United States cooperated with the central bank of Japan to halt the yen weakening. (The Bank of Japan and other central banks occasionally intervene on their own.) The foreign exchange market is the only market in the world in which governments openly intervene to try to influence prices. Coordinated intervention is therefore extremely rare. It is, however, a risk you take when investing in foreign currency denominated securities.

You will read that currencies are highly trended and it's therefore easy to apply technical analysis to foreign exchange. (See Appendix A for a primer in technical analysis.) But, just as there is more than one fundamental theory about what determines exchange rates, there are several technical approaches. For example, the Elliott Wave theory happens to be popular in the foreign exchange market at the moment, but other ideas are important, too, including longer-term moving averages and support-and-resistance. Big financial institutions—Goldman

Sachs, Deutsche Bank, Citibank, Merrill Lynch, and others—forecast exchange rates for their clients, using both fundamental and technical approaches. Some of this proprietary research makes its way into the financial press. You can find it incorporated into the foreign exchange market reviews from the Far East, Europe, and the United States at www.marketcenter.com. Bridge News Service provides these reviews, along with real-time quotes. www.bloomberg.com is another site that lists all the currencies with updated quotes every few minutes.

HOW CURRENCY WOES HAVE AFFECTED CORPORATE AND PROFESSIONAL INVESTORS

The earnings of many global titans were hit by currency woes in 2000. They arose chiefly from the unexpected 25 percent fall in the euro from its launch at the beginning of 1999 to the spring of 2000. These companies include IBM, Coca-Cola Enterprises, McDonald's, Xerox, Eastman Kodak, Lexmark International, and Unisys. In 1997 and 1998, Asian currency devaluations hit many companies, including Procter & Gamble and Gillette. Companies take a hit two ways: (1) in lower sales and earnings when translated and transmitted into dollars, and (2) from competing foreign suppliers whose costs are lower. According to S&P Compustat, 220 companies of the S&P 500 have high enough foreign sales and earnings to break out the amount in their financial statements.

The negative impact of adverse foreign exchange movements can be costly. For example, in 1988, 3M caused an uproar among its shareholders when it admitted that the strong dollar had cost it $1.8 billion in revenue and $330 million in profits over the prior three years. 3M doesn't hedge at all. The company figures it all comes out even in the end, and hedging is not only hard to do, but expensive. Only about one-third of U.S. multinationals hedge currency exposure. Honeywell and Merck are two that do, in an effort to reduce the volatility of earnings.

The same picture can be seen among fund managers. Some feel that currency risk is part and parcel of any foreign investment and should not be hedged away. To some extent, this is a function of a very long time frame. Global funds allocate their investments according to the MSCI benchmarks. Prominent among them is the "EAFE" (Europe/Africa/Far East) index, against which their performance is judged. The benchmark takes foreign currency-denominated values of fixed income and equity investments, and translates them back into dollars when the accounting period ends. The fund managers want to beat the index by their asset selection, not through some accident of currency pricing at quarter-ends and year-ends.

Fund managers have more or less discretion in maintaining their allocations to different countries and regions, but, over time, they will always have some capital allocated to each area. For example, if investments in country A are failing to come up to snuff, fund managers can shift capital to country B in the same region, without changing the allocation. To a large extent, the permanence of the investment makes the professional fund managers indifferent to currency changes.

Other global fund managers, however, care passionately about currency valuation and take care to select countries in which currency risk is either minimal or can be managed. These managers perform some very sophisticated analyses, and they are more likely to use complex currency options than outright forwards.

One form of currency management is the **carry trade.** Here, fund managers borrow in a currency with a very low interest rate (say, Japan) and invest in a currency with a higher interest rate (say, the United States). They are therefore short the currency borrowed, and long the asset denominated in the other currency. The risk in a carry trade manifests itself when the currency borrowed starts becoming expensive in terms of the currency in which the fund manager has invested. Fund managers who execute carry trades will always have a break-even exchange rate calculated

> **carry trade**
>
> A form of currency trading in which one borrows in a currency with a low rate of interest for a fixed period of time and uses the borrowed currency to invest in a different currency that yields a higher rate of interest. The higher currency instrument is used as collateral for the low-interest borrowing. The risk is that currency values that make a carry trade profitable will change and make it unprofitable before the fixed period of time expires.

in advance, to tell them where the carry trade stops being profitable. Then they have to liquidate the asset in order to pay back the now appreciating currency loan—and so does everybody else engaged in the same carry trade.

The process of buying back the borrowed currency raises its price, which then induces others to buy the currency too. Soon, the price is snowballing. Carry trades have been blamed for some of the very big one-day and one-week moves in the Japanese yen and Swiss franc in recent years. From the outside, it looks like a mania or a panic, when in fact the currency move is based on a sound rationale: market discipline and careful calculations.

SUMMING UP

Allocating your investments to foreign assets, hedging or not hedging the foreign exchange component—all of this activity is the pinnacle of international finance. To do it well, you need to have a grasp of basic economics and a political and institutional environment that will determine interest rates. It is from interest rates that much other economic activity derives its direction. In the absence of a single coherent theory of exchange rates, you also have to know what ideas are uppermost at any one time. They will be a key influence (even if they are wrong). It is an endlessly fascinating process, but to add currency hedging more than doubles the work of international investing.

CNBC provides comprehensive business and financial news Monday through Friday from 5:00 A.M. to 8:00 P.M. EST, with real-time market coverage to more than 160 million homes worldwide, including more than 77 million households in the United States and Canada. The network's Business Day programming is produced at CNBC's headquarters in Fort Lee, N.J., with reports from CNBC news bureaus in Midtown Manhattan, the New York Stock Exchange, Washington, D.C., Chicago, Los Angeles, Palo Alto, London, and Singapore.

CNBC Pre-Market (5:00 A.M.–9:30 A.M./EST) programming gives you a head start on the business day, delivering breaking business news from overseas, a look at the day's top stories and a comprehensive rundown of what's in store for the day ahead.

- *Today's Business* (5:00 A.M.–7:00 A.M., Monday–Friday). The breakfast business briefing on important overnight developments such as mergers, earnings, and overseas action with live updates from CNBC's London and Singapore bureaus.

- *Squawk Box* (7:00 A.M.–10:00 A.M., Monday–Friday). The daily word on the street leading up to, and after, the opening bell. Host Mark Haines and CNBC analysts track the strategies of investment professionals, interview prominent business figures, and debate the latest insight from the street.

During Market Hours (9:30 A.M.–4:00 P.M./EST), CNBC is the only place to go for real-time financial news and information and in-depth play-by-play analysis of what's moving the markets and why.

- *Market Watch* (10:00 A.M.–12 Noon, Monday–Friday). Delivers the play-by-play on the daily tug-of-war between buyers and sellers from the worlds of business and finance.

- *Power Lunch* (12 Noon–2:00 P.M., Monday–Friday). An up-close and personal look at the companies, CEOs, and category trends impacting business.

- *Street Signs* (2:00 P.M.–4:00 P.M., Monday–Friday). The suspenseful last two hours of trading. Every twist and turn, winner and loser, is covered, along with the next day's potential. Features live location reports from traders on the floor and industry insiders.

After the Bell (4:00 P.M.–8:00 P.M./EST), CNBC provides a complete wrap-up of the day's events, plus a close look at extended trading hour activity in real time.

- *Market Wrap* (4:00 P.M.–6:00 P.M., Monday–Friday). A comprehensive analysis of the day, covering everything from hot stocks and corporate shake-ups to breaking news after the close. Includes in-studio interviews and extended hours updates.

- *The Edge* (6:00 P.M.–6:30 P.M., Monday–Friday). The first program of CNBC's broadcast day that advises viewers how to adjust their portfolios in anticipation of the next day's opening bell. Emerging trends, cutting-edge products, and extended hours trading are covered while top market analysts and business leaders share their views.

- *Business Center* (6:30 P.M.–8:00 P.M., Monday–Thursday; 6:30 P.M.–7:00 P.M., Friday). Direct from the floor of the New York Stock Exchange, a complete overview of the day's business and financial news.

- *Market Week* (7:30 P.M.–8:00 P.M., Friday). A decisive, reflective wrap-up of the business week in preparation for the next.

Features a wide range of guests, including analysts, traders, and CEOs to give viewers perspective and predictions from the inside.

CNBC.com is a fully integrated interactive Web site that reports original news, provides summaries of on-air news stories and guides to CNBC programming, and contains a full range of investment and personal finance tools including:

- Quotes
- Charts
- Personalized Ticker
- Message Boards
- Company Conference Calls
- Company News and Information
- Analyst Reports
- Insider Trading
- Industry Groups
- Advisor Newsletters
- Personal Resources such as Career Center, Women's Investment Center, Mortgage Center, Auto Loan Center, Home Equity Center, Small Biz Center, Loan Center, and Tax Center.

The CNBC Portfolio Tracker can help you follow your stocks quickly and easily from your computer. Portfolio Tracker can also alert you before the CEO of a company you've invested in appears on CNBC TV. In addition, you can receive real-time quotes (25 a day), a personalized ticker, and the CNBC.com daily newsletter (Money Mail). Portfolio Tracker allows you to keep tabs on all your investments and provides you with current quotes, insider trading information, valuations, and analyst and technical ratings. Called "Best of the Web" by *Money* magazine, Portfolio Tracker monitors market changes and news events related to your stocks, but it also keeps you updated throughout the day via e-mail alerts. And when a guest related to a company in your portfolio appears on CNBC TV, you will be alerted so you can watch firsthand as newsmakers discuss important issues that could affect your picks.

Portfolio Tracker can also send you price breakout alerts. Enter a low or high breakout price for your securities or enter percent price moves, and you'll receive e-mail alerts when a stock in your portfolio reaches the price.

With Portfolio Tracker, you will also have access to Account Tracker, a free service that securely keeps all your personal account balances and activities in one place with one password. And with Stock Screener, you can screen and scan for stocks and mutual funds that meet specific criteria you search on. From projected growth stocks to undervalued stock to stocks with insider buying, you can find the stocks that meet your investment criteria.

INDEX